YOUR MEMORY

KENNETH L. HIGBEE has done extensive research in memory training and lectures frequently on the subject. He is Associate Professor of Psychology at Brigham Young University, where he teaches, among other subjects, a course on memory improvement that he developed. He has written many articles and papers on various topics, including memory, for professional journals and conventions and is listed in *American Men and Women of Science*.

YOUR MEMORY

How It Works
and How to Improve It

KENNETH L. HIGBEE, Ph.D.

A SPECTRUM BOOK

PRENTICE-HALL, INC. Englewood Cliffs, New Jersey 07632

Library of Congress Cataloging in Publication Data

HIGBEE, KENNETH L (date).
  Your memory.

  (A Spectrum Book)
  Includes bibliographical references and index.
  1. Mnemonics. I. Title.
BF385.H48   153.1'4   76-43059
ISBN 0-13-980144-8
ISBN 0-13-980136-7 (pbk.)

©1977 by Prentice-Hall, Inc.
Englewood Cliffs, New Jersey 07632

A SPECTRUM BOOK

20 19 18 17 16 15 14

Printed in the United States of America

Prentice-Hall International, Inc , *London*
Prentice-Hall of Australia Pty. Limited, *Sydney*
Prentice-Hall of Canada, Ltd., *Toronto*
Prentice-Hall of India Private Limited, *New Delhi*
Prentice-Hall of Japan, Inc., *Tokyo*
Prentice-Hall of Southeast Asia Pte. Ltd., *Singapore*
Whitehall Books Limited, *Wellington, New Zealand*

To Pat, of course

Table of Contents

YOUR MEMORY

CHAPTER 1

Introduction
to Memory Training

People can learn an amazing number of different things. We can learn to walk, dance, and swim. We can learn to type, repair watches, and program computers. We can learn to drive cars, ride bikes, and fly airplanes. We can learn languages, chemical formulas, and mathematical proofs. We can learn to read road maps, make out income tax returns, and balance checkbooks. The list of things we can learn to do could be continued almost indefinitely.

Of course, all this learning would be useless if we could not remember. Without memory we would have to respond to every situation as if we had never experienced it. The value of memory is also illustrated by the fact that we reason and make judgments with remembered facts. In addition, we are able to deal with time, relating the present to the past and making predictions about the future, because of what is stored in our memories. Even our own self-perceptions depend on our memories of our past.

The uses and the capacity of the human memory are indeed amazing. You can store billions of items of information in your memory. Your two-pound brain can store more than today's most advanced computers.

But people also forget. They forget things they would like to remember. They forget other people's names. They forget anniversaries, birthdays, and appointments. They forget what they learned in school (usually within a short time after an exam, and sometimes before the exam).

What is memory? Why do you remember some things and forget others? What can you do about it? Does it depend on the kind of information learned? Does it depend on *how* you learned the information? Does it depend on whether you were born with a good memory? Can a poor memory be improved? What is mnemonics?* Can mnemonics improve your memory in everyday life? These are some of the questions that will be answered in this book.

WHY WAS THIS BOOK WRITTEN?

My interest in questions such as the ones above began when I first read a book on memory improvement as a student in high school. I was amazed at the things I could do with my memory by using mnemonic techniques. I began acquiring additional books and applying the techniques. Through the years I have continued to add memory books to my personal library, and to learn and use new memory systems and techniques. My reading of popular books on memory improvement has been supplemented by my academic and professional training as a psychologist, giving me a balanced perspective between the popularized treatments of memory training and the empirical research on learning and memory. I have tried to reflect this balanced perspective in this book.

It has been my pleasure to have the opportunity of lecturing to numerous groups about memory improvement. In addition, for several years I have been teaching a college course which I have titled, "Understanding and Improving Your Memory." My experiences in developing and teaching this course have given me an idea of what things people want to know and need to know about memory. Each time I teach the course I revise it to make it more beneficial to the students. The main reason this book was written is that I have not been able to find any one textbook for my course that covers all the things I feel students of memory training should know.

On one hand, there are textbooks on learning and memory that are generally oriented toward an academic understanding of memory and have little information on improving memory. Most of them either do not discuss mnemonic techniques or discuss them only in passing as interesting oddities that are of little practical value. Also, most of the textbooks on learning and memory are too technical to be interesting and understandable to a person who does not have a background in psychology, and who may try to read the book on his own.

---

*Mnemonic systems are defined and discussed in Chapter 5. However, since the word *mnemonic* is used several times in the first four chapters, a brief definition will be given at this point also. The word *mnemonic* means "aiding the memory." Thus, a mnemonic system or technique is literally a system or technique that aids the memory. Typically, however, the term *mnemonics* refers to rather unusual, artificial memory techniques.

On the other hand, there are the popular books on mnemonics and memory training. They tend to have the opposite limitations from the textbooks. They are usually rather limited in scope, not giving the reader any memorizing principles and guides other than mnemonic techniques. In addition, they usually do not give the reader an understanding of *how* or *why* mnemonic techniques work, but only how to use the techniques. Thus, many people tend to associate mnemonics with gimmickry and showmanship. They do not realize that most mnemonic techniques are based on sound principles of learning, and can make a significant contribution to practical memory tasks in everyday life.

This book is intended to provide a reasonable balance between the technical textbooks on learning and the sometimes oversimplified popular books on mnemonics. The methods, principles, and systems are related to relevant research literature in such a way as to make the book accurate (so that it will be acceptable to the professional), but also understandable (so that it will be useful to the layman). The book is intended to be a practical guide to understanding and improving your memory. The emphasis is more on how to do it than on academic and theoretical issues of memory. Thus, only one chapter is devoted to understanding memory, and it covers only what is necessary to make the rest of the book useful.

Even though the original impetus for this book came from my desire to provide a textbook for students in my memory class, I have written the book so that it can be used by anyone who is interested in improving his memory. This consideration has determined my choice of what subjects to cover, what to say about them, and in what order to cover them. The book is a self-contained guide that you can study on your own to understand and improve your memory.

WHAT CAN YOU EXPECT
FROM YOUR MEMORY?

Some people have misconceptions about what is involved in improving their memories. It may be helpful to clear up some of these misconceptions, so that you will have a realistic idea of what to expect from your memory. The following are some considerations you should keep in mind with respect to improving your memory.

Remembering Is Hard Work

You probably do not need to be told that remembering is hard work, that it takes effort to learn and remember. But what many people do not realize is that principles and techniques for learning and remembering do not necessarily make remembering any *easier*; they just make it more *effective*.[1] You will still have to work at it, but you will get more for your efforts.

Some people hope that memory training will reveal to them a simple "key"—one thing that they can do (with little effort) so they will never forget anything they see, hear, or do. There is no one key that provides a really easy way to improve memory. Remembering is a skill. Improving your memory is like acquiring any other skill. You have to learn the techniques and practice them.

Suppose you wanted to be good at golf, chess, math, or playing the piano. You would not expect to learn just one secret that would give you the skill. Rather, you would expect to learn techniques and principles, practice them, apply them, and thereby improve your skill. However, when it comes to memory, some people do not reason the same way. They do not want to work at it. When such a person finds out that improving memory takes effort, he may decide that he can make do with his memory as it is. You should plan to put forth some effort if you really want to benefit from the principles and systems discussed in this book.

There Is No One Best Method for Remembering Everything

This consideration is closely related to the previous one, but warrants separate attention. It has been noted that there is no single key to remember everything. We will also see in Chapter 2 that a "good" memory may refer to several different things. There are a number of circumstances that determine what method is best to learn material. For example: (a) Who is doing the learning? A chemistry professor and a beginning chemistry student may use different methods to study a new book on chemistry. (b) What is to be learned? Different methods may be used for learning word lists, nonsense syllables, numbers, poems, speeches, and book chapters. (c) How will remembering be measured? Preparing for a recognition task may require different methods than preparing for a recall task. (d) What kind of remembering is required? Rote remembering of facts may require a different method than understanding and applying the facts, and word-for-word memorizing may require a different method than remembering ideas and concepts. (e) How long will remembering be required? Preparing to recall the material immediately after learning it may require a different method than preparing to recall it a week later.

The practical implication of this consideration is that when a person asks how he can improve his memory, he cannot be given any useful answer until he makes his question more specific.[2] What kinds of material does he want to remember? In what way? Under what circumstances? For how long? There are methods and principles in this book that apply to almost any kind of learning situation, but they do not all apply to all situations.

Memory Is Not a Muscle

Some books on memory training suggest that memory is like a muscle. If you want your muscles to become stronger, all you do is exercise them. Similarly, they say that if you want your memory to become stronger, all you have to do is exercise it: practice memorizing. In fact, some people believe that practice is one of the simple "keys" to memory improvement— all you have to do is practice memorizing things and your memory will become stronger. This is a form of the "doctrine of formal discipline."

The doctrine of formal discipline says that the mind can be strengthened through exercise. This notion was prevalent in education around the turn of the century, and was used as an argument for teaching subjects such as Greek and Latin in school. It was argued that the study of such subjects exercised and disciplined the mind, so the student would do better in his other subjects. The doctrine of formal discipline is not supported by research evidence.[3]

William James, often referred to as the father of American psychology, tested whether he could improve his memory by exercising it. He spent eight days memorizing 158 lines of Victor Hugo's works and found that he required an average of 50 seconds per line. He then practiced memorizing Milton for thirty-eight days. After this practice, he memorized another 158 lines from Hugo, using the same procedures as earlier. He found that he memorized at a rate of 57 seconds per line, a bit slower than previously, and reported similar results for several other people who tried the same task.[4]

In an experiment by W. G. Sleight, 12-year-old girls practiced memorizing poetry, scientific formulas, and geographical distances for 30 minutes a day, four days a week, for six weeks. The practice did not result in any improvement whatever in their ability to memorize.[5]

There is no substantial evidence that practice by itself makes a significant difference in improving memory. It is true that practicing memorizing can help improve memory, but what you *do* during practice is more important than the *amount* of practice. One classic study, discussed in Chapter 4, found that three hours of practicing memorizing did not improve memory, but that three hours of practicing using certain techniques did improve memory.[6]

Anyone Can Remember

Remembering is a basic psychological process that is common to all people, barring brain damage or severe mental or psychological disturbances.[7] "I have a poor memory" may be a convenient excuse for poor remembering, but it is a poor excuse. The capacity of your memory is a function of the memory techniques you use. Thus, improving the techniques improves the capacity.

To illustrate this point, let us compare a large cardboard box to a small 3 × 5 file box. Which one has more "capacity" in terms of how much it can hold? The cardboard box does. But suppose that one person writes notes on 3 × 5 cards and throws them in the cardboard box. A second person writes his notes on 3 × 5 cards, and files them behind the appropriate index cards in the small file box. Now, suppose each person wants to find a specific card. Which one will be able to find it more easily? Even though the cardboard box can hold more, the file box actually has a larger useable capacity because the material is stored in such a way that it can be found when needed. Similarly, the useable capacity of your memory depends more on techniques you use for filing than on any innate "capacity." In fact, we will see in Chapter 2 that your long-term memory has a virtually unlimited capacity.

Some popular books on memory training suggest that there is no such thing as a good memory or bad memory, there are only trained memories or untrained memories. While there may be some truth to this statement, it is not completely accurate. There are probably small variations among people in innate memory abilities; in this sense there may be such a thing as a good memory and a bad memory. However, the important point is that even if there are such innate differences in memory, these differences are not nearly as important in your ability to remember as are differences in learned memory skills. Remembering does take effort, but if you are willing to put forth the effort, you *can* improve your memory. You can make a "bad" memory good and a good memory better.

A Trained Memory
Does Not Remember Everything

One memory performer, Harry Lorayne, noted that people sometimes asked him to repeat a previous conversation word for word, or to recite a newspaper word for word. These people do not realize that a person who has a trained memory does not necessarily remember everything. In fact, he does not *want* to remember everything. One of the advantages of a trained memory is that you can remember what you want to remember. Lorayne did not engage in conversation for the purpose of memorizing it, and did not read the newspaper for the purpose of memorizing it.[8]

Related to this point is the belief of some people that remembering too much can clutter their minds. Actually, the problem of most people is just the opposite. Their minds are already cluttered and they do not remember enough! It is not only how much you put into your memory that affects remembering, but also *what* you put in and *how* you put it in. In some ways the more you learn about something, the more it may actually help memory; we will see in Chapter 3 that the more you learn about a particular topic the easier it is to learn new things about it. We will also see in Chapter 5 that most mnemonic systems actually add to the amount you need to remember, but they do so in such a way as to increase your memory ability.

WHAT CAN YOU EXPECT
FROM THIS BOOK?

This book has five characteristics that should help make it useful:

1. *It is less technical than textbooks on learning and memory.* This book was not written for other psychologists who are familiar with research on memory. It was written for the intelligent student and layman who does not have a background in psychological research on learning and memory, and it is intended to bridge the communication gap that sometimes exists between scientists and laymen. Thus, technical terms and professional jargon used in the psychology journals are avoided as much as possible, and such terms are explained whenever introduced. The book also avoids discussion of many technical theories and side issues that are of interest to the academician and researcher, but not to most other people.

2. *It is more technical than popular books on memory training.* The book is intended primarily to instruct, not to entertain (although I have nothing against entertaining, and I try to combine the two whenever possible). Thus, it is not intended to be read like a novel or a newspaper article. It is intended more for people who are serious about wanting to improve their memories than for people who want to do some light reading.

3. *It is more objective than popular books on memory training.* Many popular books on memory training give the reader the impression that the mnemonic techniques discussed will help in every possible kind of learning task. In addition, they give the impression that mnemonics are all-powerful, and have no limitations. The books are sprinkled with such sensationalistic terms as "super-power memory," "computer mind," and "amazing mental powers." This book presents a more balanced perspective. Mnemonics can make a significant contribution to memory in many situations, but there are also other principles and guides that can be applied in other situations. In addition, although mnemonic techniques

are very powerful for many kinds of learning, they do have limitations; this book presents both the strengths and limitations of mnemonics. I cannot promise you that after reading this book (or any other book) you will be able to learn everything the first time you see or hear it, and that you will never forget anything you learn. However, I can promise you that if you apply the methods described in this book, you can significantly improve your memory.

4. *It is more comprehensive than most books on memory.* Most textbooks on memory are concerned primarily with understanding memory, and a few give a little attention to improving memory. On the other hand, most popular books on memory training are primarily concerned with improving memory, and give no attention to understanding memory. In fact, many popular books on memory training do not even give any attention to principles of learning other than mnemonic techniques. The primary emphasis of this book is on improving memory (my experiences in lecturing to various groups and teaching the class on memory improvement have taught me that people are more concerned with improving their memories than with understanding their memories). However, some attention is also given to understanding your memory, both in terms of the kinds of questions people frequently ask about memory and the kinds of things that will help you understand how and why memory improvement techniques work.

5. *It is based on current research findings.* Most popular books on memory training do not present any sound evidence that the techniques really work. As a result, many people get the impression that the techniques are only for show, or that they are not practical, or that they are not worth the effort. After reading such a book, people may say, "Well, that's interesting," and go on their way unchanged. This book presents research evidence illustrating the strengths and weaknesses of the guides, principles, techniques, and systems discussed. Thus, this book discusses what has been found to work, not what someone *says* should work, or what *seems* like it should work.

In addition, the book is based on research evidence that is current, not on what was known ten or twenty years ago about memory. Much of the really good research on memory improvement, and virtually all of the research on mnemonics, has been published since 1965. About 70 percent of the references cited in this book have been published in the 1970s, and about 85 percent of the references have been published since 1965. There are literally hundreds of research articles and dozens of books that are relevant to the topics covered in this book. More than 150 years ago, in 1813, a bibliography of memory listed sixty references; in 1961 a comprehensive bibliography of memory listed about 7,000 references; and in 1972 a bibliography limited to only research articles on memory for pictures listed 685 references.[9] To cite all of the relevant research would be unduly burdensome (both to me and to you), so two strategies have been used to limit the number of references. First, when several studies are relevant to a certain point, one or two of the most recent studies have usually been selected to cite. Second, articles that review a number of studies have frequently been cited, rather than citing the original studies.

Comments made by students after completing my memory course suggest some of the ways in which the contents of this book may be valuable. The following are some examples of written comments made anonymously by students after finishing the class:

> I learned more than just techniques. I gained the desire to organize my daily life and be a more useful person.
>
> If I could have learned these things early in my college career, I would have saved many hours and probably had a higher grade point average.
>
> I have heard of using mnemonic systems before but I was never before convinced of their worth or practicality. Now I know that these things can be useful.
>
> I am now aware of some of the capabilities of the human mind (mine specifically) which I previously thought were out of reach.

Similarly, when you finish studying this book, you will have a better understanding of what your memory is and what it can do; you will be aware of basic principles to guide you in improving your memory; and you will have an extensive repertoire of learning strategies and mnemonic systems that will enable you to use some of the capabilities of your mind which you also may have previously thought were "out of reach."

In this chapter you have been introduced to memory training and to what you can expect from your memory. Chapter 2 gives a basic understanding of the nature of memory and answers some questions you may have about memory, to serve as a foundation for understanding and using the rest of the book. Chapter 3 discusses some principles on which effective learning strategies (including most mnemonic techniques) are based. Chapter 4 describes learning strategies that can help you improve your ability to learn material that is not especially suited for mnemonic techniques. Chapter 5 gives an introduction to mnemonics, including the strengths and limitations of mnemonic systems. Chapters 6 to 9 explain the nature and uses of specific mnemonic systems. Chapter 10 suggests some additional practical uses of mnemonics in everyday life.

SUMMARY

This book is intended to provide a balanced perspective between popular books on memory training and textbooks on memory and learning. It is a self-study guide that you can use to understand and improve your memory.

Misconceptions that some people have regarding memory improvement are cleared up by the following principles of memory training: (1) Remembering is hard work; memory training does not make it easier, just more effective. (2) There is no one best method for remembering everything. (3) Memory is not a muscle; it does not improve significantly through exercise as a muscle would. (4) Anyone can remember; regardless how "bad" or "good" your memory is, you can make it better. (5) A trained memory does not remember everything.

This book has the following characteristics: (1) It is less technical than textbooks on learning and memory. (2) It is more technical than popular books on memory training. (3) It is more objective than popular books on memory training. (4) It is more comprehensive than most books on memory. (5) It is based on current research findings.

When you finish studying this book you will have a better understanding of what your memory is and what it can do; you will know basic principles to guide you in improving your memory; and you will have an extensive repertoire of learning strategies and mnemonic systems that you can apply in almost any learning situation to increase your memory ability.

CHAPTER 2

Meet
Your Memory

What is memory? The use of the word "memory" in everyday speech suggests that a memory is some *thing* that we have, like a heart or an eye. A person says he has a bad memory, or his memory is failing him, just like he would say he has a bad heart, or his eyes are failing him.

There is no such thing as a memory, in the sense of some object that exists in itself, and that can be seen, touched, or weighed. Memory cannot be located in a specific part of the brain, and even the extensive studies on chemical changes in the brain that accompany memory (for example, changes in RNA) have not revealed very striking or consistent findings.[1] Memory is an abstraction. It refers to a set of attributes, activities, and skills rather than to an object. These skills may be of quite a wide variety; there is no single standard by which to judge a "good" or "poor" memory. Ian Hunter has noted that a person who claims to have a good memory may mean that he can do any one of a number of things: read a book and tell you everything that is in it; read a paragraph and recite it word for word; tell you anything you want to know about a given topic; recall many experiences from his early childhood; never forget anniversaries and appointments; or still do something (like play chess or speak a foreign language) that he has not done for years.[2]

The fact that there is no single standard by which to judge a "good" or "poor" memory is also indicated by several of the topics discussed in this chapter. For example, there are different ways of measuring memory, and a person may have a good memory by one measure but not by another. Or a person may have a good memory for pictures but not for words.

Most of this chapter is concerned with answering the question, What is memory? For the reader who would like a more complete understanding of the nature of memory, a more comprehensive (and more technical) coverage is given in a number of recent books.[3]

The aspects of memory that have been selected to discuss in this chapter are those that will give you an understanding of memory that is sufficient to make the rest of the book meaningful. Thus, the information in this chapter provides a basic foundation for understanding and using the principles, methods, and systems discussed in the rest of the book.

WHAT ARE THE STAGES OF MEMORY?

The process of remembering is generally viewed as consisting of three stages: (1) *acquisition* or encoding is learning the material in the first place; (2) *storage* is keeping the material until it is needed; and (3) *retrieval* is getting the material back out when it is needed. To help remember these three stages, they can be referred to as the "Three R's of Remembering:" Recording (acquisition), Retaining (storage), and Retrieving (retrieval).

Another way to remember the three stages of memory is by referring to the "Three F's of Forgetting" (or more accurately, the three F's of *not* forgetting). Corresponding with Recording, Retaining, and Retrieving are, respectively, Fixating, Filing, and Finding.

The three stages can be illustrated by comparing the memory to a filing cabinet. You first type the desired information on a piece of paper (Recording). Next you put it in a file cabinet drawer under the appropriate heading (Retaining). Later you go to the file cabinet, look it up, and get it out (Retrieving).

Sometimes when a person cannot locate what he wants in a file cabinet it may be because the information was never recorded; sometimes it may be because the recorded information was never put in the cabinet; but often it is because the information was not put in the cabinet in such a way as to be easy to find.

Suppose a person using the file cabinet just throws letters and documents haphazardly into the drawers. A few months later he goes to the cabinet to retrieve a specific document. He would likely have a problem getting it. Why? Because it was not recorded? No, the document had been typed. Because it was not retained? No, the document had been put in the cabinet. Rather, his problem is a result of *how* it was stored. Similarly, most problems in remembering come in retrieval rather than in storage.

There is a difference between material that is *inaccessible* and material that is *unavailable*.[4] For example, material that is misplaced in your filing cabinet is available because it is stored, but it is inaccessible because it cannot be retrieved. However, if the material is not even in the filing cabinet, then it is not only inaccessible but is also unavailable. Likewise, material that is recorded and retained in your memory may be inaccessible, but not necessarily unavailable; you know it is in there somewhere, but you just cannot find it.

We are all very aware that memory is limited more in getting things out than in getting them in. More can be stored in memory than can be retrieved. There is not much we can do to improve retrieval directly, but retrieval is a function of how the material is recorded and retained. Therefore, improved methods of recording and retaining will improve retrieval, both from a filing cabinet and from your memory.

The principles and methods discussed in this book will help you record and retain material more effectively. We will see in Chapter 5 that mnemonic systems may be viewed quite literally as mental filing systems. They help you record and retain information in such a way as to be able to retrieve it at will.

WHAT ARE SHORT-TERM AND LONG-TERM MEMORY?

There appear to be at least two different processes involved in memory, *short-term memory* (also called *primary memory*) and *long-term memory* (also called *secondary memory*). The distinction between short-term memory and long-term memory is more than just a semantic distinction between remembering for a short time vs. remembering for a long time. Most psychologists view short-term and long-term memory as being two separate storage mechanisms that differ in several ways, although some psychologists have suggested that they are not really different mechanisms, but merely different levels of processing in the same mechanism. We will avoid this theoretical issue and merely refer to them as two different processes.[5]

Some of the differences between the processes of short-term and long-term memory are the following: (1) the nerve changes that take place in the brain may be different for short-term memory and long-term memory. (2) Short-term memory is an active, ongoing process that is easily disrupted by other activities; long-term memory is not as easily disrupted. (3) Short-term memory has a limited capacity; the capacity of long-term memory is virtually unlimited. (4) Retrieval from short-term memory is an automatic,

dumping-out process; retrieval problems come in long-term memory. (5)
Some drugs and diseases can affect short-term memory without affecting
long-term memory, and vice versa. Let us consider some of these points
further.

Short-Term Memory

Short-term memory refers to how many items can be perceived at one
time—how much a person can consciously pay attention to at once. It is
similar to the older concept of "attention span." Short-term memory has a
rapid forgetting rate. Information stored in short-term memory is forgotten in less than 30 seconds, unless you rehearse the information. (Rehearsing, which consists of repeating the information over and over, can
serve at least two functions: (1) It can keep the information in short-term
memory, and (2) it can help you transfer the information into long-term
memory by giving you time to code it.)

The rapid forgetting rate of short-term memory is shown in an experience that may be familiar to you. Have you ever looked up a telephone
number and forgotten it before you got to the phone to dial it? Or perhaps
you remembered it (by rehearsing it) long enough to dial it, but you
received a busy signal. Then you had to look up the number again to dial it
a few seconds or a few minutes later. The ease with which short-term
memory can be disrupted is shown if someone asks you a question, such as,
"What time is it?" right after you look up a number. You answer, then find
you have to go back to the phone book.

It should be noted that rapid forgetting in short-term memory is not
necessarily undesirable. Imagine how cluttered and jumbled your mind
would be if you were consciously aware of every little bit of information it
recorded. It would be almost impossible to concentrate on one thing or to
select useful information. For example, add the following numbers
mentally: 1, 8, 4, 6, 3, 5. In doing this problem, something like the following probably went through your mind: "1 plus 8 is 9, plus 4 is 13, plus 6 is
19, plus 3 is 22, plus 5 is 27." Of all the numbers that went through your
mind the only one that is necessary to remember for any length of time is
27. All the others needed to be remembered only long enough to use them.
Imagine how difficult it would be to keep track of your addition if each
subtotal did not disappear as soon as you reached the next one. Similarly,
think how hard it would be for a short-order cook to keep track of what he
was doing if he did not forget each order as soon as it had been filled.

Besides having a rapid forgetting rate and being easily disrupted,
short-term memory also has a limited capacity. George A. Miller suggested
that this capacity is around seven items for most people, although subse-

quent research has suggested that the capacity may be slightly less.[6] You can demonstrate the limited capacity of short-term memory by having someone read to you a list of digits one at a time at the rate of about one digit per second. Then you repeat them back. Start with a list of four digits (for example, 8293). Next try a list of five digits (for example, 27136). Add one digit each time, building up to a list of twelve digits (for example, 382749562860). Most people find that when they get much above seven digits they cannot remember all of them long enough to repeat them back. It seems as if they must lose the first few digits to "make room" for the last few. A few people can remember ten or eleven digits, but hardly anyone can go past eleven digits. This demonstration can also be used to illustrate the rapid forgetting rate of short-term memory. Instead of repeating the digits as soon as they are read to you, wait for 10 to 15 seconds to repeat them. If you do not rehearse the digits during this delay, you will find that the numbers of digits you can remember decreases considerably.

We can increase the limited capacity of short-term memory by a process that Miller referred to as "chunking." Chunking consists of grouping separate bits of information into larger chunks. For example, a person can remember the following eight letters, c-o-m-p-l-e-t-e, by chunking them into one word, "complete." Numbers are also easier to remember if they are grouped into chunks. A number such as 266315374264 can be remembered as twelve separate digits, but is easier to remember as four chunks of three digits each—266-315-374-264. Similarly, a phone number can be better remembered as 601/394-1217 than as 6013941217 and a social security number of 513-63-2748 is easier to remember than 513632748.

Miller compared short-term memory to a purse that can hold seven coins. If the coins are pennies, then the capacity of the purse is only 7¢. But if the coins are nickles (each representing a "chunk" of five pennies), then the capacity is 35¢. If they are dimes, the capacity is increased to 70¢. Similarly, short-term memory may be able to hold only about seven items, but we can increase the amount of information contained in these items by grouping the separate bits of information into larger chunks. For example, the capacity of short-term memory is about 8.0 for separate digits, about 7.3 for consonants, about 5.8 for concrete words, and about 1.8 for six-word sentences[7]; assuming that the nouns contain an average of about 4 letters each, we increase the capacity from 7.3 letters using only consonants, to about 23 letters using concrete words, and over 40 letters using sentences.

The principle of chunking suggests that long words would not necessarily be harder to remember than shorter words, even though they contain more letters to remember, if they are remembered as a chunk. One study has, in fact, found that two-syllable, six-letter words were recalled better than one-syllable, four-letter words, when they were equated for frequency, concreteness, and meaningfulness.[8]

Chunking is illustrated also by an interesting phenomenon in chess. An excellent chess player can look for 5 seconds at the board of a chess game in progress, then look away and recall the position of every piece. This suggests that chess masters have unusual memories. However, if the chess pieces are placed randomly on the board, rather than in the positions one would find in a game, then the chess master cannot remember the positions of any more pieces than can the beginning chess player. What makes the difference? The chess master makes use of his vast chess experience to recognize familiar visual patterns and interrelations among the pieces. Rather than remembering the position of each separate piece, he remembers groups (chunks) of pieces. He can only remember about seven chunks, but each of his chunks consists of several pieces.[9]

Long-Term Memory

Long-term memory is what most people mean when they talk about memory. There is evidence that more is stored in our memories, and that memories are more permanently recorded in our brains, than we might assume. Long-term memory is relatively permanent, and has a virtually unlimited capacity. When you really try to remember a specific event, you sometimes find that you can recall more than you thought possible. On repeated recall attempts people can recall more material than they did on the first recall attempt, without having the material presented again.[10] Recall of "forgotten" information (such as early childhood experiences) under drugs or hypnosis also illustrates the large capacity and permanent nature of long-term memory.

Some of the most striking evidence for the large capacity and permanent nature of memory comes from electrical stimulation of the brain. When they are preparing patients for brain surgery, surgeons may touch parts of the brain with an electric probe. The patient is conscious and can report what he experiences as different parts of the brain are electrically stimulated. Under such conditions, patients have reported reliving a previous event, complete with all the sensations experienced at that earlier time. These memories are much more vivid than ordinary memories, as if the electric probe started a film strip or a tape recording on which the details of the event were registered. One man saw himself in his childhood home laughing and talking with his cousins. A woman reported that she heard a song playing that she had not heard since her youth; and she believed that there was a phonograph in the room playing the song. These people are not just reminded of the event, but their memory of the event seems very real, even though they know that they are on the operating table; it is as if they are experiencing a double-consciousness. The experience stops when the probe is removed, and may be repeated if the probe is replaced.[11]

Memory was compared earlier to a filing cabinet. We can now refine the analogy. Short-term memory is like the in-basket on an office desk. Long-term memory is like the large file cabinets in the office. The in-basket has a limited capacity; it can only hold so much, then has to be emptied to make room for more. Some of what is taken out is thrown away and some is put into the file cabinets. But nothing is put into the file cabinets without first going through the in-basket.

Similarly, information goes through short-term memory to reach long-term memory. This makes short-term memory the bottleneck in storing information. Not only does short-term memory have a limited capacity, but information in short-term memory must be coded in some way to be transferred to long-term memory. This coding takes time, which limits the amount of information that can be sent into long-term memory in a given period.

Getting information out of short-term memory is not too hard; everything is dumped out at once. Getting information out of long-term memory is where the problems arise. Some kind of systematic search is necessary. As we saw previously, if the information is not stored in some orderly way, it will be hard to find. The principles and methods discussed in later chapters provide ways to code and categorize information so that it can be efficiently transferred from short-term memory.

Evidence that nerve changes in the brain may be different for short-term memory and long-term memory is provided by brain-damaged patients. One patient had a defective short-term memory with a normal long-term memory. His retention of events in everyday life was not impaired, indicating that his long-term learning ability was normal. However, he could not repeat back number sequences of more than two digits.[12]

Another patient could not form new long-term memory traces, although his short-term memory and his existing long-term memory appeared to be normal. He performed well on tests involving knowledge acquired before his brain damage, and had no apparent personality changes as a result of the brain damage. However, he could not remember any new information for very long. He read the same magazines over and over, and worked the same jigsaw puzzles without realizing he had seen them before. As long as information was held in short-term memory he behaved normally, but when his attention was distracted the contents of his short-term memory were lost. The connecting link between short-term memory and long-term memory seemed to have been broken; he could not transfer information from short-term memory into long-term memory.[13]

The following diagram summarizes many of the points discussed in this section, and pictorally illustrates the relationship between short-term and long-term memory:

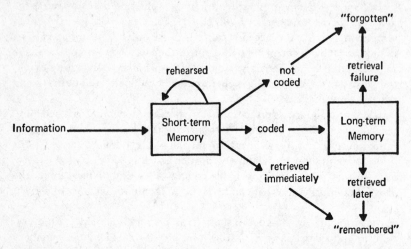

HOW CAN WE MEASURE MEMORY?

There are three main ways to measure how much a person remembers. We can ask him to tell us everything he remembers; we can ask him to pick out the items he remembers from a group of items; or we can see how easily he learns the material a second time. These three approaches are referred to as recall, recognition, and relearning.

Recall

Most people are thinking of recall when they talk about remembering. Recall requires producing information by searching the memory for it. In school, recall is the task you are given in test questions such as "Name the first five presidents of the U.S.," or "Name the capital of Argentina," or "Recite the Gettysburg Address." When most people say they do not remember something, what they mean is that they do not recall it.

A person who is unable to recall something may be able to recall it if he is given some cues. This is called *aided recall*. For example, it is noted in Chapter 3 that giving people the first letters of words they have learned improves their recall of the words. If you are unable to recall the names of the first five presidents, try it again with the first letter of the last name of each president given to you as cues: W, A, J, M, M.

There are several different methods that psychologists use to study recall. In the *free-recall* method a person is presented a list of words one at a time and required to learn the list so that he can recall as many words as possible, in any order. Examples of free recall in everyday life are remembering a shopping list and remembering what movies are playing in town. In the *serial learning* method the person is presented a list of words one at a time, and is required to learn the list so that he can recall the words in the same order they were presented. Serial learning differs from free recall in that the order of recall is important, and each word serves as the cue for the next word. Examples of serial learning in everyday life are learning the alphabet and learning a speech. A third method for studying recall is the *paired-associate* method. In this method pairs of words are shown and the person is required to associate them, so that later when he is given the first word he will recall the second word. Examples of paired-associate learning in everyday life are learning the capitals of states, and learning a foreign language with flash cards. The Link method discussed in Chapter 6 is especially appropriate for improving memory in serial learning tasks. The methods discussed in Chapters 7 to 9 involve also paired-associate learning. All the methods can help in free-recall tasks.

Recognition

A person may be unable to recall something, even when given cues, but may still show evidence of remembering if recognition is used as the measure of memory.[14] When we recognize something, we acknowledge that it is familiar, that we have met it before ("recognition" means literally "to know again"). In recall the test is, "What was the item?", whereas in recognition the test is, "Is this the item?" An example of a recognition task in school is a multiple-choice question such as: Which of the following is the capital of Argentina? (a) Lima, (b) Rio de Janeiro, (c) Santiago, (d) Buenos Aires.

Recognition is usually easier than recall. The reason is that we do not have to search for the information; it is given to us and all we have to do is be able to identify it as something we learned. Most people remember other people's faces better than their names (do you often hear people say, "Your name is familiar but I don't remember your face?"). One reason for this is because remembering the face is usually a recognition task and remembering the name is usually a recall task. Suppose you had to recall the face and describe it, while you merely had to recognize the name from a list of names. In a study in which memory for faces was measured by recall and memory for names was measured by recognition, names were remembered better than faces.[15] Another possible reason why we remember faces better than names is that we see the faces, but only hear the names.

The high sensitivity of recognition as a measure of memory was demonstrated by showing people 600 pairs of items (words, sentences, or pictures). Later the people were shown some of these items paired with new items and were asked to indicate which member of the pair was the one they had seen previously. The average correct recognition score was about 88 percent for sentences, 90 percent for words, and over 98 percent for pictures.[16]

Relearning

A person may be unable to recall something, to recall it with cues, or even to recognize it, but may still show evidence of remembering by the third measure—relearning. Suppose you measure how long it takes you to learn something the first time. Later you measure how long it takes you to learn it again. If you learn it faster the second time, then that is evidence that you still have some memory of the material.

Relearning may be illustrated by the common experience of a person who studies a foreign language that he learned many years ago. He may not be able to recall any of it. He may recognize very little. But when he starts studying it, he may find that it comes back to him rather easily. Similarly, you may not be able to recite the Gettysburg Address or the Declaration of Independence, or something else that you learned in school, but you could probably relearn them faster than someone who has never seen them before.

An interesting study that a psychologist conducted on his own son illustrates that relearning is a very sensitive measure of memory, and also that relearning may show evidence of memory even when the material was not fully learned originally. The psychologist read passages of Greek to his son from the age of 15 months to 3 years. He later tested the boy for retention at the ages of 8, 14, and 18 by having him memorize the original passages and some other comparable new passages. At age 8 it took the boy 27 percent fewer trials to memorize the original passages than the new passages, suggesting a considerable savings in relearning effort as a result of retention of the earlier learning. The methods of recall and recognition would likely have shown no evidence of remembering. The savings decreased from 27 percent at age 8, to 8 percent by age 14, and to only 1 percent by age 18.[17]

In summary, it is not accurate to say that you do not remember something merely because you do not recall it. Information that is available in memory may be inaccessible by recall, but may be accessible by recognition or relearning. Recognition is generally a more sensitive measure of memory than is recall in the sense of detecting retention where recall does not. Likewise, relearning is more sensitive than recognition. If you can recognize something, or can relearn it faster than you learned it the first time, then that indicates that you have some memory of it even though you cannot recall it. This is one answer to the person who says that it does not do any good for him to read something because he cannot "remember" (recall) it anyway.

Similarly, students who criticize school exams because they forget most of what they learn soon after the exam are basing their complaint solely on recall. It is interesting to note that some of these same college students may complain that a certain course is a waste of time because they have had the same material in another course. This suggests that they have not forgotten the material, because they can still recognize it.

Of course, practically speaking, most people are more concerned with recall than with recognition or relearning because most of us have the greatest problems with recall. One way in which the mnemonic systems discussed in Chapters 6 to 9 help recall is to change recall to aided recall by providing you with cues that you can use to cue yourself.

With respect to measuring memory, a method that is frequently used to study memory should be noted. One of the problems in studying memory is that people have different degrees of familiarity with different words. Thus, if one person learns a list of words faster than another person, it might be because he has seen those words more often. To control for this difference in familiarity, much research on learning has used *nonsense syllables* that are unfamiliar to virtually everyone who participates in the study. A nonsense syllable is a three-letter "word" such as CEJ, JUL, ZIB, LOF, or TAF.

HOW DO WE REMEMBER PICTURES VERSUS WORDS?

Information may be recorded in memory either in visual form (pictures) or in verbal form (words). For example, you may see in your mind's eye a visual image (a mental picture) of a chair or you may think of the word "chair." These two types of recording processes may be referred to as, respectively, an *imagery process* and a *verbal process*. Research shows that there are several ways in which visual material, such as scenes, faces, and pictures, is remembered differently from verbal material, such as words, names, and numbers.

The imagery process appears to be best suited for representing concrete events and objects and concrete words, whereas the verbal process may be best suited for representing abstract verbal information. One reason for this is that concrete nouns are better able than abstract nouns to produce mental images. (The following four words illustrate the difference between concrete and abstract nouns: *apple* is more concrete than *fruit*, *fruit* is more concrete than *food,* and *food* is more concrete than *nourishment.* It is easier to picture an apple in your mind than it is to picture nourishment.)[18]

There is some evidence that concrete words are processed in the memory differently from abstract words. Concrete words and their associated images may be processed by the visual system, whereas abstract words may be processed by an auditory-linguistic system.[19] Not only may visual and verbal memories be different *processes,* but they may also occur in different *places.* There is evidence that visual memory and verbal memory are located in different parts of the brain. The right half of the brain seems to play the predominant role in the visual imagery process; while the left half seems to predominate in the verbal process.[20] There is even evidence that words we hear are stored differently from words we see.[21]

Further evidence for a difference between verbal and visual memory is suggested by the finding that verbal and visual memory processes may operate at different speeds. The average person can generate the twenty-six letters of the alphabet (speaking to himself) in about 4 seconds, but it takes about 13 seconds to generate visual images of the twenty-six letters. Also, it takes longer to name a picture than to read the corresponding printed word.[22]

The capacity of memory for pictures may be almost unlimited. We saw earlier that recognition memory for 600 pictures was very high (98 percent). Another study illustrates this fact even more strikingly. People were shown 2,560 different pictures over a period of several days. They were later shown 280 pairs of pictures. One of each pair was a picture the person had seen before and the other was not. The people were asked to indicate which of the two pictures they had seen before. In this recognition task they correctly identified about 90 percent of the pictures. Later research has found equally striking results with as many as 10,000 pictures, and also found that picture memory exceeds word memory when measured by recall as well as by recognition.[23]

The saying that "one picture is worth a thousand words" is usually applied to the effectiveness of a picture in communicating an idea that would take many words to express; it may also apply to the effectiveness of a picture in remembering what was communicated. For example, pictures of objects are remembered better than verbal descriptions of the objects, and better than the names of the objects, both by young children and by adults.[24] Similarly, one reason why visual imagery may be a powerful aid in recalling verbal material is because images are apparently more memorable than words alone.[25]

Another reason why imagery may help in recalling verbal material is that imagery may be processed in a nonverbal location as well as in a verbal location.[26] This means that a word that can be visualized can be processed both in a verbal location and a visual location. This dual representation (verbal and visual) of concrete words may make them recalled better than abstract terms which are only verbal, because any information that is represented in two ways is more likely to be recalled than if it is represented in only one way.[27] You are more likely to remember words plus images better than words alone for the same reason that it is better to leave two notes for yourself than to leave only one, or that it is better to cross-reference a paper under two headings in a file cabinet: it is twice as likely that you will be able to retrieve the message.

Of course the two explanations above for why images may help memory are not mutually exclusive. It may be that pictures are inherently more memorable than words *and* that pictures are coded both visually and verbally.[28]

In the nineteenth century, one researcher who found that visual images of objects were remembered better than their written names suggested that

> the fact that mental images of objects are remembered better than their names is of great pedagogical significance, indicating that if objects are shown children, or when that is impracticable, if they are led to form mental images of them, they can obtain a genuine knowledge of things more readily than they can be crammed with the verbal appearance of knowledge.[29]

Almost eighty years later Ralph Haber similarly suggested that one implication of the findings on visual vs. verbal memory "is that if techniques could be found to facilitate an attaching of words to visual images, recall might dramatically improve."[30] This is, in fact, what most mnemonic systems do. We will see in Chapter 3 that visual imagery can indeed improve recall dramatically. We will also see in later chapters that visual imagery plays a central role in mnemonic systems.

WHY DO WE FORGET?

In discussing short-term memory it was noted that forgetting is not all bad. If you did not forget, your mind would be cluttered with so many trivial things that it would be impossible to select the useful and relevant items you need for decisions. Thus, it is not desirable to clutter your mind with unimportant things. Forgetting the unimportant may help you remember the important. The trick is, of course, to be able to forget the unimportant, not the important. Research on "intentional forgetting" indicates that people can forget what they want to forget, [31] but unfortunately we also sometimes forget what we do not want to forget.

You probably do not have to be told that forgetting is easier than remembering. But why is it? One way of answering this question is to consider again the 3 R's of Remembering. To forget something you only have to fail at any one of the three stages, recording, retaining, or retrieving. But to remember something you have to be successful at all three of these stages. It is as if there is only one chance to remember and three chances to forget.

Several explanations have been suggested for why we forget. Let us briefly consider four of the classical explanations:

1. Passive decay. This explanation says that memories cause some kind of a physical "trace" in the brain which gradually fades away with time, much as a pathway across a meadow will become overgrown if not used. The basis of forgetting is disuse. This is one of the oldest and most widespread explanations of forgetting.

2. Repression. This explanation was suggested by the work of Sigmund Freud on the unconscious mind. According to Freud, unpleasant or unacceptable memories may be forgotten intentionally. They are pushed into the unconscious on purpose so the person will not have to live with them. Although some of the details of Freud's elaborate theories are not widely accepted, most psychologists do believe that such motivated forgetting can occur.

3. Systematic distortion. Memories may be affected by our values and interests, so that we remember some things the way we *want* to remember them. This explanation suggests that we change our memories to fit with what we want them to be or how we feel they should be.

To demonstrate such distortion, read the following list of words aloud to someone: bed, rest, awake, tired, dream, wake, night, eat, comfort, sound, slumber, snore. Now ask the person to list as many of the words as he can remember. Usually, at least half of the people's lists include the word "sleep." Why? Because most of the words are related to sleep, so it seems like "sleep" *should* be on the list.[32]

Some people were asked to wait in a room that had a poster on the wall. They were then taken into another room where some of them were asked to describe the poster in as much detail as possible. All of them were later shown the poster and were asked whether it was the one they had seen before. The people who had tried to recall the poster were more likely to say that it was *not* the one they had seen before. Why? Because it did not match the somewhat distorted perception they had recalled; in fact, some of them defended their judgment by noting details they had mentioned in recall that were not in the poster.[33]

Systematic distortion has some interesting implications for courtroom practices and eyewitness investigations. For example, by asking leading questions, a questioner can cause a person to "remember" an event that never occurred; "What color was the victim's coat?" may cause a person to remember a coat that did not exist. Similarly, statements that only imply a conclusion may cause a person to remember the conclusion as if it had happened; "I ran up to the burglar alarm" may lead the person to later "remember" that I rang the alarm.[34]

4. Interference. Forgetting may not be affected so much by how much time passes (as is suggested by the passive delay explanation) as it is by what happens during that time. Much forgetting is likely due to interference by other learning. Interference does not imply a limited memory capacity, where new information that is stuffed into our heads pushes the old information out. It is not so much the *amount* we learn as it is *what* we learn that determines forgetting by interference.

Information you have learned in the past may interfere with your memory for something you have learned recently. Psychologists refer to this as "proactive inhibition." It is "proactive" because the interference is in a forward direction; learned material affects memory for material learned later. It is "inhibition" because the effect is to hinder or inhibit the memory for the later material. Likewise, information you have recently learned may interfere with your memory for something you learned in the past. This is called "retroactive inhibition." Suppose that you met a number of people at a business meeting last week, then met some more people at a party last night. If you try to recall the names of the people at the party you may find the names from the business meeting getting in the way. This is proactive inhibition. If you try to recall the names of the people at the business meeting you may find that the names of the party-goers get in the way. This is retroactive inhibition.

To illustrate these four explanations of forgetting, let us compare your memory to the attic of a house. You store things in your memory and in your attic. Now let us suppose that you go to the attic to find a specific item. The passive-decay explanation of forgetting would be like a "deteriorating room"; you cannot find your item because it has been left in the attic so long that it has deteriorated and disappeared. The repression explanation would be like a "walled-up room"; the attic is blocked off, so you cannot get into it to find the item. The systematic distortion explanation would be somewhat like a "rearranged room"; objects in the attic are all mixed up so you cannot find your item because things are not arranged as you thought you left them. The interference explanation would be like a "cluttered room"; the room has become cluttered with other things that get in the way when you try to find your item.[35]

This book will not deal much with the first three explanations of forgetting. Passive decay is not well-substantiated by research. It may apply to short-term memory, but probably not to long-term memory. Repression, although fairly well-substantiated by clinical experiences, primarily involves memories of traumatic, unpleasant, personal experiences. These kinds of memories are not of central concern in this book. Systematic distortion is substantiated by some research evidence, but there is not a lot we can do about it except perhaps to be aware of it and guard against it. There is research evidence to indicate that interference is responsible for much of our forgetting. We will discuss some ways to reduce interference in Chapter 4. We will also see in Chapter 5 how mnemonic systems may help reduce interference.

There is one other explanation of forgetting that is more recent than the four that have been discussed. It attributes forgetting to retrieval failure. The memory does not fade away, nor is it interfered with by other information, but is merely dependent on your finding the right cue to get it. This explanation is thus referred to as *cue-dependent forgetting*. It says that if you can find the right cue, you can retrieve a desired item from memory; if you "forget" the item it is because you have not found the right cue. There is a considerable amount of research support for this explanation.[36] The mnemonic systems in Chapters 6 to 9 help by providing cues to find the information.

HOW FAST DO WE FORGET?

What is the rate of forgetting? Research on memory indicates that we do not forget at a constant rate but that most forgetting occurs fairly soon after learning, then the rate of forgetting levels off as time passes. Thus, most of what we forget about something will occur shortly after we have learned it. Of course, not all learning follows this pattern. Material that is learned very thoroughly, or that is very important to us, may be retained all our lives.

What is the difference between a slow learner and a fast learner in their forgetting rates? Will a slow learner forget more rapidly than a fast learner? Contrary to the belief of many people, the answer to this question appears to be no. An analogy used by Benton Underwood illustrates why this is so.[37] He compares the learning process to the pumping of water into a pyramid-shaped beaker (see the diagram below). Learning is represented by the level of water. Forgetting is indicated by evaporation. As the level of water rises, the surface area decreases, so there is less evaporation. Fast input (beaker A) represents the fast learner; his beaker fills up faster. However, in time the slow input (beaker B) will fill the beaker just as full. If we run water into each beaker for the same amount of time, less evaporation will occur from beaker A because it will be fuller and thus have less surface area. But if we let the water continue to run into B until it reaches the same level as A, then there will be no difference between the two in the rate of evaporation.

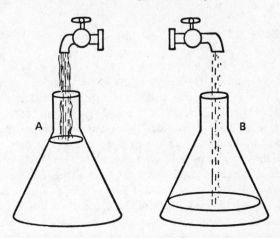

Similarly, if a slow learner is allowed enough time to study something so that he can reproduce it as readily as a fast learner, he will score just as high as the fast learner in later tests of remembering. The ultimate *degree* of learning rather than the *rate* of learning is the critical factor in the rate of forgetting.[38]

Underwood has suggested an implication of the beaker analogy for students in school. A bright student may do better on an examination than a dull one because he has learned the material more effectively, not because he has a better memory. If both students study a lesson for an hour, the bright student will master the lesson more fully—he will have filled his beaker to a higher level. But if the dull student fills his beaker to the same level by studying two or three hours, then he is likely to do equally well on the examination. Thus, students of average learning ability can do as well in school as students with greater learning ability by spending more time studying.

The beaker analogy can also illustrate the rate of forgetting for meaningful material vs. meaningless material. Let beaker A represent the meaningful material and beaker B the meaningless material. The more meaningful the material is, the faster it is learned. Does this mean that it is remembered longer? Not necessarily. If the less meaningful material is studied until it is learned as well as the meaningful material, then there will be no significant difference in how fast the two are forgotten. Again, the rate of forgetting is determined more by how well the material is learned than by how fast it is learned.

One implication of the principle underlying the beaker analogy is that techniques that help you learn material faster will not necessarily help you remember it longer. Research evidence indicates that this can happen.[39]

IS IT "ON THE TIP OF YOUR TONGUE"?

Have you ever had the experience of almost being able to recall a specific word, but not quite being able to get it? You feel that you know the word but are unable to recall it. You may have had this experience when trying to recall a name. Perhaps you could tell what letter it started with, or even what it rhymed with, but could not quite get the name. It is from such a situation that we get the expression, "It's on the tip of my tongue."

I had such an experience when trying to recall the last name of a person I knew many years ago. I could picture him in my mind, but could not think of his name. In searching my mind for the name, I thought of Scotland and of hillbillies. It seemed that the name had two syllables, and was rather short. Finally it came to me. The name was "McCoy." Now the associations were obvious. The Scottish association came from the "Mc" prefix (McDuff, McDougall, etc.). The hillbilly association came from a past television show about hillbillies entitled "The Real McCoys."

You might expect that psychologists would have tried to study such an interesting and widespread phenomenon, and you would be right. One way to study the "tip-of-the-tongue," or "feeling-of-knowing," phenomenon has been to ask people questions of general information. Some people could not recall the answers, but still felt they knew them. Later recognition tests showed that they were right. In other research on the tip-of-the-tongue phenomenon, the definitions of words that are infrequently used (such as *sextant, nepotism, sampan*) were read to college students. The students were asked to say what the word was. If they could not think of the exact word, they were to tell everything they could about the word. Some people could give other words with a similar meaning or similar sounds (sound being more frequent than meaning), tell the first or last letter of the word, and even tell how many syllables it had, but could not quite tell the word itself. For example, when tying to remember *sampan* (a small Chinese boat), they thought of such words as *Saipan, Siam*, and *sarong* ; they also thought of words similar in meaning such as *barge* and *junk*.[40]

The initial studies on the tip-of-the-tongue phenomenon were published in the mid-1960s. Research interest in this topic has recently been revived; several studies published during the 1970s have duplicated the initial findings, and have investigated possible theoretical explanations and implications of the phenomenon. The phenomenon has also been studied in memory for people's names. For example, when people are shown pictures of famous persons and asked to recall their names, some can recall the first letter of a name, other names that sound like the name, and the number of syllables in the name, without recalling the name itself. More frequently, however, people recall the famous person's profession and where they have seen the person's face most recently, without recalling the person's name.[41]

The tip-of-the-tongue phenomenon has at least four implications for understanding memory. First, it suggests that memory is not an all-or-none phenomenon. Memory is a matter of degree; it is a continuum, not a dichotomy. We do not necessarily remember something either completely or not at all. Rather, we can remember a part of something without remembering all of it. A second implication of the tip-of-the-tongue phenomenon is that most memory is generative, not duplicative. Memory is not an automatic picture-taking process. Most memories do not appear as fullblown, exact duplicates of the information learned, but are generated through a process of reconstruction. A third implication is that words may be stored in memory in more than one way. They may be stored in auditory terms (how many syllables, and how they are pronounced), in visual terms (the first and last letters of the word), and in terms of meaning (cross-referenced with other words of similar meaning). Finally, the tip-of-the-tongue effect illustrates the difference between availability and accessibility of information. That the information is available is shown by the fact that the people know when they know the answer to a question, or they can produce part of the word they are trying to recall. But although the information is available, it is not accessible by unaided recall.

WHAT IS A PHOTOGRAPHIC MEMORY?

Wouldn't it be great to have a photographic memory, working like a camera taking a snapshot? You could take a quick picture of a page of print, or of a scene, then describe it in complete detail any time later by conjuring up the snapshot in your mind. Are there people who can do this? Would it solve all your memory problems if you could do it?

Most psychologists do not believe in this popular notion of a photographic memory. However, there is a phenomenon that is somewhat similar to the notion of photographic memory. Psychologists call it "eidetic imagery."[42] The word *eidetic* means "identical" or "duplicative." Eidetic imagery is a very strong visual after-image that enables a person to duplicate the picture mentally and describe it in detail shortly after looking at it. Eidetic imagery has been very hard to study objectively, but most research indicates that it differs from normal imagery in *degree* but not in *kind* — it is merely a more powerful version of the capacity for visual imagery that we all possess. No more than 5 to 10 percent of children possess eidetic imagery, and it is even rarer after adolescence.

Eidetic imagery differs from the popular notion of photographic memory in several ways: First, the eidetic image fades away soon after viewing the scene. It does not stay with a person over a prolonged period of time, but lasts for a few seconds to a few minutes. Second, the eidetic image is affected by the subjective state of the viewer. The image may contain additions, omissions, or distortions, and the aspects of the scene that are of most interest to the person tend to be reproduced in most detail. The image is not an objective reproduction like a camera photograph. Third, the person does not take a split-second snapshot, but requires a viewing time of several seconds to scan the scene. Fourth, images cannot be brought back once they have faded away. Thus, people with eidetic imagery do not seem to be able to use their eidetic images to improve long-term memory.

Some researchers have studied people who seem to have photographic memories that are not subject to all of the above limitations. One 23-year-old woman reportedly could look at a page of poetry in a foreign language and years later repeat it verbatim, reading either forward or backward. She could retain a pattern of 10,000 black-and-white squares in her mind for as long as three months. However, she did not just take a snapshot like a camera would, but required some time to scan the pattern.[43]

A well-known example of another person who seemed to have a photographic memory is given in the account of a Russian newspaper reporter, S, by Alexandr Luria. S was able to recall perfectly as many as seventy words or numbers presented once, and could later produce them in reverse order (you can get an idea of how difficult this is by trying to repeat the alphabet backwards). He invariably performed successfully in experiments to test his retention (without being given any warning) fifteen or sixteen *years* after the session in which he had originally recalled the words. Luria's description of these test sessions is interesting:

> During these test sessions S would sit with his eyes closed, pause, then comment: "Yes, yes . . . This was a series you gave me once when we were in your apartment . . . You were sitting at the table and I in the rocking chair . . . You were wearing a gray suit and you looked at me like this . . . Now, then, I can

see you saying . . ." And with that he would reel off the series precisely as I had given it to him at the earlier session. If one takes into account that S had by then become a well-known mnemonist, who had to remember hundreds and thousands of series, the feat seems even more remarkable.[44]

Like the 23-year-old woman just described, S did not just take a snapshot of the information, but required time to study it. For example, memorizing a table of fifty numbers required 2½ to 3 minutes of study. One of the methods S used to perform such feats is similar to the Loci system discussed in Chapter 7 of this book.

My main concern with the popular notion of photographic memory is that it leads people to believe that a person who remembers well has some *thing* that others do not. Seeing a person perform a fantastic memory feat, they shrug their shoulders and say, "I sure wish I had a photographic memory." The fact that this person has a photographic memory seems to give them a convenient excuse for not being able to remember as well as he can.

There may possibly be such a thing as photographic memory — I cannot completely discount the possibility of its existence, because of rare examples like the two just described that seem to confirm its existence. More generally, there are likely innate differences between people in their memory ability. But whatever innate differences there may be between people, they are not nearly as important as learned memory skills. And most of what people attribute to "photographic memory" is probably not something innate, but merely the application of powerful memory techniques such as those discussed in Chapters 6 to 9.

A photographic memory is not necessary to perform amazing feats of memory. One man, VP, who apparently relied on verbal memory rather than visual memory, could look at a 6×8 matrix of forty-eight digits for about 4 minutes and recall all forty-eight digits in any order two weeks later. A nineteenth-century memory prodigy could memorize a hundred digit number in 12 minutes if the digits were read to him, but he became confused if the digits were shown in him in writing; another person could recite two and a half pages of material after reading it only once, although he had poor visual imagery.[45]

I have done a demonstration several times that illustrates the difference between photographic memory and the application of powerful memory techniques. The demonstration consists of memorizing a fifty-page magazine completely enough to be able to answer such questions as: What is on page 32? On what page is the article about communication? What is on the page opposite the picture of a tower? How many pictures are on page 46? How many people are in the lower left picture on page 9, and what are they doing? Who wrote the article about tolerance? What is the name of the main character in the story that begins on page 17, and what happened to her on page 19?

When I finish such a demonstration someone usually asks if I have a photographic memory. I explain to them that I possess no such power, but merely use powerful mnemonic techniques explained in this book. The fact that I do not have a photographic memory is shown by an occasional question that I cannot answer, such as How many of the people in the picture on page 21 are wearing glasses?, or What is the third word on page 42? If I did not consciously record this information when studying the magazine in the first place, I cannot answer the question. On the other hand, if I had a photographic memory I could merely conjure up in my mind a picture of page 21 or page 42 and count how many people are wearing glasses, or read the third word.

There is another interesting memory phenomenon that is somewhat related to the notion of photographic memory. Some people possess one outstanding mental ability, such as a so-called photographic memory, a chess-playing ability, or the ability to do complex mathematical calculations in their heads, but lack general intelligence. Such a person is called an *idiot savant*, a term meaning "wise idiot."

Having a so-called photographic memory, or any other outstanding mental skill, is not necessarily a blessing. Idiot savants are generally incompetent at anything other than their one feat, being unable to reason or to comprehend meaning. In some cases they may even be retarded in areas others than that of their feat. Similarly, S's photographic memory was in many ways more of a burden than a blessing. When he tried to read, every word brought forth an image; these images cluttered his mind and prevented him from understanding what he was reading. He also found it hard to erase images that were no longer useful (remember our earlier discussion of how difficult it would be to select relevant information if all the information were constantly at the fore of our awareness). In addition, S could only understand what was concrete enough to visualize. Thus, abstract ideas presented problems and torments to him, as did metaphors and synonyms (when a person was called a "baby" on one page and a "child" on another, it was hard for him to understand that the words were referring to the same person). Thus, it was very difficult for S to understand the overall meaning of material he read.

CAN YOU LEARN IN YOUR SLEEP?

Think how much time and effort you would save in learning if you could just play a tape recording of the material while you were asleep and learn it. Isn't it a shame to waste all that time sleeping, when you could be learning something useful at the same time? This is the kind of argument offered in advertisements for sleep-learning machines. Some radio stations have even broadcast messages during the night to help sleeping people lose weight, quit smoking, and reduce tension.[46] Can you really learn in your sleep? Dozens of studies have been conducted on sleep learning in the United States and in the USSR. Extensive reviews of these studies are available elsewhere, so we will just briefly consider a few representative studies.[47]

A central issue in determining whether you can learn in your sleep is what we mean by *sleep*. There are several stages of sleep, ranging from very light to very deep. Early studies that showed positive effects of sleep learning did not determine whether a person was really asleep, and, if so, how deeply asleep he was.

Two controlled studies were done in which the level of sleep was measured by observing the people's brain-wave patterns on an electroencephalograph. In one study, questions and answers were read to people while they were sound asleep. When the people were questioned after waking, it was found that the more deeply asleep they were when it was presented, the less they remembered of the material. Their answers to questions that were read to them in deep sleep showed no evidence of being remembered. In a second study, a recording of ten words was played as many as eighty-two times to people when the electroencephalograph indicated that they were sound asleep. After waking, they were asked to choose the ten words from a list of fifty. They showed no evidence of remembering the ten words.[48]

In a similar study conducted more recently, the people were awakened and tested immediately after the material was presented, rather than waiting until the next day. Again, there was no evidence that they remembered any of the material presented to them.[49] These studies, plus most other evidence, indicate that you cannot learn while you are sound asleep. In 1970 the New York attorney general banned the advertising of a language-learning machine that claimed to teach a person in his sleep, on the grounds that there was no evidence that a language could be learned in one's sleep.[50]

What about light sleep? Is it possible to remember material that is read to you when you are just barely asleep? There is some evidence that people may learn while in states of drowsiness or of very light sleep. Most of this research has been conducted in the USSR. In one study that was conducted in the United States, people were read statements like "A is for Apple" during different stages of sleep. After they awoke, they were asked to check any familiar word on a list of ten words beginning with "A." Correct words were recognized from 28 percent of the statements presented in the lightest stage of sleep, 10 percent in the next lightest stage, and none in deep sleep.[51]

The suggestion that it may be possible to learn in very light sleep s subject to several conditions. (1) The material must be presented at just the right level of drowsiness or light sleep. If the person is not asleep enough, the material will wake him up. If he is too deeply asleep, he will not remember any of it. (2) No complex material or material involving reasoning or understanding can be learned. Only material such as nonsense syllables, Morse code, technical expressions, facts, dates, foreign languages, and formulas constitute potential materials for sleep learning. (3) Even when both of these conditions are met, sleep learning is not sufficient by itself, but only as an aid to daytime studies. Thus, it appears that even if it may be possible to learn some kinds of material in some stages of sleep, it is an inefficient way to learn. You are better off to stay awake while you are studying or listening to a lecture.

There is research evidence that indicates that people can remember more if they go to sleep immediately after learning than if they stay awake during the same period of time. However, the learning itself took place when the people were awake.[52]

Related research has been done on subliminal learning and advertising. "Subliminal" means below the level of conscious awareness, and refers to messages that are too fast or too weak for us to be aware of them. During the 1950s "subliminal advertising" became publicized and people became concerned about its implications for mind control. A famous case indicated that messages saying "Eat popcorn" and "Drink Coca-Cola" were flashed on a movie screen during a movie. They were flashed so fast that no one was consciously aware of them. Popcorn sales reportedly shot up 50 percent and Coke sales went up 18 percent. Many people were justifiably concerned at the implications of this report. However, well-controlled research studies have found no evidence that subliminal messages have significant effects on either learning or behavior.[53]

Thus, whether you are asleep or awake, you are not likely to learn and remember material if you are not consciously aware that it is being presented to you.

SUMMARY

There is no such thing as a memory in the sense of some *thing* that can be seen, touched, or weighed. Memory is an abstraction referring to a set of skills rather than to an object. Neither is there a single standard for judging a good or poor memory. There are a number of different ways in which a person may have a "good" memory.

Memory is generally viewed as consisting of three stages: (1) acquisition refers to learning the material; (2) storage refers to keeping the material in the brain until it is needed; and (3) retrieval refers to getting the material back out when it is needed. These three stages may be viewed as the 3 R's of Remembering: Recording, Retaining, and Retrieving. Retrieving is where most problems come. We cannot do much about retrieval directly; but since retrieval is a function of recording, we can improve it by improving our methods of recording.

Memory consists of at least two different processes: short-term memory and long-term memory. Short-term memory has a limited capacity and a rapid forgetting rate. Its capacity can be increased by chunking, or grouping separate bits of information into larger chunks. Long-term memory has a virtually unlimited capacity. Short-term memory and long-term memory also differ in several other ways.

One measure of memory is recall, which requires you to produce information by searching the memory for it. In aided recall, you are given cues to help you produce the information. In free-recall learning you recall the material in any order; in serial learning you recall it in the order it was presented; and in paired-associate learning you learn pairs of words so that when the first word is given you can recall the second word. A second measure of memory is recognition, in which you do not have to produce the information from memory, but must be able to identify it when it is presented to you. In a third measure of memory, relearning, the difference between how long it took to learn the material the first time and how long it takes to learn it again indicates how much you remember. Relearning is generally a more sensitive measure of memory than is recognition, in the sense of showing retention where recognition does not; recognition is generally a more sensitive measure than recall.

Some material may be remembered in visual form (pictures), and other material may be remembered in verbal form (words). Some research evidence indicates that there are two different memory processes for these two kinds of material. Pictures may be processed differently from words, and concrete words high in imagery may be processed differently from abstract words low in imagery. Visual images are easier to remember than words alone, leading some researchers to suggest that we should try to use visual images as much as possible in memory.

There are several explanations of why we forget. Passive-decay theory says that learning causes a physical "trace" in the brain that decays with time. Repression theory says that we purposely push unpleasant or unacceptable memories into our unconscious mind. Systematic-distortion theory says that our memories may be distorted by our values and interests, to be consistent with how we want the memories to be or how we think they should be. Interference theory says that forgetting is due to interference by other learning. Retrieval failure theory says that forgetting is due to problems in retrieving the information, and that we can remember almost anything if given the right cues. The last two of these explanations are the ones of most interest in this book.

Most research on memory indicates that we forget much of what we have learned immediately after learning it, then the rate of forgetting levels off. Slow learners and fast learners do not differ in their rate of forgetting if the slow learner is allowed more time to study the material originally so he can learn it as well as the fast learner. It is the *degree* of learning rather than the *rate* of learning that is critical in rate of forgetting. Similarly, meaningless material may take longer to learn than meaningful material, but it is not forgotten faster if learned equally well. Methods to help you learn material faster do not necessarily help you remember it longer.

The tip-of-the-tongue phenomenon refers to being *almost* able to recall something. You feel that it is on the tip of your tongue. Research on this phenomenon suggests that memory is not an all-or-none matter, that much memory is generative rather than duplicative, that material may be stored in memory in more than one way, and that material in memory may be available without being accessible.

Eidetic imagery differs from the popular notion of photographic memory in several ways. The eidetic image fades away soon after viewing the scene; it is affected by the subjective state of the viewer; it requires a viewing time of several seconds or minutes; and it cannot be brought back once it has faded away. Some researchers have reported very striking cases of people with strong eidetic imagery.

The main problem with the popular notion of photographic memory is that it leads people to believe that a person who remembers well has some *thing* that they do not have. Even if there are innate differences in memory ability, these differences are not as important as learned memory skills. Much of what people attribute to "photographic memory" is really the application of powerful mnemonic techniques. Having one outstanding mental skill is not necessarily a blessing. Some people, called *idiot savants,* have a photographic memory or some other outstanding mental skill, but lack general intelligence.

Despite popular notions and some advertising claims, research evidence does not support the claim that people can learn in their sleep, although there is some evidence for learning certain kinds of materials in very light sleep. There is no substantial evidence to support the claim that people can learn, or be influenced by, material that is presented too fast or too weakly for them to be consciously aware of it.

CHAPTER 3

Principles
of Memory Improvement

Psychologists have done a considerable amount of research on principles of learning. The basic principles on which learning and memory are based include: meaningfulness, organization, association, visualization, attention, interest, and feedback. The mnemonic systems discussed in later chapters use many of these principles. Many people seem to be aware of at least some of the principles, because in memorizing people try various techniques to recode the material, reorganize it, give it meaning, and in some way make sense of it.[1]

MEANINGFULNESS:
"THAT DOESN'T MAKE SENSE"

One of the determinants of how easy something is to learn is how meaningful it is to the learner. If it doesn't make sense, it will be hard to learn; the more meaningful it is, the easier it will be to learn. Words are easier to remember than nonsense syllables. Concrete words are easier to remember than abstract words. Words grouped into meaningful categories are easier to remember than words given in meaningless order. Sentences are easier to remember than words in ungrammatical order. And well-organized paragraphs are easier to remember than disorganized ones. At all levels, meaningfulness affects memory.[2]

In an old study that shows the effect of meaning on learning, people memorized a list of 200 nonsense syllables, a 200-word passage of prose, and 200 words of poetry. The nonsense syllables took about 1½ hours to memorize, while the prose took less than ½ hour, and the poetry took about 10 minutes.[3]

People who participate in experiments on learning sometimes try various personal strategies to give meaning to a list of words or nonsense syllables so they can learn them easier. They may try converting a nonsense syllable into a meaningful word by using a substitute word (HAWK for HOK), adding a letter (TACK for TAC), or substituting a letter (CUT for KUT). Others try organizing material into meaningful units or looking for a pattern. These people realize that in order to remember something, you should try to make it meaningful.[4]

Many of the principles discussed later in this chapter (for example, association, visualization, organization) help to make material meaningful. In addition to these other principles, familiarity, rhymes, patterns, acronyms, and acrostics can help to make material meaningful.

Familiarity

Generally, the more you know about a particular subject the easier it is to learn new information about it. Learning builds upon learning. If you already know something about a topic, if you are already familiar with it, then not only will the new information be more meaningful, but you will also have something with which to associate it (association is discussed later). For example, if you gave a list of cooking terms and sports terms to a group of men and women, the women would likely memorize the cooking terms faster, and the men the sports terms; these terms are more familiar, and thus more meaningful, to them. Familiar items are not only more likely than unfamiliar items to be recalled correctly, but are also recalled more quickly.[5]

Joyce Brothers described how she prepared for a TV quiz show on the subject of boxing. She started by spending five weeks studying a boxing encyclopedia. She read every other book and magazine article she could find on boxing. She associated with people who were interested in boxing and attended boxing matches. She immersed herself in boxing. The more she learned about boxing, the easier it was to learn and remember new things because they were more meaningful to her.[6]

The study described in Chapter 2 in which a 3-year-old child who was read passages of Greek showed some memory of the Greek at age 8 suggests another advantage of familiarity. Exposure to something may result in partial learning of it, even without intent to learn.[7] Thus, the child whose parents read to him may later learn to read more easily, or the child with music in his house may later learn music more easily.

One reason children from low-income families have a difficult time in school may be that they have not had as much exposure as middle-class children to words and concepts that they could build on in school. To illustrate how learning can build on learning, suppose a kindergarten teacher who has gone to Europe for the summer takes two coins to her class. She shows the first one to her students and says, "This is an Austrian shilling." Then she shows the other one and says, "This is a French franc."

Now, suppose there is a boy in the class whose family has been to Europe. He has heard his parents talk about Austria and France, and about exchanging American dollars for foreign money. In addition, he has been given money to spend for himself; he knows the difference between various United States coins. On the other hand, there is a little girl in the class who has never heard of Austria and France. She has never had any money of her own to spend, so that she has only a vague idea of what a coin is.

Which of these two children is more likely to remember, on the following day, which of the two coins the teacher holds up is the shilling and which is the franc? Naturally the boy is more likely to learn and remember, because he possesses some knowledge to which the words "shilling" and "franc" can be attached. The girl has nothing inside her to which the words can readily be attached.[8]

Rhymes

Do you remember when Columbus discovered America? In fourteen-hundred and ninety-two, what happened? Most likely you learned this rhyme at one time: "In 1492, Columbus sailed the ocean blue." Similarly, "*i* before *e* except after *c*; or when sounded as *a*, as in neighbor and weigh," helps to remember how to spell words with *ie* in them. Many people rely on a rhyme to help remember how many days are in each month: "30 days hath September, April, June, and November. . . ." Rhythm and rhyme are used by children in learning the alphabet with the following jingle:

> ABCDEFG
> HI-JK-LMNOP
> QRS and TUV
> WX, Y and Z
> Now I've said my ABC's
> Tell me what you think of me

These are examples of the value of rhymes in remembering. If you can make up a rhyme involving the material to be learned it will make the material more meaningful and thus easier to learn.

Research has shown that when you are trying to recall a word, other words that rhyme with it may be effective cues to help recall it, and that when a list of words is recalled, words that rhyme tend to be recalled together, even though they were not together in the original list.[9]

Patterns

If you can find a pattern, rule, or general principle in the material you will likely be able to learn it easier. In fact, one educational psychology textbook suggests that "the most universally effective organizing strategy is the student's active search for patterns, principles, or other significant relationships in the subjects he studies."[10] One study found that when a paired-associate list had a pattern underlying the associations, the associations were remembered better a week later than when the list was tested without an underlying pattern.[11] We saw in Chapter 2 how a chess master can memorize the positions of pieces on a board at a glance because they form a pattern; but if the pieces are arranged randomly, then he does not do much better than the beginner.

It was noted in Chapter 2 that the number 266-315-374-264 is easier to remember if you arrange it in four groups of three. The task is even easier if you can see some pattern of relationships among the four groups. For example, the first and last groups each start with 26; the middle two groups each start with 3, and end only one digit apart (5 and 4); the second digits in the last two groups are only one digit apart (7 and 6), and the last digit is the same. Noticing such patterns helps make the number more meaningful. Similarly, looking for patterns in phone numbers, addresses, dates, or any other numbers will help you remember them. For example, the phone number 575-2553 might be analyzed as follows: 3 into 75 gives 25, followed by another 5 (2 fives), and ending with the same number it starts with.

Some people tried to memorize the following twenty-four-digit number: 581215192226293336404347. Try it yourself before you read any further. Do you see any pattern in the number? Some of the people were asked to learn the number by rote repetition, without any regard to meaning. Others learned a pattern. Three weeks later none of the people in the first group could recall the number, but 23 percent of the people who learned the pattern could recall the number. You may have figured out by now that the pattern is to start with 5, add 3 to get 8, then add 4 to get 12, then add 3, then add 4, etc. Once you find the pattern, all you have to do is remember the pattern and use it to generate the sequence.[12]

This last example illustrates chunking as well as meaning. If you can find a pattern, you only have to remember one piece of information (5 plus 3 and 4 alternately) rather than twenty-four pieces of information. Finding a pattern is one way to code a number to put it in long-term memory; you no longer have to keep rehearsing it to remember it. Thus, one of the values of patterns, in addition to making material more meaningful, is that they serve to chunk the material so there is less to remember. If you can see a pattern, then all you have to remember is the pattern, and you can generate the original material.

Acronyms and Acrostics

Can you name the five Great Lakes? Try it now before you read any further. What you have just attempted was a recall task. Let us now change it to an aided recall task. The following word is composed of the first letters of each of the five lakes: HOMES. Using this word as a cue, if you were not able to name all five lakes, can you now? Many people who cannot recall the names of the lakes can do so when given this cue. The cue is what is known as an acronym — a word that is made out of the first letters, or first few letters, of the items to be remembered. In this example the acronym HOMES stands for Huron, Ontario, Michigan, Erie, and Superior.

Acronyms are widely used to represent corporations (for example, NABISCO for National Biscuit Company), associations (CORE for Congress of Racial Equality), organizations (NOW for National Organization of Women), government agencies (CAB for Civil Aeronautics Board), military titles and terms (WAVES for Women Accepted for Voluntary Emergency Service, and SNAFU for "Situation normal, all fouled up"), and many other uses. Collections of at least 10,000 such acronyms used on a national level have been compiled.[13] One reason that so many groups identify themselves with an acronym is that it serves as an aid to help people remember them.

A well-known acronym that is used as an aid to remember the colors of the visible spectrum is the name ROY G. BIV. This name represents Red, Orange, Yellow, Green, Blue, Indigo, and Violet. Similarly, suppose you have a shopping list of bananas, oranges, milk, and bread. The word BOMB could be used to help remember the list. An acronym does not even have to be a real word. What are the only four states in the United States that come together at a single point? The coined word, CANU, will help you remember Colorado, Arizona, New Mexico, and Utah.

Research studies have found that acronyms can significantly improve memory for lists of items.[14] There are at least three ways in which an acronym can help memory: First, it makes the material meaningful; it gives you something meaningful to remember, such as "HOMES," "ROY G. BIV," and "BOMB." Second, it chunks the information, so that you do not have to remember so much. Instead of seven colors, for example, you only have to remember one name. Of course the acronym itself is not the original information (a physics professor may not be particularly impressed if you said on an exam that the colors of the visible spectrum were ROY G. BIV); the acronym merely cues you to help you retrieve the original information. Research has shown that the first letter of a word is the most important cue in recognizing words for young children, and that the first letter also helps adults to recall words.[15] This leads to the third advantage of acronyms; they change a recall task to an aided recall task by providing cues to help you retrieve the items.

A closely related strategy for making something meaningful is the acrostic, which is a series of words, lines, or verses in which the first or last letters form a word, phase, or something else. An example is Psalm 119, which is divided into twenty-two eight-verse sections corresponding to the twenty-two letters of the Greek alphabet. The first word of every verse in each section begins with the same one of the twenty-two Greek letters, in order. A similar example is: On Old Olympus' Towering Top, A Finn and German Viewed Some Hops, to remember the cranial nerves, Olfactory, Optic, Oculomotor, Trochlear, Trigeminal, Abducens, Facial, Auditory, Glossopharyngeal, Vagus, Spinal Accessory, and Hypoglossal. Another well-known example of a similar technique is "Every Good Boy Does Fine," to remember the notes on the lines of the treble clef on a musical scale, EGBDF.

ORGANIZATION: "GET IT ALL TOGETHER"

How useful would a dictionary be if the words were listed in random order rather than alphabetically? One of the reasons you can find a particular word in a dictionary is because the words are organized in alphabetical order. Similarly, one of the reasons you can find a book in a library, or a particular document in a filing cabinet, is because the information is organized. You do not have to search through all the words in the dictionary, all the books in the library, or all the documents in the filing cabinet, but can merely go to the section where the desired item is stored. Of course, not only must the information be organized, but if there is a large amount of information then you also need a cataloging system. You could not find much in a library without the card catalog. And the usefulness is even greater if the materials in the card catalog are cross-referenced.

Material is also organized in long-term memory. A simple demonstration of this fact is to try recalling the names of all the states. You likely make a systematic search of memory. You do not randomly start naming states. Most likely you will name them geographically, starting with the states in a certain part of the country, and working across the country. Another possibility is that you may name them alphabetically, starting with the "A" states. The important point is that your recall will be in some organized manner, not just haphazard.

Similarly, if you try to make a list of men's names that begin with the letter "R," you do not just start recalling words randomly (names and non-names, men's names and women's names, "R" names and "A" names, etc.) but immediately go right to the section of your memory where "men's R names' are stored. Even within this section, your recall does not occur randomly. You may try to think of all your friends whose names begin with R; you may proceed alphabetically—Ra, Re, etc.; or you may try to think of famous people whose names begin with R.

These examples of state names and R names show that information is organized in memory. The more you consciously organize material at the time of recording, the easier it is to retrieve. If you put it into memory in some organized way, then it will be easier to find when you want it. The role of sequential organization in recall can be illustrated by trying to say all the letters in the alphabet. This is an easy task for most people. But now try reciting all the letters in random order: W, C, A, M, etc. You will soon find that you have a hard time keeping track of how many letters you have named and which ones.

The value of categories in memorizing is shown in a study in which people were presented a list of 112 words four times. For some of the people the list was organized in categories. For other people the list was not organized in categories, but the words were merely presented in random order. After one presentation the first group could recall 65 percent of the words, and the second group could recall only 19 percent of the words. By the third and fourth presentations the first group recalled all 112 words, whereas the second group recalled only about 62 percent of them—about the same as the first group had done after one presentation. This study shows that presenting information organized into categories definitely helps in learning the information.[16] Learning and memory are helped even when the words are presented in random order rather than grouped into categories, but the people are told the categories into which the words *could* be organized.[17]

On a list that is not presented in categories, people may impose their own organization to help learn it. For example, if you gave people the following list of words to learn: man, rose, dog, pansy, woman, horse, child, cat, carnation—they would likely recall the words grouped in similar categories: man, woman, child; dog, cat, horse; rose, pansy, carnation. Even children as young as 6 years old have been taught to use this organizing strategy well enough to significantly improve their memories for eighteen-item lists. If the items to be remembered could not be grouped by categories, they would likely be grouped by other criteria, such as same first letters.[18]

It has even been found that people who are instructed to organize material remember it as well as people who are instructed to learn the material.

The value of organization is not limited to word lists; organized paragraphs are also recalled better than unorganized ones. Nor is the value of organization in memory limited to verbal material. Objects that are organized in a meaningful, coherent picture are remembered better than objects in a jumbled picture.[19]

One value of organization is that it can be used to make material meaningful. Consider the number 5812151922262933640404347 discussed earlier in this chapter. If the number were reorganized as follows—5 8 12 15 19 22 26 29 33 36 40 43 47—then you are much more likely to see the pattern and thus learn the number faster. Similarly, the following set of letters may not be too easy to memorize; BUS HAW OR THIS T WOBIR DH AND INT HE INT HE. But if we reorganize the letters (not the order, but just the grouping) we get BUSH A WORTH IS TWO BIRD HAND IN THE IN THE. Reorganizing the *order* of the words gives A BIRD IN THE HAND IS WORTH TWO IN THE BUSH. What makes this last set of letters so much easier to remember? It consists of the same elements; but they are reorganized to give them more meaning.

Another value of organization is that it can involve chunking. The previous example of the twelve-digit number divided into three-digit chunks (266-315-374-264) involved organizing the numbers by grouping them. People who are just learning to type may begin by coding each letter as a separate chunk. Soon they are able to group the letters into words: then maybe even phrases are perceived as chunks. Thus, more efficient organization reduces the amount of material to be learned, which increases the length of the message that can be remembered.

A somewhat similar situation exists for a child who knows the letters of the alphabet but does not know the word "automobile." To remember this word he has to remember ten things; the adult has to remember only one. Adults can chunk even further and remember phrases ("I beg your pardon") and even longer sentences ("A bird in the hand is worth two in the bush") as one chunk.

When lists of digits are presented one at a time to people, they can remember them better if they chunk the digits into groups of two or three than if they try to remember them individually. Of course, chunking takes time; if items are presented too fast (for example, one per second), then chunking is less effective than if they are presented more slowly (for example, one every 5 seconds).[20]

As a practical example of the use of organization, suppose you had the following items to remember for a shopping list: cookies, milk, grapes, cheese, can opener, chicken, pie, butter, bananas, bread, pork, and gum. It may help you to reorganize the items by categories: dairy—milk, butter, cheese; bakery goods—cookies, pie bread; meat—chicken, pork;

fruit—grapes, bananas; and other—can opener, gum. You now have five chunks of two or three items each rather than twelve separate items to remember. Another possibility is to group the items by same first letters: C—cheese, cookies, chicken, can opener; B—butter, bread, bananas; G—grapes, gum; P—pie, pork; and M—milk. Then you could cue your memory by remembering "four C's, three B's, two G's, two P's, and an M."

ASSOCIATION:
"THAT REMINDS ME..."

Can you draw a rough outline of Italy? How about Denmark? Most likely you can do better with Italy. Why? One reason is that at some time it was probably pointed out to you that Italy looks like a boot. This illustrates the use of association. Association refers to taking the material you want to learn and relating it to something you already know. This can be done with analogies (which is why I have used several analogies throughout this book), metaphors, and examples; and by comparing, contrasting, or rewording.

One way to remember the difference in spelling between "principle" and "principal" is that a principal is a pal; to remember how to spell "believe," never believe a lie; to remember the difference between "port" and "starboard," remember that "port" and "left" both have four letters; to remember the difference between stalactites and stalagmites, remember that stalactites grow from the ceiling and stalagmites from the ground. All of these simple examples illustrate the principle of associating something you want to remember with something you already know. You already know how to spell "pal" and "lie," how many letters are in "left," and what letters "ceiling" and "ground" start with.

In memorizing a number you might try to associate it with familiar numbers, dates, or events. For example, the phone number 375-2553 might associate for one person as follows: 3 is the number of digits before the hyphen, 75 is the middle of the 1970 decade, 25 is his age, and 53 represents his parents' anniversary (May 3).

Association can even occur at the unconscious level. Have you ever seen or heard something and said, "Oh, that reminds me. . . ?" The reason for such an experience is that somehow in the past those two particular things became associated with each other, so that bringing one of them from memory drew the other with it. I had an interesting experience in college that illustrates unconscious association. A fellow student in one of my classes came up to me about halfway through the semester and said, "I just figured out why I don't like you." Naturally, that caught my attention, so I asked him why. He said, "Every time I looked at you I felt that I didn't like you, but I could never really figure out why. Today it suddenly dawned on me. I saw a movie on venereal disease a few years ago in a health class, and you remind me of the bad guy in the movie." This shows that we can form associations and have them affect us, without even being consciously aware of them.

It was noted earlier in this chapter that learning builds on learning. Association plays an important role in this fact. The following quote from William James describes the process:

> The more other facts a fact is associated with in the mind, the better posses-sion of it our memory retains. Each of its associates becomes a hook to which it hangs, a means to fish it up by when sunk beneath the surface. Together, they form a network of attachments by which it is woven into the entire tissue of our thought. The "secret of a good memory" is thus the secret of forming diverse and multiple associations with every fact we care to retain. . . .
>
> Most men have a good memory for facts connected with their own pursuits. The college athlete who remains a dunce at his books will astonish you by his knowl-edge of men's records in various feats and games, and will be a walking dic-tionary of sporting statistics. The reason is that he is constantly going over these things in his mind, and comparing and making series of them. They form for him not so many odd facts but a concept-system — so they stick.[21]

One way that association helps memory is to make material meaningful. In fact, in research on learning, the meaningfulness of a word is frequently defined in terms of the number of associations it has.[22] Another way in which association helps memory is to give us cross-referencing in our memories. You will have a greater likelihood of finding a letter from a bookstore con-cerning your account if it is filed under "correspondence," "books," and "charge accounts" than it if is filed under only one category. Similarly, the more other information an item is associated with in your memory, the more pathways you have to find it.

VISUALIZATION:
"I CAN SEE IT ALL NOW ..."

How many windows are in your house? In answering such a question your memory search is more likely visual than verbal. You conjure up a mental image of each room and count the windows, then move on to the next room. This task, which is not too hard for most people, illustrates a use of images in memory.

There is research evidence from as long ago as the 1800s indicating that imagery can improve memory for verbal material.[23] However, imagery was not considered an appropriate field of study for most psychologists from the early 1900s until the 1960s; it was viewed as being something going on inside the person that could not be objectively studied.[24] In fact, in an extensive survey of the field of human learning published in 1952, mental imagery and visualization were not even mentioned.[25]

The number of references appearing under "Imagery" in *Psychological Abstracts* (a journal that publishes summaries of all the research articles published in psychology) increased from eight in 1960, to nineteen in 1965, to sixty-two in 1970, and ninety-eight in 1975. Considerable research done during the 1960s on the effectiveness of imagery in memory has been summarized in several books published in the early 1970s.[26]

In Chapter 2 we saw that memory for pictures is very powerful, and that imagery is also effective for verbal material. Two possible reasons suggested in Chapter 2 are that images are inherently more memorable than words, and that words which evoke images are coded dually (in both verbal and visual memory) so there is twice as great a likelihood of remembering them. There are other theories about *why* imagery is such a powerful memory aid, but regardless of what the reason is, the important point for our purposes is that visual imagery *does* help memory. We can take advantage of this fact by visualizing material we want to remember.[27]

Visualization refers not to picturing the word itself in your mind, but picturing the object the word stands for. There are several lines of evidence to indicate that such mental imagery helps in learning verbal material. First, concrete words are almost always learned faster than abstract words (we saw in Chapter 2 that concrete words are more easily visualized). Second, people report spontaneous use of mental pictures in learning particular paired-associate word pairs, and tend to learn these pairs the quickest. Third, instructing people to use mental pictures relating two words of a pair greatly helps paired-associate learning of nouns. Fourth, people who report vivid visual imagery perform better in tests of recall than people who report poor visual imagery.[28]

There are literally dozens of studies showing the effectiveness of visual imagery in remembering. Most of them have used a paired-associate learning task. Some of the studies that have involved mnemonic systems will be discussed in later chapters. In this section some studies that have used a paired-associate learning task will be discussed. Many real-life learning situations involve paired-associate learning: capitals of states, names and faces, foreign languages, vocabulary words, names and sounds of letters. In addition, some mnemonic systems involve paired-associate learning, so this research is relevant to their use also.

The general approach of studies on imagery in paired-associate learning is to instruct some people to use verbal techniques to associate the words, and others to form images representing the words and associate the images for each pair of words. For example, for "dog-broom" you might picture a dog sweeping the house with a broom; for "door-baby" you might picture a baby climbing a door or hanging onto a doorknob. The general finding of these studies is that the imagers learn and remember much more effectively than the verbalizers. In fact, in many of these studies, the effect of using imagery may be underestimated because people who are instructed to verbalize sometimes report using imagery spontaneously.

Of the many paired-associate studies that show the effectiveness of visualization, the results of only five will be briefly described here.[29] In one study, pairs of common nouns were read to people at their own pace (they indicated when they were ready for the next pair), and they formed bizarre mental images combining each of the pairs of words. The people's memories were tested by giving the first word and having them recall the second word for each pair. They were able to accurately recall 99 percent of 500 pairs of words, and 95 percent of 700 pairs. In a second study, people who were instructed to use imagery were compared with people who were simply told to study and rehearse the word pairs. Both groups spent the same amount of time studying the material, but the imagery group showed 80 percent recall whereas the control group showed only 33 percent recall. In a third study, people learned six different lists of ten pairs of words. At the end of the six lists, they were tested on recall of all sixty words. The imagers recalled an average of 63 percent, while the nonimagers recalled an average of 22 percent.

While many studies on imagery in paired-associate learning have found that people who used imagery remembered better than other people who did not use imagery, the fourth study described here compared the same people with themselves. They used imagery to learn some words and repetition to learn others. Their recall averaged between 80 and 90 percent of the words they learned by imagery, and between 30 and 40 percent of the words they learned by rote repetition. A fifth study shows that visualization can be effective in young children, increasing paired-associate recall by two times in first-graders and four times in fourth-graders. The advantages of visual imagery in verbal memory may still be apparent after several days, or even several weeks.[30]

Learning a foreign language is an example of paired-associate learning. Would imagery help in this task? People who did not know Spanish studied a list of Spanish words for a fixed time period; they heard each word pronounced and saw its English equivalent on a screen. They were later tested by giving the English translation as each Spanish word was pronounced. The people who used rote repetition averaged 28 percent correct, whereas the people who used mental imagery averaged 88 percent.[31] Foreign languages are discussed further in Chapter 10.

Of course the main advantage of imagery is that it can make learning more effective. Another advantage is that it can make learning more fun. Most people find it more interesting to picture images and associate them than to merely repeat words over and over by rote methods to memorize them.

Most of this section has discussed the use of imagery to learn words, because that is where most of the research has been done. However, the value of imagery is not limited to nouns. Imagery has also been found to aid memory for verbs and adverbs. Nor is the value of imagery limited to memory for single words. Visual imagery has been found to help in learning sentences, prose material, and even concepts.[32] The effective use of imagery, and its strengths and limitations, is discussed further in Chapter 5.

ATTENTION: "I DON'T GET IT"

An important principle of memory is suggested by a statement that has been attributed to Oliver Wendell Holmes: "A man must *get* a thing before he can *forget* it."[33] Frequently when we say we forgot something, what we should really say is that we never actually *got* it in the first place; we were never consciously paying attention to it. The following quiz may help you recognize this distinction:

1. Which color is on top on a stoplight?
2. In his image on a penny, does Lincoln wear a tie?
3. What four words besides "In God We Trust" appear on most U. S. coins?
4. When water goes down the drain, does it swirl clockwise or counterclockwise?
5. What letters, if any, are missing on a phone dial?

Can you answer all of these questions? If you were not able to answer some of them, the reason is probably not because you forgot. Although you have seen pennies, watched water go down the drain, and used the phone many times, you most likely have never consciously paid attention to these things. Thus, you cannot accurately say that you do not remember what letters are missing on a phone dial. A more accurate answer is that you never really knew in the first place. The correct answers to the questions are: (1) Red; (2) Yes, a bow tie; (3) United States of America; (4) Counterclockwise (in this hemisphere); (5) Q, Z.

Some of the difficulty people report with "poor memories" is not a matter of forgetting, but simply of not learning in the first place. People blame their memories for something that is not their memories' fault. If you want to remember something, you must pay attention to it, concentrate on it, and make sure you get it in the first place. Although it is possible to learn some things that we are not paying attention to and are not trying to learn, it is not too surprising that nearly every comparison of such incidental learning with intentional learning shows that intentional learning is superior.[34] We can talk about forgetting only if there is some evidence of learning.

Sometimes when students complain about forgetting things they studied, it may be true that they do not know what they studied; but it may also be true that they did not really study the material enough for it to be considered learned in the first place. They might not have remembered much more immediately after study than they did later. Just because people sat through a lecture or ran their eyes over a textbook does not mean that they learned. If they were not paying attention, then the later recall failure (a flunked test) is due to the fact that they never *got* the material in the first place.

The failure to pay attention is a common reason for "forgetting" the names of people we meet. Frequently when we are introduced to someone we are not really paying attention; we never really get the name in the first place. We are waiting for our own name to be said, or trying to think of something to say to the person. Thus, one way to reduce the problem of forgetting names is to make a special effort to concentrate on the name.

Failure to pay attention is a reason also for absentmindedness. Usually when you forget where you parked your car, or left your umbrella, it is because you were not consciously paying attention to what you were doing when you parked the car or put your umbrella down. Your mind was on something else. Thus, one way to reduce absentmindedness is to pay attention to what you are doing. You might even tell yourself as you put the umbrella on the store counter, "I am putting the umbrella on the store counter." This will focus your attention on what you are doing and reduce the likelihood that you will walk off and forget it. One girl in my memory class was always forgetting where she put her car keys, so she told herself out loud whenever she put them down, "I am now putting my keys on the kitchen counter," or "I am putting my keys in my desk." Her roommates thought she was crazy—but she remembered where she put her keys. Absentmindedness is discussed further in Chapter 10.

INTEREST:
"WHAT'S IT TO YA?"

Attention is influenced by interest. We pay attention to the things we are most interested in, and thus we are most likely to remember those things. If it is not important to you, you are not likely to remember it. Any two people who walk through a department store, read a restaurant menu, or read a book are likely to remember different things because of their different interests. The influence of interest on attention and memory is illustrated by the story of the returning serviceman who was greeted at the airport by his girlfriend, and casually mentioned as the attractive stewardess walked by, "That's Miss Nelson." His girlfriend asked him how he happened to know her name. "Oh," he said, "the names of all the crew members were posted at the front of the plane." She stumped him with the next question, "What was the pilot's name?"[35]

The value of interest in memory may be illustrated by comparing two people who are studying French. Suppose that one of them is planning to take a trip to France in a few months. Other things being equal, which one would be more likely to learn and remember the French? Similarly, suppose you are introduced to two people, and one of them then borrows $5 from you. Which person's name are you more likely to remember? Or suppose you have been told that pericholecystitis is an inflammation of tissue around the gall bladder. You may not remember this fact. But suppose that you were told by your doctor that *you* have pericholecystitis. Now would you not be much more likely to remember it? These simple examples show that we tend to remember the things that interest us.

Some people complain that they are "just no good" at such subjects as math or mechanics. Frequently the reason for this is that they have no interest in those subjects; they see no value in them, and thus have not, and do not want to, put forth effort to learn them.[36] Women who claim to have bad memories may be able to remember the birthdays and anniversaries that their husbands have a hard time keeping track of, or may be able to describe in detail what other women at a party were wearing. Boys who cannot seem to learn in school may be able to tell you everything you want to know (and more) about sports or cars. The reason is simply interest.

The last section suggested that one reason some people do not remember names is because they do not pay attention to them. We may take this one step further and suggest that one reason they do not pay attention to the names is because they are not as interested in the other person as they are in themselves. Most people are more interested in what they are going to say, or what the other person will think of them, than they are in the other person.

Two ways in which interest helps in memory have been suggested: it helps us pay attention and it motivates us to try to remember. Another way interest helps memory is that people spend more time thinking about things that interest them than they do thinking about things that do not interest them. As we will see in Chapter 4, repetition and review aid learning.

The importance of interest can be illustrated by referring again to the twelve-digit number that has been used to illustrate several points: 266-315-374-264. You may not have learned this number by now. It is not especially easy to learn, but more importantly you see no reason for doing so. Therefore, you are not motivated to learn it. But I did not just make up that number from nowhere; I have been using that particular number on purpose. If you memorize that number you will in effect have the calendar for all of 1977 memorized (you can do the same for any other year with the appropriate twelve-digit number). You will be able to answer questions such as, "What day of the week is June 18?", "How many Mondays are in November?", or "What date is the second Sunday in April?" Now are you interested? Do you now think that you could learn the number? Having a reason for learning it may have increased interest, which will make it easier to learn. In Chapter 5 I will describe how it can be used.

The principle of interest suggests that if you are having trouble learning and remembering certain things, you should increase your interest in them. The logical questions is, how? If you are not interested in something it probably will not work to just say to yourself, "From now on I am going to be interested in that." One way to develop an interest in something you need to learn is to try to find ways to relate it to your present motives and interests. Try to find some use for the material. The housewife who has a difficult time in math may be able to learn it better if she can see some ways to use the information to make measurements in cooking and sewing. The carpenter who has a hard time learning math may improve if he can see how it will help him be faster and more accurate in his carpentry work. The salesperson who has a hard time remembering names may be able to improve after realizing how important people's names are to them, and how much remembering their names may help sales.

FEEDBACK:
"HOW ARE YOU DOING?"

Suppose you were shooting with a rifle at a target that was too far away for you to see where you hit. You take a total of fifty shots without ever looking at the target to see where they are hitting, so you have no idea how you are doing. How interesting would this kind of target practice be? How much do you think you would improve? On the other hand, if you looked through a spotting scope after every few shots, this would not only help maintain your interest in what you are doing, but would also give you information about how you are doing so that you could make adjustments to improve.

Feedback in learning serves the same two functions: First, knowing how you are progressing in learning something helps sustain your interest in the task. If you constantly study and never know whether you are remembering any of the material, you will soon grow bored and lose interest. Second, if you get feedback on how much you can remember you will be able to make adjustments to improve. You can correct your recall errors and put more effort into the parts you cannot remember.[37]

Some people were tested on written material right after they finished reading it, and received feedback as to how they did on the test. Others received no feedback. The people who received feedback remembered the material better a week later than did the people who did not receive feedback.[38]

You can apply the principle of feedback by using any technique that gives you information about how you are doing. One method is to study with a friend and quiz each other. Another method is recitation. Recitation in effect involves testing yourself. If you are memorizing a poem or learning a speech, try saying it to yourself after a few readings and look at it only when you get stuck. If you are studying a chapter, glance at the headings and words in italics and try to explain to yourself what they mean. You might even make up test questions. This gives you feedback on how you are doing. It will help to sustain your interest, and to make adjustments to improve your learning. Recitation is discussed further in Chapter 4.

SUMMARY

Psychological research has shown that there are a number of basic principles that help learning and memory: meaningfulness, organization, association, visualization, attention, interest, and feedback.

The more meaningful something is to you, the easier it will be to learn. Thus, anything you can do to make material meaningful will help you learn it. You can take advantage of familiarity; merely exposing yourself to something without purposely trying to learn it may make it more meaningful to you. If you can make a rhyme of the material, or find a pattern in it, it will be more meaningful. Acronyms and acrostics, making words or phrases out of the first letters of the items to be remembered, also help make the items meaningful.

Organization makes a difference in your ability to remember. Most of the information in your memory is organized in some way. The more you organize it purposely when you are learning it, the easier it will be to remember. Organization includes grouping by categories, rearranging to find a pattern, and chunking.

Association refers to relating the material you want to remember to something you already know. This can be done by analogies, metaphors, examples, comparing, contrasting, or rewording. Learning builds upon learning, and the more you know about a subject, the easier it is to learn new things because you have more to associate new information with.

Much research has been done on visual imagery since the 1960s. The research has shown that very striking improvement can be seen in many kinds of memory tasks when people are asked to visualize the items to be remembered, as compared with learning them through rote repetition. Not only is visualization effective, but it is also a more interesting way to remember than is rote repetition.

Failure to pay attention is frequently the real reason why we "forget." We are blaming our memory for something that is really the fault of our concentration. You must *get* something before you can *forget* it, and frequently when we say "I forget" what we really should be saying is, "I never really knew in the first place; I was not consciously paying attention." This may be the single most important reason why we "forget" the names of people to whom we are introduced. It is also a common reason for absentmindedness — you may "forget" where you put your car keys because you were not consciously paying attention to what you were doing at the time you put them down.

Interest influences whether or not we will pay attention to something. We attend to, and thus are more likely to remember, things that we are interested in. We also are more motivated to remember them, and we spend more time thinking about them. Finding some way to relate material to your interests will help you learn the material more effectively.

Feedback in learning serves two important functions: (1) it helps sustain your interest in the task; and (2) it enables you to make adjustments to improve, to study further the parts you cannot remember as well.

CHAPTER 4

Strategies
for Effective Learning

Although we all learn, and presumably use various strategies in learning, we may not be sure which strategies work and which do not. In fact, we may not even be sure which strategies we use. In discussing strategies in learning, a recent textbook notes that "if there is one message that is common to all these chapters on learning and retention in human beings, it is that people cannot correctly identify the processes that go on in themselves as they learn."[1]

There are a number of strategies that can help you learn and remember more effectively: take steps to reduce interference; space your learning sessions out over time; use whole learning and part learning in appropriate circumstances; use repetition, recitation, and tne SQ3R study technique. Each of these strategies will be discussed in this chapter. You have probably used some of the strategies, but you may have used them without knowing for sure what you were doing or why you were doing it. You may have used others without knowing whether they were really doing any good. And you may have used others in such a way that they did not do much good.

The learning strategies are discussed from the viewpoint of a student in school; they may help a student develop good study habits (the *quality* of your study habits is more important than the *quantity* of study — good students do not necessarily study more than poor students, but they use their study time more effectively[2]). However, the scope of the chapter is broader than just the school setting. These strategies will help not only in remembering material for an exam but also in tasks such as remembering names of people you meet, learning a foreign language, learning a speech, or memorizing a poem, a song, or lines for a play. Thus, even if you are not currently in school you will still find that you can use some of the learning strategies to help improve your memory.

REDUCE INTERFERENCE

In Chapter 2 we saw that interference from other learning is one of the main causes of forgetting. What are some factors that affect interference and what can you do about them?

How Well the Material is Learned

The more thoroughly something is learned, the less it will be affected by interference.[3] Material that is just barely learned is more subject to interference than is material that is learned very well. Thus, if you want to remember something, overlearn it (overlearning is discussed later in the chapter).

Meaningfulness of the Material

The more meaningful the material is, the less subject it is to interference. This does not mean that interference occurs only with meaningless material, such as nonsense syllables (which have been used in much of the research on interference). Interference can also occur with meaningful connected discourse,[4] but the effects of interference are generally not as great for meaningful material as for less meaningful material. Thus, any of the principles you can use from Chapter 3 to make the material meaningful will help reduce interference.

Amount of Interpolated Activity

How much you do, especially in terms of mental activity, between the time of learning and the time of recall can affect interference. Generally, the more you do the more opportunity there is for interference to occur. Suppose one student studied for an exam, then went to a movie, read the newspaper, read a magazine, and studied another subject before the exam. Suppose a second student studied, then slept or rested until the exam. Other things being equal, there would be more interference for the first student than for the second. Minimum interference should occur if you sleep between studying and testing (assuming you studied well and are not sleeping *instead* of studying). As we noted in Chapter 2, there is research evidence that a person who goes to sleep right after learning will remember more than a person who stays awake.

Similarity of Interpolated Activity

The previous item referred to *how much* you do between learning and recall. *What* you do can also affect interference. Two kinds of information that are similar will interfere with each other more than two that are dissimilar.[5] If you cannot sleep all the time after study, then you should do something that is different from what you have studied. It is best not to study two similar subjects close together when you can help it. For example, if you had to study French, Spanish, and Biology in the next few days it would be better to study Biology in between French and Spanish. French and Spanish are more similar, and thus more likely to interfere with each other. (Of course, a student who has two tests tomorrow and has not studied either one by tonight does not have much choice.)

Similarity of Learning Contexts

The context in which you learn something affects your ability to remember it. For example, you are more likely to recognize a person you have met only once, and to remember her name, if you see her in her office where you first met her than if you see her walking down the street. Similarly, other recall will be helped if it occurs in the same context in which the material was learned.[6] This suggests that *where* you study can make a difference in interference. Studying two different subjects in two different rooms can reduce the interference between the subjects by as much as half.[7]

This fact has at least two practical implications. First, ideally you should study each subject in the same place where recall will be tested, so that all the contextual cues that were present at study will be there at recall. In other words, study each subject in the classroom where the exam will be given. Usually, of course, this is not possible, but the research evidence suggests that it would help. Similarly, if you are learning a speech, for example, it would be helpful to practice it in the exact place where you will be giving it.

The second implication of this fact is that if you need to study subjects that are likely to interfere with each other, you should study them in different places. For example, having one place to study your French and another place to study your Spanish will help you keep the two subjects separate when you recall them.

When teachers teach two different sections of the same class covering the same subject matter during one semester, a common problem is that they cannot remember what they talked about in one class and what they talked about in the other class. I find that it helps me to teach the classes in different rooms, rather than in the same room.

Time Between Learning Sessions

If you have more than one subject to study, you may have less interference if you study each one in a separate study session, rather than studying them all in one session. Some people learned two paired-associate lists on Thursday and were tested on the second one on Friday. Others learned the first list on Monday, the second one on Thursday, and were also tested on the second one on Friday. The first group recalled 38 percent while the second group recalled 65 percent.[8] In another similar study, people learned four different sets of words paired to the same key words, then recalled the fourth set later. This situation is also very susceptible to proactive interference. Some people studied all four sets in one session, while others studied them on a spaced-out basis over a period of three days. Those who did all their studying in one session could recall only 31 percent of the fourth set of words after one day, and 7 percent after a week. Those who had learned the four lists separately in the spaced schedule recalled 89 percent after one day, 72 percent after a week, and 34 percent even after a month.[9]

What if you don't have several days? Suppose you have to know the material tomorrow. It will still help to take a break. The time between study sessions does not have to be very long. Merely going to get a drink of water between two learning sessions has been found to reduce the interference (in fact, taking such a break and coming back to the same room reduced interference as much as going to a different room for the second session[10]). Suppose you need to study French and Spanish for two hours in one night. You could study French and Spanish intermittently for the two hours; or you could study French for an hour, take a break, then study Spanish for an hour. The second strategy would be preferable.

SPACE IT OUT

Suppose you have allotted a given amount of time to study your material. Should you do all of your studying in one session, or should you distribute your study time across shorter time periods? For example, if you can allot three hours to study it then you could either spend one three-hour session studying the material or you could space it out over three one-hour periods.

The first strategy will be easily identified as "cramming" by almost anyone who has been a student. Psychologists call it "massed learning." They call the second strategy "distributed learning." The latter is what teachers tell students to do, but few students follow that advice—probably because they do not start studying for a test far enough ahead to be able to space their study. They study by the "brush-fire" method, stamping the fire out wherever it flames up, with little stopping to plan ahead. This is probably one reason why most books on studying for students include a chapter on budgeting your time.

In the previous section we saw that spacing of study sessions helps reduce interference among different sets of material. How effective is spacing in terms of efficiency in learning a given set of material? Research evidence indicates that spaced learning is generally more effective than massed learning, for a number of different kinds of learning tasks.[11] Spaced learning reduces the amount of actual study time it takes to learn the material. Of course, the *total* amount of time between the beginning of study and final mastery increases with spaced learning, because it consists of both actual study time and time between study sessions.

When reviewing material that you have already learned, it has been found that spaced reviews are more effective than contiguous reviews in helping retention.[12] For example, it would be better to review the material for a half-hour each day for three days than to review it three times during a 1½-hour period.

There are at least two possible reasons why spaced learning is generally better than massed learning. First, you can only concentrate for so long before your attention wanders. Thus, if you try to do all your studying in one session, you may not be able to pay attention for the whole time. Second, there is evidence that what you have learned during a study session may consolidate in your mind during a break.[13] You can even help the process along by consciously reviewing the material in your mind between study sessions.

There is a limit to the improvements in performance with spacing. As the interval between the two sessions is increased, performance improves to a point, then declines. For example, distributing your three hours into eighteen 10-minute periods may be worse than cramming for one three-hour period. Thus, one of the practical problems is deciding what is the best length for the study periods, and for the intervals between periods. It has been recommended that with difficult tasks, young inexperienced learners, and in early stages of learning, the study period should be shorter than with easier tasks, more mature learners, and tasks that are in an advanced stage of learning.[14]

Massed learning may be better for a task that requires a lot of preparation or for certain problem-solving tasks. Massed learning may also be more efficient if recall is going to be required right after learning. Fifth-graders studied some spelling words during a single study session and then were given other words for the same amount of study time distributed over several study sessions. The children spelled more words correctly right after the massed session, but ten and twenty days later the words learned under the distributed sessions were remembered better.[15] This suggests one reason why many students are not able to recall material for very long after an exam — they have learned it by cramming the night before the exam.

In a study of people's memory for names and faces of high school colleagues, the relatively high level of recall (40 percent even after forty-eight years) was attributed in part to the effects of distributed learning — we learn the other students' names over a period of four years.[16] You might have a hard time remembering the names of ten people you met in one evening, but would probably do better if you met one person each day for ten days.

BREAK IT UP?

Another choice you are faced with in learning your material is whether you should study it by the part method or by the whole method. In the part method you would break the material up into smaller parts, then study the first part (section, verse, paragraph, stanza, etc.) until you had it learned. You would then study the second part until you had it learned, then the third part, etc. In the whole method you would study the whole thing from beginning to end, all the parts together, over and over until you had it learned.

There are several conditions that determine whether whole learning or part learning is more efficient.[17]

1. One of the main advantages of the whole method is that it gives a context of meaning to each part and prompts recall of the next part. This holds especially for material in which there is developing theme (such as a poem or speech). Whole learning gives you an overall picture of how the parts fit together, and an overview of the context helps to remember the material.[18] Learning the parts without having an overall picture of how they go together is somewhat like putting a jigsaw puzzle together without knowing what it is supposed to be. In the part method, putting the parts together will take up as much as half the total learning time and will be the source of most errors. Thus, the difficulty in the part method is not in learning the parts, but in putting them together.[19]

2. One of the main advantages of the part method is that the learners get feedback on how much they are learning sooner than do people using the whole method. If you keep studying the whole thing over and over you may not realize that you are learning anything. However, the person who is studying the separate parts may be able to recite each part as he finishes it. He gets concrete feedback. If the whole learner keeps studying, he will soon find that he can recite most of the material. But without feedback on progress along the way he may give up before he reaches this point. As we saw in Chapter 2, feedback helps sustain interest.

For example, suppose that it takes a person an hour to memorize a passage of 500 words. A hundred-word portion of this passage requires only 9 minutes to memorize. After 9 minutes of study part learners have something to show for their efforts, while whole learners may not be able to recall even a single sentence correctly. This may discourage the whole learners and they may give up. For this reason, the part method may be better for adults who are not used to the whole method, and for children who need feedback to keep them going.

3. Continued practice using the whole method will improve its efficiency, whereas continued practice with the part method will not. Let us consider further the above example of memorizing a 500-word passage. The 9 minutes spent by the whole learner is not wasted, but is leading toward mastery. The part learner still has four portions left to memorize and may forget some of each while memorizing the others. In addition, he still has to work on putting the parts together (see no. 1 above). People who have had practice using the whole method realize these things, and realize that they are learning even though it does not show yet. Because of past experience, they know that even though they may not be getting feedback for some time, the final results will justify their patience and endurance.

4. The more mature and intelligent the learner is, the more efficient the whole method will be for him.

5. The advantages of the whole method are greater for distributed learning than for massed learning.

6. The more material there is to be learned, the more efficient the part method will be. Incidentally, it is interesting to note that regardless of whether you use the whole or part method, a passage that is twice as long as another requires more than twice as long to learn. For example, in one study a passage of 100 words required a total learning time of 9 minutes, 200 words required 24 minutes, 500 words required 65 minutes, and 1,000 words required 165 minutes.[20] Thus, if it takes you one hour to master a thirty-page chapter, it will probably take you more than two hours to master a sixty-page chapter.

7. The more distinctive the parts are, the more efficient the part method will be. For example, the part method may be more appropriate for learning the constitutional amendments than for learning the Gettysburg Address.

For much of your learning you would probably want to use a combination of whole and part learning. For example, you might study by the whole method, but select certain parts for extra study. Or you might try using a compromise between the whole and part methods that has been called the "progressive part" method.[21] In the progressive part method, you learn the first part, then the second part, then study the first two parts together. After you know the first two parts, you learn the third part, then study all three parts together, etc. The progressive part method has an advantage over the part method in that you connect the parts together as you learn them, rather than learning them as disconnected parts. It has an advantage over the whole method in that you get feedback to realize that you are really learning something. Another combination method is the "whole-part-whole" method, in which you first go through the whole thing once or twice, then break it up into logical parts and learn them, and finally review the material as a whole. This method is very effective for long, difficult material.[22]

REPEAT IT, REPEAT IT

One of the basic principles of learning that almost everyone is familiar with is repetition. We may learn some things in only one trial, but most learning requires repeating the material over and over; and, of course, repetition does help learning. But some people do not realize that although repetition is *necessary* for learning, it is not *sufficient* for most learning. That is, it is necessary that you repeat most material to learn it, but repetition alone is not sufficient to assure that you will learn it. Repetition should be combined with other principles and strategies of learning to be effective.[23]

The insufficiency of repetition alone is illustrated by the story of the young boy who used the phrase "I have went" in a paper he wrote in school. The teacher made him stay after school and write on the board 100 times, "I have gone." She went to a faculty meeting, and told him that when he finished he could go home. When she returned to the classroom later she found "I have gone" written 100 times on the board, and scrawled at the end of it, "I have finished, so I have went."[24]

What about continued repetition *after* you have learned something? Suppose you reach the point in your study where you can recite your poem, or give your speech once, without any mistakes. You may think that you now have it learned, so you might as well stop studying; further study would be inefficient. This is not true. *Overlearning,* continued learning beyond the point of bare mastery or of mere recall, has been shown to be effective.

Three groups of people memorized a list of nouns. One group quit studying as soon as they could recall the list perfectly once (0 percent overlearning). The second group continued to study the list for half as many trials as they had needed to reach one perfect recall of the list (50 percent overlearning). The third group continued to study the list for as many more trials as they had needed to reach one perfect recall (100 percent overlearning). For example, if it took ten repetitions to reach the criterion, the second group studied the list for five more repetitions, and the third group studied the list for ten more repetitions. Memory for the lists was measured by recall and relearning at various intervals from one to twenty-eight days later. The greater the degree of overlearning, the better the memory at all time intervals (although the improvement from 0 percent to 50 percent overlearning was greater than the improvement from 50 to 100 percent overlearning). Other studies have also found that overlearning is beneficial.[25]

Overlearning accounts for the fact that you can still remember some things you learned as a child (such as the multiplication tables, the alphabet, and how to ride a bicycle), even though you may not have used them for a long time. Overlearning also shows one reason why cramming for an exam does not result in retention of the material for very long after the exam—you have barely learned the material, so it is forgotten quickly. We have seen that distributed learning is one reason suggested for the good memory of most people for their high school colleagues. The other reason suggested by the researchers is overlearning; we learned most of our colleagues' names very thoroughly.[26]

RECITE IT

Reciting means repeating to yourself what you have learned, without looking at it. In recitation you recall as much of what you are trying to memorize as you can, looking at the material only when necessary, after you have read it once or twice. For example, if you are studying a book chapter you might look at the headings and try to tell yourself what they are about; if you are studying a poem you might look at the first few words of each line or stanza and try to recall the rest; if you are studying a foreign language you might look at each English word and try to recall the foreign word.

Suppose you have two hours to study a textbook chapter that takes a half-hour to read. Would it be more effective to read it four times or to read it once or twice and spend the rest of the time reciting, testing yourself, and rereading to clear up the points you could not recall? Research evidence suggests that it would be more effective to spend as much of the time as possible reciting.

In one study, people benefitted in learning biographies and nonsense syllables by increased recitation up to 80 percent of the total study time. In a second study high school students read passages of prose. Some of the students recited what they could remember twice, immediately after reading. Three weeks later the recitation group remembered six times what the other group remembered about what they had learned from the reading. In fact, the recitation group remembered more after sixty-three days than the other group did after one day. Some other people were given 5 minutes to memorize a poem in a third study. Half of them were instructed to read the material over and over, while the other half were instructed to read it once and spend the rest of the time reading and reciting line by line. The reading group recalled an average of thirty-three words, while the recitation group recalled an average of forty-six words, an increase of 40 percent.[27]

You have probably noticed that the effectiveness of most of the strategies in this chapter is affected by various conditions, such as the kind of material learned or who is doing the learning. The effectiveness of recitation does not depend on whether the learners are dull or bright, whether the material is long or short, whether the material is meaningful or not—in virtually every case it is more efficient to read and recite than to just read. A recent introductory psychology textbook discussing learning strategies concluded that "recitation is the most powerful tool of all in learning." One book on effective study noted that recitation is "one of the most effective devices to retard forgetting" and another one emphasized, "Don't think though that this is merely a good but rather incidental rule. Recitation can make all the difference in the world in how much you remember."[28]

One reason recitation is so effective is that it forces you to use many of the other principles and strategies discussed in Chapters 3 and 4. For example, recitation forces active learning; it gives you feedback on how you are doing; it involves repetition; and it forces you to pay attention to what you are doing.

Also, in reciting you are practicing the very thing that will be required of you later—recall. You are actually rehearsing retrieval. In one study, people who were given a test on the material right after reading it remembered it better a week later than did people who were not given the test. These results are due in part to the fact that the first group had practiced retrieving the material.[29]

Many students have reported a saving in study effort by the following rule: Never finish a reading session without reviewing in outline the main points of what has just been read. This rule has been found by many students to be the most important single step to reduce forgetting.[30] Not only does it help you see what you have learned, but it also helps you learn the material further before forgetting it. In addition, such recitation saves time and effort; you remember more, so you do not have to spend so much time rereading and reviewing the material for the exam later. (This also applies to reviewing lecture notes. The mere act of taking notes does not necessarily help you remember the lecture better, but the notes give you something to review later.[31])

If recitation is so helpful, why do more people not do it? Why do some people spend all of their study time reading the material over and over?

There are at least two possible reasons. First, some people probably do not realize the value of recitation. Second, recitation takes more work than reading. It is easier to let your eyes wander down the page (while your mind may be wandering somewhere else) than to concentrate on trying to recall what you have read.

Of course, recitation can be done by yourself, but you can also use the principle of recitation by studying with another person. You ask the other person questions about the material to give her a chance to rehearse retrieval, then she does the same for you. Not only do you benefit by *answering* questions, but your recall will also benefit from making up questions to *ask* the other person.[32]

USE SQ3R

An effective study method should (1) be based on the strategies for effective learning, (2) help you identify and understand the important parts of the material, (3) help you remember these important parts, (4) be more efficient than merely reading the material over and over, and (5) be easy to learn.

SQ3R is a classic, widely recommended study method that meets these criteria. SQ3R consists of five steps: Survey, Question, Read, Recite, Review. SQ3R benefits both good and poor students. The following is a brief description of the SQ3R method, based on more extensive discussions in books on study habits by Francis Robinson and by Clifford Morgan and James Deese.[33]

Survey

To survey a book, read the preface, table of contents, and chapter summaries. To survey a chapter, study the outline and skim the chapter, especially the headings, pictures, and graphs. Surveying consists of getting an overview of what the book or chapter is about, and should not take more than a few minutes. Many books have a summary at the end of each chapter; reading this summary *before* you read the chapter may also help you get an overview. The overview is somewhat like looking at a map before taking a trip, or at a picture of the finished product before starting a jigsaw puzzle. Surveying gives a framework within which to place the parts as you learn them, which in turn speeds up your reading time by allowing you to comprehend the parts more rapidly.

Memory for reading material can be increased significantly merely by giving the reader a short title reflecting the main idea of the material.[34] The reason authors of textbooks organize their material under different chapters and headings is to tell the readers the main idea of each chapter and section, how the material is put together, and how the topics relate to each other. If you do not use the headings you are failing to take advantage of an important source for learning the material.

The same holds true for pictures and graphs. The reason pictures are included in a textbook is not to take up space, to make the book thicker, or to give the reader something to look at to break up the monotony of reading. Rather, including pictures that illustrate material in the text has been found in a number of studies to increase learning and memory for the text material.[35]

Question

Skim again, asking yourself questions based on the headings, so you will know some things to look for when reading. Several studies have found that inserting written questions before, within, or after text material helps in learning and remembering the material; since most material you read does not have questions inserted, you may benefit by asking your own as you read.[36] Questions can maintain interest, foster active involvement in learning, and give a purpose to your reading, all of which help you learn the material. Also, some textbooks provide review questions at the end of the chapter; you might try reading them *before* reading the chapter so you will know what to look for as you read the chapter.

Read

Read the chapter without taking notes. Answer the questions you have asked. Read everything. Sometimes tables, charts, and graphs convey more information than the text does. Note that this is the *third* step in SQ3R; for most students it is the *first* step in studying. In fact, for some students it is the only step—some students think that when they have run their eyes over the textbook they have studied it. The characteristic strategy of freshmen who flunk out of college is that they read a chapter and underline, then in studying for a test they review the underlined parts;[37] one problem with this approach is that you usually do not know what is important, or what relates to what, the first time you read a chapter. Thus, when you review the underlined parts you may miss much of what is important.

Underlining while you are reading material for the first time also has other problems. It is easy to do, so most students underline too much; this results in their reviewing pages that have heavily marked not only the important points but also repeated and conflicting points. Another problem with underlining the first time through is that some students may develop the habit of reading to *mark* important points rather than reading to *understand*

and *remember* the points; thus, a student may underline an italicized sentence and continue reading without having even read the italicized sentence! To use underlining properly, you should wait until reaching the end of a section before underlining, think about what the important points were, then underline only the key phrases. Underlining the wrong things may actually *interfere* with learning.[38]

Recite

Recitation has already been discussed. Reread, asking yourself questions about the headings and italicized words, and answering the questions as much as you can. This can be done after each section or after each chapter, depending on their length. How much of your study time should you spend reciting? For most textbooks about half of your study time should be spent reciting. You may want to spend more of your study time reciting for disconnected, meaningless material such as lists of rules and formulas; but somewhat less for storylike, connected material.

Review

Survey again, reviewing what you could recite and noting what you could not. Question yourself again. Like the Survey, the Review should take only a few minutes. In Chapter 2 we saw that it takes fewer trials to relearn old material (even when it has apparently been forgotten when measured by recall) than to learn new material. Thus it pays to review the material occasionally to refresh your memory so that you will have to spend less time going over the material for the final exam. The best times to review are: (1) during study, by reciting after each major section, (2) immediately after studying, and (3) just before the exam. A review immediately after studying helps consolidate the material in your memory, and a later review helps in relearning forgotten material. Having one review immediately after learning and one a week later has been found to be more effective than only one review, or two reviews immediately after learning, or two reviews a week later.[39]

SQ3R has been found to increase rate of reading, level of comprehension, and performance on examinations. In addition, the principles of SQ3R can be used not only for textbooks but also for such tasks as outside reading assignments, English literature, and charts, tables, maps, and drawings.[40]

Most other study strategies that have been suggested offer essentially the same suggestions as SQ3R. For example, Ian Hunter suggested three steps: (1) Survey the task. What is to be remembered? For what purpose? How much effort will it take? When will you do it? (2) Organize the material.

Relate things to each other; relate them to other knowledge; note similarities and differences. (3) Repeat what was learned. Step 1 of Hunter's procedure corresponds to Survey; step 2 corresponds to Question and Read; step 3 corresponds to Recite and Review. Wayne Bartz also suggested three steps in studying. (1) Glance through the chapter. (2) Read it rapidly. (3) Rehearse retrieval — the most important step. Step 1 of Bartz's procedure corresponds to Survey and Question; step 2 corresponds to Read; step 3 corresponds to Recite and Review.[41]

HOW WELL DO THE PRINCIPLES AND STRATEGIES WORK?

Do the principles and strategies discussed in Chapters 3 and 4 really help? One classic study suggests that they do. In the study, people were taught seven simple rules for memorizing. One group was instructed in the seven rules, then given three hours of practice using the rules. A second group also practiced memorizing for three hours, but they were given no instruction. Both groups were then given a memorizing test involving many different kinds of material, such as poetry, prose, facts, foreign languages, and historical dates. The instructed group improved about eight times as much in their memorizing ability as did the uninstructed group — an average of 36 percent compared with about 4.5 percent for the uninstructed group.[42]

The seven rules that the students were taught are listed below as they were given in the original study. Following each rule, in parentheses, are the principles and strategies in Chapters 3 and 4 that are related to the rule:

1. Learn by wholes. (Whole learning; "Survey" of SQ3R)
2. Use active self-testing. (Recite it)
3. Use rhythm and grouping. (Meaningfulness; Organization)
4. Attention to meaning and advantages of picturing. (Meaningfulness; Visualization)
5. Mental alertness and concentration. (Attention)
6. Use of secondary associations. (Association)
7. Confidence in ability to memorize.

SUMMARY

Many of the learning strategies in this chapter make up what are referred to as "study habits." Studying is usually associated with school, but these strategies can be beneficial to anyone who has something to learn and remember.

Some forgetting is due to interference by other material. You can reduce this interference in several ways: (1) Learn the material thoroughly. (2) Make the material meaningful. (3) Engage in as little mental activity as possible between study and recall. (4) Do not study other similar material between study and recall. (5) Study in the same context where recall will occur, and study each set of material in a different context. (6) Study each set of material in a separate study session.

Should you try to learn the material all in one long study session (called "massed learning" by psychologists, and "cramming" by students), or should you divide your study up into several shorter study sessions (disbributed learning)? Studying for several shorter sessions is generally more effective than studying for one long session. One possible reason is that you can only concentrate for so long on one thing. A second reason is that what you have learned has a chance to consolidate in your mind during a break. In some situations, however, cramming may be more appropriate (for example, where recall will be required immediately after study, or where there is a time limitation).

Should you study all of the material over and over (whole learning) or should you divide it into parts and learn a part at a time (part learning)? Whole learning is better than part learning for the practiced learner, for material of moderate length, and for distributed learning. Whole learning gives an overall context to the parts. However, where the parts are very distinctive, where the material is very long, or where feedback is needed to keep going, part learning may be more appropriate. Compromise methods that combine whole and part learning may be the most effective for many learning tasks.

Repetition is one of the basic elements of almost all learning. We may learn some things with only one trial, but most learning requires us to repeat the material over and over. Although repetition is necessary, it is not sufficient; that is, repetition alone does not assure that you will remember the material. Once you have learned the material to the point of being able to recall it once perfectly, continued repetitions can still be beneficial; overlearning (continued learning beyond the point of mere recall) results in increased retention.

Recitation refers to repeating to yourself the material you have learned, without looking at it. In recitation you are practicing what will be required of you — recall. Recitation forces active learning, gives you feedback, involves repetition, and forces you to pay attention to what you are doing. Generally, it is advisable to spend as much of your study time as possible reciting, rather than rereading the material many times. Regardless of the nature of the material or of the learner, it is more effective to read and recite than to keep rereading.

SQ3R is a widely recommended study method that consists of five steps: Survey, Question, Read, Recite, Review. Suppose you are studying a chapter of a book. You should first survey the chapter by skimming it and noting the outline, headings, pictures, and graphs to get an overall view of what the chapter is about. Next you should skim again and ask yourself questions based on the headings, so that you will have something to look for when you are reading. Third, you should read the chapter without taking notes (for many students, reading is the first step, and for some it is the only step). After reading the chapter, recite to yourself what you could remember; quiz yourself and look up the answers to the questions you cannot remember. Finally, review what you have studied. Most study procedures that have been suggested fall within the SQ3R framework.

There is research evidence that the learning principles and strategies discussed in Chapters 3 and 4 really do make a significant contribution to learning. People who were given three hours of practice using these principles improved their memorizing ability eight times as much as did people who practiced memorizing for three hours without being instructed in the principles.

CHAPTER 5

Working Miracles
with Mnemonics

Can you remember a list of 50 words, or a 30-digit number, after hearing them only once? Can you look through a shuffled deck of cards once and remember all 52 cards in order? These are the kinds of demonstrations performed by mnemonists in public performances. In addition to duplicating these memory feats, and others that were discussed under "photographic memory" in Chapter 2, I have memorized the 136 phone numbers of everyone in a group to which I belong, and have memorized the major contents of each of 239 chapters in a book.

Such feats seem like miracles to people who are unfamiliar with the mnemonic systems involved, and they *are* miracles when compared with the abilities of the unaided memory. But most people could do such feats if they made the effort to learn and practice the mnemonic systems involved. You may not want to be able to perform these particular feats, but the important point is that you *can* — they are not beyond the reach of a normal memory. If you can do these feats, this means that you can also accomplish other memory tasks you *do* want to do, but may have thought were beyond your capacity.

Donald Norman introduced a chapter on mnemonics as follows:

> Throughout the centuries man has been concerned with the practical art of memory. Everyone knows that normally it is difficult to memorize things. Yet a few people have always known special techniques that make the task possible with apparent ease. We tend to ignore these techniques today because they are mere tricks and sophistry — the practitioners exhibit themselves as stage entertainers or advertise themselves and their methods in unrespectable classified

advertisements—but we cannot deny that the techniques work. In fact, we ought to examine procedures that simplify the job of memorizing with great care. Not only might they be useful in our lives, but the secrets of those who practice the art of memory ought to shed some light on the organization and operation of the mechanisms involved in memory.[1]

Gordon Bower has similarly observed that people have always searched for various rituals, tricks, gimmicks, and methods to improve their memories. He noted that the search has produced a few reasonably successful methods, which are advertised in sensationalistic terms in newspapers and magazines by commercial memory courses. He notes: "Although such hard-sell tactics are somewhat repugnant to respectable scholars (who view their grant proposals and fund-raising speeches in a different light), we should not be deterred by these commercial trappings from investigating scientifically some of the mnemonic devices."[2]

Fortunately, these commercial trappings have not deterred psychologists from scientifically investigating mnemonic devices in recent years. Their research has supported some of the commercial claims and refuted others. Research on mnemonics has provided new theories about memory processes, and also has practical implications for memory improvement.

The research evidence discussed in this chapter, as well as in the rest of the book, frequently does not lead to clear-cut, unambiguous conclusions. Often there are some studies that suggest one conclusion and others that suggest another conclusion. There are a number of differences among studies that make it hard to make direct comparisons between studies: the meaningfulness of the material learned (for example, nonsense syllables vs. prose); the ages of the learners (for example, one may use preschool children while another uses college students);* the kind of learning task (for example, paired-associate vs. serial learning); the time of memory measurement (for example, immediately after learning vs. a week later); the kind of memory measure (for example, recall vs. recognition); and the rate of presentation of material to be learned (for example, 2 seconds per item vs. 10 seconds per item). These are some of the factors that make it difficult to compare studies directly and to draw clear-cut conclusions. I have suggested conclusions that seem to be indicated by the evidence, without devoting too much space to discussing all the studies that would make us qualify the conclusion in some way; at the same time, I have given a little consideration to conflicting evidence, so that the conclusions will not be grossly oversimplified.

---

*While studies have been done on people ranging from 3-year-olds through adults, most of the research discussed in this book has been on college students. In describing the research, I have generally noted when the people participating in the studies were *not* college students.

WHAT IS MNEMONICS?

The word *mnemonic* may be briefly defined as "aiding the memory." A mnemonic system or technique is thus any system or technique that aids the memory. *Mnemonics* is used both as a singular word ("Mnemonics is an interesting field") and as a plural word ("Different mnemonics can be used for different learning tasks"). Mnemonics refers in general to the process or technique of improving the memory, but typically is used to refer more specifically to rather unusual, artificial memory techniques. For example, the strategies discussed in Chapter 4 aid the memory, but they are not usually referred to as mnemonic strategies.

The word *mnemonics* is derived from *Mnemosyne,* the ancient Greek goddess of memory. The use of mnemonics to aid the memory is not new; the Loci system described in Chapter 7 dates back to about 500 B.C., and was used by Greek orators to remember long speeches. An interesting book by Frances Yates traces the history of mnemonics from ancient times through the Renaissance.[3]

Some Examples

The rhymes, patterns, acrostics, and acronymns discussed in Chapter 3 in the section on "Meaningfulness" may properly be referred to as mnemonic techniques. "Thirty days hath September..." uses rhyme to help us remember the lengths of the months. ROY G. BIV is an artificial aid to help us remember the colors of the visible spectrum. "In 1492..." helps us remember when Columbus discovered America. Some of the examples discussed in Chapter 3 in the section on "Association" are also mnemonic techniques (for example, remembering "port" vs. "starboard" and "stalactite" vs. "stalagmite").

Some additional examples of specific-purpose mnemonic techniques using acrostics, and acronyms, rhymes, and other devices may help give a feeling for what a mnemonic technique is.[4]

An acrostic for remembering the order of plants from the sun is: Men Very Easily Make Jugs Serve Useful Nocturnal Purposes (Mercury, Venus, Earth, Mars, Jupiter, Saturn, Uranus, Neptune, Pluto). An acrostic that helped one woman line up baking ingredients in their proper order is: Shirley Shouldn't Eat Fresh Mushrooms (sugar, shortening, eggs, flour, milk).

SKILL (Skin, Kidneys, Intestines, Liver, Lungs). An acronym that may help a French student remember most of the verbs that are conjugated with the helping verb "to be" is the name of a lady—MRS. VANDERTAMP—to remember "Monter, Rester, Sortir, Venir, Aller, Naître, Descendre, Entrer, Rentrer, Tomber, Arriver, Mourir, Partir."

A rhyme for remembering the books of the Old Testament in order begins: "That great Jehovah speaks to us, in Genesis and Exodus; Leviticus and Numbers see, Followed by Deuteronomy," and continues for the remaining thirty-four books. A rhyme I once read on a Cheerios cereal box (when I was hard-pressed for reading material at breakfast one morning) is aimed at helping children remember what each vitamin does for us. Part of the rhyme went as follows:

> The vitamin called A has important connections
> It aids in our vision and helps stop infections.
> To vitamin C this ditty now comes,
> Important for healing and strong healthy gums.
> Done with both of these?
> Here come the B's:
>
> B_1 for the nerves.
> B_2 helps cells energize.
> Digesting the Protein's
> B_6's prize.

Rhymes have helped women in their cooking chores: "A pint's a pound, the world around" helps us remember a useful equivalence; "Cooking rice? Water's twice" helps us remember to cook one cup of raw rice in two cups of water; and "One big T equals teaspoons 3" helps us remember that there are three teaspoons in a tablespoon. A well-known mnemonic that is used to remember which way to set the clock for daylight savings time is, "Spring forward, fall back" (set the clock forward one hour in the spring, and back one hour in the fall).

To remember long numbers, sentences may be constructed so that the number of letters in each word corresponds with each of the digits in order. (If the first digit is "3," the first word would have three letters, etc.) For example, to remember Pi (π) to four decimal places (3.1416) remember: "Yes, I know a number." For the ambitious memorizer, this technique can be combined with the use of rhyme to remember π to thirty decimal places, as the following example from the *Mensa Journal* shows:

> Sir, I send a rhyme excelling
> In sacred truth and rigid spelling
> Numerical sprites elucidate
> All my own striving can't relate
> If nature gain
> Not you complain
> Though Doctor Johnson fulminate.

It has been noted that a rhyme ("Thirty days has September. . .") may help us remember how many days are in each month. If you have a hard time remembering the rhyme, you can use another mnemonic technique for remembering the number of days in the months (see the following diagram). Hold your hands out in front of you in a fist, with the palms down, the hands together. The knuckle of the left little finger represents January, the valley between it and the ring finger represents February, the knuckle of the ring finger represents March, and so on until you reach the knuckle of the right ring finger, which represents December. All the knuckle months have thirty-one days, and the valley months are the short months.

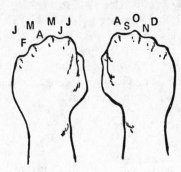

Memorizing the Calendar

While we are on the topic of calendars, let us consider again the twelve-digit number that we have encountered several times in the book: 266-315-374-264. In Chapter 3 you were told that if you memorize this twelve-digit number you will, in effect, have the calendar for the whole year of 1977 memorized. Here is how it works. Each digit represents the date of the first Sunday in each month; the first Sunday in January is the 2nd, the first Sunday in June is the 5th, and the first Sunday in December is the 4th.

Knowing that, all you have to know in addition is the months and the days of the week. If you can also add and subtract up to 7, then you can give the day of the week for any date. What day of the week is July 4, 1977? The seventh digit is 3, so the first Sunday in July is the 3rd. Add one day to determine that July 4, 1977 is a Monday. Try another one. What day is June 18, 1977? The sixth digit is 5, so the first Sunday in June is the 5th. Add 7 to get the second Sunday, the 12th, and add six more days to get the 18th, which is a Saturday. In this example, it may be simpler to add 7 more to the second Sunday to get the third Sunday, the 19th, then subtract one day.

Try a question like the following: How many Mondays are in May, 1977? The digit for May is 1, so the first Monday is May 2. Add sevens to get the other Mondays—May 9, 16, 23, 30; there are five Mondays in May. Try the following: What date is the fourth Thursday in November (Thanksgiving)? The digit for November is 6. This means the first Thursday (counting backward) is November 3, making the second Thursday November 10, the third Thursday November 17, and the fourth Thursday November 24.

Can you see how the principle of chunking is involved in this mnemonic? For all practical purposes you have 365 things memorized, when in fact you really have only 12 things memorized, but each of the 12 chunks represents about 30 bits of information (dates). Of course, you can adapt the technique to any year merely by memorizing the appropriate number for that year. The following are the key numbers for 1978 to 1980: 1978: 155-274-263-153; 1979: 744-163-152-742; 1980: 632-641-637-527. If you do not want to memorize a new number every year, you could use the 1977 number for 1978, with each number representing the first Monday of the month rather than the first Sunday of the month, and for 1979 with the number representing the first Tuesday of the month. For 1980, which is a leap year, it is probably simplest to memorize a new number again. Then, in 1981 you could memorize a new number to use for 1981 to 1983.

Specific Mnemonics

Many people make up their own specific mnemonic devices to help them in various learning tasks. One study found that about a third of psychology students studying for their final examinations sometimes used mnemonic techniques to remember points. The most frequent mnemonic technique used spontaneously by a group of college students to learn a list of words was the acronym, or some variation using the first letters of the words; a little over one-third of the students used this technique. The other two mnemonic techniques they used frequently were grouping the words by similar sounds or meanings, and making a story out of the words.[5]

When college students were given the task of learning paired associates, two-thirds of them used some kind of *verbal mediator* to relate the pairs of words.[6] A verbal mediator is the use of words to mediate, or associate, items to be remembered. For example, the pair "cats-rats" might yield verbal mediators such as "*cats* like to eat *rats*," or "*cats* sounds like *rats*," or "*cats* has the same three last letters as *rats*."

Most of the examples of mnemonic techniques discussed in this section are specific-purpose techniques. The "1492. . ." verse helps us remember when Columbus discovered America, but is not much good for remembering other dates. And "*i* before *e*. . ." helps us remember how to spell words with *ie* in them, but it is not much good for spelling other words. ROY G. BIV helps us remember the colors of the spectrum, but is not much good for anything else. Of course, other rhymes and acrostics may be constructed to help remember other dates, spelling words, etc., but these particular mnemonic techniques lack generality; they can be applied only for one purpose.

The mnemonic systems discussed in subsequent chapters are more general. They are not one-purpose techniques, but are more general-purpose systems that can be applied to different kinds of memory tasks. I will refer to the kinds of specific-purpose mnemonics discussed in this section as mnemonic "techniques," and will refer to the more general mnemonics discussed in Chapters 6 to 9 as mnemonic "systems." These are the Link, Loci, Peg, and Phonetic systems. The mnemonic systems are not limited to only one set of material, but can be used over and over to learn different kinds of material.

YOUR MENTAL FILING SYSTEM

In Chapter 1, an organized 3 × 5 file box was compared with a larger unorganized box to discuss the capacity of memory. Then, in Chapter 2, the analogy of a mental filing system was used in discussing short-term and long-term memory. Mnemonic systems may be viewed quite literally as mental filing systems. They allow you to store information in your memory in such a way that you will be able to find it and get it back out when you want it.

Suppose you were asked to go to the library and get a certain book. Even though the library may have thousands of books, the task would not be too hard because the books are filed systematically. You would go to the card catalog and look up the number of the book, then go to the part of the library where that number was located and get the book (unless your luck is like mine, in which case the book would probably be checked out).

Now suppose all the books in that library had been dumped into one big pile in an empty field, and you were asked to get a certain book. Your task would be much more difficult. Why? The pile contains the same number of books as the library. The difference is that you now have no systematic way to locate a particular book. You have to search through all the books to find a particular one.

Similarly, suppose you are given a list of ten items to remember. Later, when the time comes for recall, you begin looking through your memory for the ten items. For most people, the task is like finding one book in a pile of thousands of books. You know the ten items were put in your memory somewhere. But you know thousands of words; how can you systematically search through these words and identify the ten you are looking for? Unless the items were originally stored in some systematic, orderly manner, you have no good way to systematically search for them. For people who use a mnemonic system to learn the ten items, the task is more like finding a book in a library. They have stored the items in such a way that they can identify them and cue themselves as to where the items are.

As a mental filing system, a mnemonic system may help in at least three ways when you are trying to find items in your memory: (1) It will give you a place to start your search, a way to locate the first item. (2) It will give you a way of proceeding systematically from one item to the next. (3) It will let you know when your recall is finished, when you have reached the last item. Even for material that you know very well, you may have a hard time without steps 2 and 3 above. For example, try to recite the alphabet in random order. You are likely to find that by the time you are halfway finished, you are lost; you do not know for sure which letters you have named, or how many you have named — problems that do not occur when you recite the letters in alphabetical order.

PRINCIPLES OF MNEMONICS

An important point not realized by some people who read popular memory-training books is that mnemonic techniques and systems do not *replace* principles of learning, but rather *use* them. It removes some of the mystical aura around mnemonics to realize that they are based upon well-established principles of learning and memory. As Ian Hunter has stressed, mnemonic techniques are oddities only insofar as they enable their users to deal with memory tasks which most people do not even attempt in everyday life: "But they are not oddities in the sense that they employ any basic procedures which are absent from everyday activities. They are merely specialized elaborations of normal memory activites."[7] Mnemonic techniques and systems make use of the principles and strategies of learning and memory that were discussed in Chapters 3 and 4.

Principles of Memory Improvement

Meaningfulness. Mnemonic techniques and systems help make material meaningful, by using rhymes, patterns, associations, etc. Perhaps the most powerful example of the use of this principle is the Phonetic system (Chapter 9), which gives meaning to one of the most abstract, meaningless, kinds of material — numbers — so they will be easier to learn.

Organization. All of the mnemonic systems inherently involve organizing the material. They give a systematic way to record and retrieve the material. The previous example of finding a library book shows the advantage of organization.

Association. The principle of association is basic to all the mnemonic systems discussed in this book. In the Link system the items are associated to each other. In the Loci, Peg, and Phonetic systems, easily remembered material that is previously memorized serves as your filing system; you associate the new material that you want to learn with the material that has been previously memorized.

Visualization. Visual imagery also plays a central role in the mnemonic systems discussed in this book, because the associations are made visually. Visualization is probably the most unusual aspect of mnemonic systems, and may also be the most misunderstood. For these reasons, it is discussed more thoroughly in this book than any other principle. Chapter 2 discussed the differences between remembering pictures and words; Chapter 3 discussed the effectiveness of visual imagery in remembering verbal material; and the next section in this chapter will offer some suggestions for the effective use of visual associations to remember verbal material.

Of course, not all mnemonic techniques involve visual imagery. The techniques described earlier in this chapter are examples of nonvisual mnemonics. We have seen that verbal mediators are frequently used by college students in paired-associate tasks. For example, to associate the words "cats" and "rats" you could either form a mental picture of cats eating rats (visual mediator), or you could form the sentence, "Cats like to eat rats" (verbal mediator). Many studies have compared the effectiveness of verbal and visual mediators. Although some studies have found no significant difference between visual and verbal mediators,[8] visual mediators are more often found to be more effective than verbal ones for remembering concrete words, whereas verbal mediators may be more effective for abstract words.[9]

Attention and interest. Mnemonic systems force you to concentrate on the material in order to form pictures and associate them. They tend to be interesting because they make the material meaningful and involve visual imagery.

Strategies for Effective Learning

In addition to using the principles of memory improvement, mnemonic systems can also be used in connection with the strategies for effective learning discussed in Chapter 4. There is a considerable amount of evidence to show that, while mnemonic systems do not completely *eliminate* interference, they do *reduce* it as compared with using only the unaided memory.[10] For example, the Peg system (Chapter 8) has been used to learn six successive ten-item lists with very little interference among the different lists.[11] You will probably still get some interference among different lists if they are learned consecutively by the same mnemonic system, but the interference will be a lot less than if you did not use a system. Of course, you can reduce the interference even further by combining the use of mnemonics with the other methods for reducing interference discussed in Chapter 4 (such as studying the lists in different rooms and in separate sessions).

The effectiveness of mnemonic techniques can be increased if you combine them with other learning strategies. Space your study sessions out. Use whole and part learning where appropriate. Repeat the material (although learning material with a mnemonic system frequently takes fewer repetitions than learning with the unaided memory, your retention of the material will still be increased if you overlearn it). Use recitation. Finally, use the SQ3R steps where appropriate. For example, just because you use a mnemonic to learn something does not mean that you do not need to review the material occasionally. Remember, mnemonic systems aid the memory by using the basic principles and strategies of learning, not by replacing them.

HOW TO MAKE
EFFECTIVE VISUAL ASSOCIATIONS

Because visual associations play a central role in the mnemonic systems, it may be useful to have some guides for using visual imagery in associations. Four suggestions may be helpful in making effective visual associations.

Picture the Items Interacting

Visual imagery by itself may not be too effective. To make visual association effective, your imagery must both be "visual" *and* involve "association." It is necessary that the two items you are associating are pictured as interacting in some way with each other, rather than merely sitting next to each other, or one on top of the other. For example, if you were associating "dog" and "broom" it would be better to picture a dog sweeping with a broom than to picture a dog standing by a broom.

There is considerable research evidence supporting this conclusion that visual imagery must involve interaction among the items if it is to be effective. Research studies in which pictures have been shown to people, rather than having them make up their own mental pictures, reveal that when the items in the picture are interacting, they are remembered better than when they are not interacting—both for young children and for college students.[12] Studies in which people made up their own mental pictures to remember words have also shown that interacting imagery is more effective than separated images in paired-associate learning.[13]

Effectiveness of interacting images over separate images has also been found by Ian Begg, who suggested that the reason for the effectiveness of interacting imagery is that images of separate items can be combined into a single image which operates as a unit in memory; the image is remembered as a unit, so that each part of the image serves as a cue for remembering the rest of the unit.[14] This suggests that chunking plays a role in the effectiveness of interacting imagery—one image represents the relationship among two or more items. It is interesting to note also that interacting imagery is rated as more vivid than separate images,[15] which leads us to the next point.

Make the Pictures Vivid

The mental pictures should be seen as clearly as possible. A vivid visual image is one that is clear, distinct, and strong. For example, if you are associating "dog" and "broom," you should not just think about the words "dog" and "broom" together, or think about a dog sweeping with a broom, but should actually try to *see* the dog sweeping with the broom in your mind. People who are not used to visualizing may find that it helps if they close their eyes when trying to see the picture. It also helps if you make the picture detailed. What kind of dog is it? What kind of broom? Where is he sweeping? What is he sweeping? Picture a dachshund sweeping mud off your porch with a pushbroom; or a bulldog sweeping food off the kitchen floor with a straw broom.

Some suggestions that are frequently recommended to help make visual associations effective are aimed at making them more vivid: *motion* (see the picture in action—the dog is sweeping with the broom, not just holding it), *substitution* (see one item in place of the other—you are sweeping with a dog instead of a broom, or a broom is coming out of a doghouse), *exaggeration* (see one or both of the items exaggerated in size or number—a chihuahua is sweeping with a giant broom, or a St. Bernard is using a small whisk broom).

There are several different kinds of studies which suggest that visual associations should be vivid to be remembered. In one study of imagery in paired-associate learning, people rated the vividness of their images as they constructed them. For every person, the more vivid the images were rated, the better they were recalled. This positive relationship between recall and vividness of imagery has also been found for sentences. In another study, students instructed to make *vivid* mental images tended to remember a list of words better than students told only to make mental images; students instructed to make *vivid, active* images tended to perform even better.[16]

People learned concrete sentences or paragraphs that described events with either high or low vividness. The vivid descriptions were more emotional, colorful, and forceful and yielded more graphic imagery. The vivid sentences and paragraphs were recalled better than the nonvivid ones. Similarly, including vivid adjectives in paragraphs can result in better recall of the paragraphs than using "dull" adjectives, and vivid pictures (like a crashed airplane) are remembered better than normal pictures (like a flying airplane).[17]

Should the Pictures be Bizarre?

Popular memory-training books typically recommend that visual associations must be bizarre (unusual, weird, implausible, incongruous, or ludicrous). The opposite of bizarre would be plausible — imagining a picture that makes sense, and could really occur. For example, a picture of a dog being chased out of a house by a person with a broom is plausible; a dog sweeping with a broom would be somewhat bizarre; and a dog riding a broom like a witch, or a person sweeping the floor with a dog tied to the end of a broomstick would be bizarre.

Three studies provide evidence that bizarre imagery can be effective, but these studies did not compare bizarre imagery directly with plausible imagery to see if it is more effective than plausible imagery.[18] Most research that has made such a direct comparison has found no difference between bizarre and plausible imagery. Studies have also found that bizarre imagery is not more effective than plausible imagery in paired-associate tasks or in tasks using the Loci system or the Link and Peg systems.[19]

Novel visual associations between objects have been found to help memory for the objects more than did common associations, as long as the novel associations were plausible. However, implausible novel associations were no more effective than common plausible associations.[20] (A man playing a harp is an example of a common plausible association; a man sitting on a harp is a novel plausible association; a harp playing a man is an implausible novel association.)

One study compared the importance of bizarreness vs. interaction. People saw pictures composed of two objects. Some of the objects were bizarre and some were common. In addition, some of the objects were interacting and some were not. Interacting pictures were recalled better than noninteracting pictures, but bizarreness did not affect recall.[21]

Thus, there is considerable evidence that bizarre visual associations are not more effective than plausible ones. There is even one study that suggests that bizarre images may be *less* effective.[22]

When bizarreness does help, it is probably because bizarre images incorporate other factors that help memory. Thus, some interacting images may almost have to be bizarre in order to involve interaction (for example, it is hard to think of a plausible picture showing an elephant and a piano inter acting). Bizarre images may be more vivid than plausible images; bizarre images tend to be unique, and the uniqueness of an image helps memory; bizarre images take more time to form than do plausible images and extra time spent on an image may increase its memorability.[23]

However, all of these factors (interaction, vividness, uniqueness, extra time) can also be used in images that are not bizarre. It is not necessary that an image be bizarre to incorporate these factors. One popular memory-training book illustrated the advantages of ridiculous, impossible, illogical associations by the following examples for associating *airplane* and *tree:* A logical picture would be an airplane parked near a tree. Since that is possible, the book said, it probably will not work; better pictures would be airplanes growing on trees, or trees boarding an airplane.[24] It is true that the latter examples would be more memorable than a plane parked near a tree. However, it is also true that more plausible pictures involving interaction, vividness, and uniqueness would also be more memorable; for example, a low-flying airplane shearing the tops off trees, or an airplane crashing into a tree.

One reason why bizarreness may be ineffective for some people is that some people have a hard time making up bizarre images.[25] For the person who finds it difficult to make up bizarre images, or who feels uncomfortable doing so, my recommendation would be to concentrate on making the images interacting and vivid, and not worry about making them bizarre. On the other hand, for the person who does not have any trouble imagining bizarre associations, and who feels comfortable with them, my recommendation is to go ahead and use them. These research findings do not mean that bizarreness does not help, but only that it is not necessary.

Make Abstract Material Concrete

In Chapter 2 we saw that concrete words are easier to visualize than abstract words. It is not hard to picture concrete words such as *apple, car, book,* and *horse,* but it is harder to picture more abstract words such as *nourishment, liberty, justice,* and *happiness.* Since most mnemonic systems use visual imagery, how can the systems be used to remember abstract material?

The procedure for using imagery to help remember abstract terms is the same as for concrete terms except that you substitute a concrete word to represent the abstract word. One way of doing this is to use objects that typify the abstract term: for *liberty,* you might picture the liberty bell; for *justice,* picture a judge; for *happiness,* a smiling face; for *education,* a schoolhouse; for *fashion,* a model; for *depth,* a hole; for *agree,* a nodding head; for *salary,* a paycheck.

A second way of substituting a concrete word for an abstract one is to use objects whose names sound like the abstract term (at least enough to remind you of the term): *celery* for *salary; fried ham* for *freedom; happy nest* for *happiness*. You can even use this technique to remember nonsense syllables: Cage for KAJ; rocks for ROX; seal for ZYL; sack for XAC. This technique is frequently recommended in memory-training books and we will see in Chapter 10 that it plays an important role in remembering names and faces. Does it help?

Pictures of concrete substitute objects have been found to help in learning abstract paired associates. For example, a picture of a hammer hitting a vacuum cleaner can help remember the pair, "impact-vacuum," and a picture of a big flower in an open doorway can help remember "bloom-portal."[26] By using concrete substitute words, people can employ visual imagery to learn abstract words almost as well as concrete words, and can even use visual imagery to help in concept learning.[27]

Another possible way to make abstract verbal material more concrete is suggested by a study on memory for abstract sentences such as "the regulations annoyed the salesman," or "the set fell off the table." Such sentences were remembered better by adding concrete modifiers to yield sentences such as, "the strict parking regulations annoyed the salesman," and "the ivory chess set fell off the table."[28]

LIMITATIONS OF MNEMONICS

It was noted in Chapter 1 that mnemonic systems are not magical, all-powerful answers to all learning tasks. In this section we will consider some of the limitations of mnemonic systems. Some of the limitations are a result of the use of visual imagery, while others would apply also to verbal mnemonics.

Time

We saw in Chapter 2 that visual memory processes may be somewhat slower than verbal processes. It may take a little longer to think up an image of the object that is represented by a word than to think of the word itself. Many studies have shown that if material is presented too fast, you may not have time to form images and associate them.[29] Thus, visual associations may not be an effective strategy when material is presented too fast.

What is "too fast?" The Peg system (Chapter 8) has been found to be effective at a learning rate of 4 or 8 seconds per item, but not at 2 seconds per item.[30] Two seconds is apparently not long enough for the unpracticed person to form effective visual associations. A difference of only 1 second per item (5 vs. 6 seconds) has been found to make a significant difference in the effectiveness of visual associations for remembering the items.[31] Studies using visual imagery in paired-associate learning typically give people at least 5 seconds per pair; when allowed to set their own rate, people average about 7 seconds per pair.[32] If material is presented to you at the rate of 1 or 2 seconds per item, you will probably not be able to use visual imagery to remember it.

However, we have noted previously that any kind of coding to transfer material from short-term memory to long-term memory takes time—whether it be visualizing, chunking, associating, organizing, or seeking meaning. Thus, the time limitation is not unique to mnemonic systems using visual imagery (although the time limitation is a more serious problem for visual imagery with abstract words than with concrete words, as discussed in the next section). Also, it may be noted that you can improve your speed of making visual associations with practice; the more you practice forming visual associations, the less time it takes for you to do it.[33] The average time of 7 seconds per association is for people who are using visualization for the first time. In addition, the time limitation does not matter in many practical learning tasks, because you can determine your own rate; the material does not come one item at a time at a set rate. Finally, it should be noted that, even though it may take longer to go through some materials once using visual associations than not using them, you usually will not have to go back through the material as many times to learn it, so that the overall learning time may be less.[34]

Abstract Material

As we saw earlier in the chapter, visual imagery may aid memory for abstract terms by using concrete substitute words. However, the use of concrete substitute words for abstract terms has at least three possible limitations. First, to form an image this way takes somewhat longer than for concrete words.[35] The process takes an additional step—thinking of a concrete word to represent the abstract term. Also, abstract words tend to have more dictionary entries than concrete words, and words with many dictionary meanings tend to be learned more slowly than words with fewer meanings, even when they are equated in imagery value.[36]

Second, the substitute word is only a cue to remind you of the abstract idea and there is always the chance that you will remember the word without remembering the idea it represents. It is possible that you might recall the picture of a liberty bell or a judge or a smiling face and not be able to recall that they represent *liberty, justice,* or *happiness.* This may be one reason why it has been found to be more difficult to decode abstract mediators than concrete mediators.[37]

A third limitation of using concrete substitute words is that there are some abstract terms and ideas for which it may be very hard to form good, representative, concrete words. For example: "assertion," "function," "theory," "necessity," "value," "analysis," "inference." Even if you can come up with some concrete words for such terms, they will likely take inordinately long to construct and will likely not be very good representations of the abstract terms they represent.

Although visual imagery can help you remember abstract material, because of the above limitations verbal mediators may be more effective than visual mediators for some abstract material. Verbal mediators are not as dependent on the concreteness of the material for their use. For example, to associate "theory" and "value" you could say "that theory has considerable value," but it would be hard to think of a good image for this association. In addition, research has shown that verbal mediators do not take more time for abstract terms than for concrete terms, as visual mediators do.[38]

Learning versus Retention

There is some debate among researchers as to whether mnemonics help only learning or also help retention. In Chapter 2 we saw that the rate of forgetting depends on how well you learn something more than on how fast you learn it. Thus, it is possible to learn material faster without necessarily retaining it longer. Some researchers say that although mnemonic techniques and systems help one learn material faster, they do not help one remember it longer.[39] For example, verbal mediators helped learning but not retention in fifth-graders, and the same result has been found for both visual and verbal mediators with college students.[40] In fact, it has even been claimed that we cannot really improve memory, but that memory systems work by improving learning.

On the other hand, there are those who say that mnemonics help a person remember material longer, as well as learn it faster. Studies have found that visual associations aid retention for days, weeks, or even months.[41] After reviewing the relevant research, Allan Paivio concluded that although a few studies do show that imagery does not help long-term retention, most studies show that imagery does help retention at least as much as it helps learning.[42]

There are two considerations that we should keep in mind concerning this issue of learning vs. retention. First, whether mnemonics help retention depends on how retention is measured, and retention has been measured different ways in different studies. To illustrate the differences, let us consider a simple hypothetical example. Suppose one group of people learned a list of twenty items using a mnemonic, and a second group learned the list without using a mnemonic. After going through the list once, the first group remembered an average of eighteen items and the second remembered an average of twelve items. This would indicate that the mnemonic helped in learning the list better with one exposure. A week later, the mnemonic group may remember twelve items and the other group eight items. Did the mnemonic help retention a week later? Using the *amount remembered,* it did—the mnemonic group remembered four more items than the other group. Using the *amount forgotten* it did not—the mnemonic group forgot two more items than the other group. Using the *percentage* remembered or forgotten, there was no difference between the two groups; they each forgot one-third of what they had learned. Such differences in measuring retention constitute one reason for conflicting findings as to whether mnemonics help retention as well as learning.

The second consideration to keep in mind is that the issue of learning vs. retention may be an important theoretical distinction to the researcher, but may not make much practical difference to the person doing the learning. Suppose that mnemonics did help learning only. Now suppose that one group used a mnemonic system to learn material and another group did not. Each group learned the material until they could recite it perfectly once. Now, if mnemonics helped learning but not retention, we would expect that they would remember the same amount a week later. But, the mnemonic group may have taken only 10 minutes to learn the material and the other group may have taken 30 minutes. This means that the mnemonics helped the people to make more efficient use of their study time—they remembered as much as the other group with only a third as much study. But suppose that both groups studied for 30 minutes. This would mean that the mnemonic group could then spend 20 minutes overlearning the material, so that they would have it learned better and thus would retain it longer.

Imagery Ability

Many adults are not used to thinking in images. Surveys of mnemonic techniques that are used spontaneously by college students in learning lists of words did not find visual imagery among the many different techniques they used.[43] Perhaps this is because visualizing is harder work than verbalizing;[44] or perhaps as children acquire language skills they rely less and less on imagery;[45] or perhaps our culture and educational system, with its emphasis on facts and its verbal orientation, destroys the childhood reliance on imagery.[46] Whatever the reason, there is evidence that children tend to rely on imagery for memory more than adults do.[47] Because many adults are not used to picturing things, visualization seems unnatural to them. Those adults who do have the ability to use imagery benefit more from instructions to make visual associations than do adults lacking this ability.[48] Thus, mnemonic systems using visual imagery may have limited usefulness for some adults.

However, even though some people may not have the *ability* to use imagery, most people do have the *capacity* to do so, and can be trained to use imagery.[49] Disadvantaged black grade-school children in a summer urban action program, very young children, and even mentally retarded children, have been trained to use mnemonic elaborations effectively.[50]

People who can visualize well can benefit from the start by the mnemonic systems. People who have difficulty visualizing may require some time to develop the ability, but if they practice they can acquire the skill. It has been suggested that some people do not do too well when they first try to use visual associations to remember, not because they are incapable of imagery but rather because they may not try as hard, or may resort to other methods because they do not trust the procedure.[51] The few people who cannot use visual imagery at all, and cannot learn to do so, may be able to use mnemonic techniques involving verbal mediation; but the visual imagery part of mnemonic systems may be less powerful for them.

Verbatim Memory

Some memory tasks require word-for-word memorizing of verses of scripture, poems, speeches, etc. Mnemonic systems are not especially appropriate for verbatim memory. When people ask me how to memorize verses of scripture, or poems, etc., I refer them to the memorizing strategies discussed in Chapter 4. We will see in subsequent chapters how mnemonic systems can help in remembering the points or ideas to be covered in a speech or poem, and in getting them in the right order, but the systems do not help as much in the word-for-word memory.

Interference

We have seen that one of the advantages of mnemonic systems is that they tend to reduce interference between different sets of material. Now I will suggest that visual images may actually increase interference. There is really no inconsistency, because we are now talking about a different kind of interference.

An image may be easy to remember, but when it is used to remember verbal material, the image must be decoded back into the appropriate verbal response. The interference problem arises in recalling a concrete noun that has synonyms that could be represented by the same picture. Thus, one picture could represent more than one word. For example, the picture of a small child could also represent "infant," or "baby"; the picture of a dog could also represent "canine," or "wolf"; and the picture of a carpet could also represent "rug."

This interference problem can arise especially when we are using imagery to learn abstract material. For example, if we use an image of a smiling face to represent "happiness," then later when we recall the smiling face we might think of "smile," "face," or "head." A number of studies indicate that while high imagery is superior to low imagery, this kind of decoding error is more likely with visual images than with verbal material alone.[52]

PSEUDO-LIMITATIONS
OF MNEMONICS

The previous section discussed some of the valid limitations and problems of mnemonics. There are also pseudo-limitations—criticisms that are based on problems and limitations that are not as valid as the ones just discussed, or that are not as serious as some critics would have us believe. Gordon Bower has observed that "like many things, mnemonic techniques are easy to parody and poke fun at." But, he noted, that makes them no less effective, "and there is nothing like success to reinforce someone in a new method of learning." He also observed that critics rarely make explicit that the alternatives to mnemonics in memorizing are either "dumb, blind repetition or simply outright failure, and no one seems to want to champion these alternatives."[53] Let us look at some of the criticisms that have been made of mnemonics.

What About Understanding?

Some people (and some textbooks on learning and memory) dismiss mnemonic systems with the comment that they are effective for certain kinds of rote memory tasks, but that many learning tasks involve understanding and reasoning more than straight memory for facts. The implication is that the systems are not worth learning because they do not help understanding and comprehension.

It is generally true that mnemonic techniques and systems are not effective in learning tasks that involve understanding (although there is evidence that visual imagery can help in *understanding* both concrete and abstract sentences, as well as *remembering* them[54]). However, to say that mnemonic systems are not worth learning because many learning tasks do not involve straight memory is somewhat like saying that French is not worth learning because many people do not speak French, or that the multiplication tables are not worth learning because many math problems do not involve multiplication. It is true that many tasks are not straight memory; however, it is also true that many tasks *are* straight memory. Whether we like it or not, everyone has many things to remember — names, phone numbers, things to do, things to buy, addresses, errands, etc.

Much of school work also involves straight memory. Gordon Bower has suggested that schools should teach memory skills just as they teach the skills of reading and writing, and he offered the following insightful analysis of the role of memory in education:

> Although teachers typically describe educational goals in such lofty terms as teaching their students to be critical, insightful, curious, and deeply appreciative of the subject matter, these are usually only extra requirements beyond the learning of basic facts that is demanded as a minimum. Any geography student who thinks Istanbul is in France, or any art-history student who thinks Salvador Dali painted the Sistine Chapel, is going to flunk his exams if he pulls such boners often enough.
>
> The point is that we do demand that students learn a lot of facts just as we are constantly required to do in our daily life. You can get a feel for this if you try to carry on an intelligent conversation about some current event. . .without having learned some facts about the topic.
>
> But the solution to the problem is probably at hand. By systematically applying the knowledge that we now have about learning, we should be able to improve our skills so that we spend less time memorizing facts. By the strategic use of mnemonics, we might free ourselves for those tasks we consider more important than memorization.[55]

People who are more concerned with understanding and reasoning than with memorizing may still benefit in at least two ways by using mnemonics: (1) They can memorize the necessary routine things more efficiently, and thus free their minds to spend more time on tasks that involve understanding and reasoning. (2) They can better remember the facts that they use for understanding and creating; even those tasks that involve reasoning and understanding require that one remember the facts in order to reason with them and understand them.

You Have More to Remember

Most mnemonic systems actually increase the amount of material you must remember. They require you to memorize material constituting a mental filing system in addition to the information you want to remember. This leads some critics to suggest that the systems are actually more work than it would be to just learn the information by itself (something like determining the number of horses in a herd by counting the number of legs and dividing by four).

It is true that most mnemonic systems do add to the material to be remembered, and as a result, they may be extra effort at first. But this extra effort may be illusory for two reasons.

First, it was noted in Chapter 1 that remembering is hard work, and that memory training does not make it any easier, just more effective. Mnemonic systems are not supposed to take the effort out of learning; they are supposed to give you more for the effort you put in. Learning to use mnemonics is a skill, and requires some practice. When a person is first learning to type, typing may be slower than writing, and it may seem that typing is more trouble than it is worth. But after the person masters the skill, then typing is faster than writing.

Or a person who plays golf may find that learning a new grip or a new swing may actually hinder her game at first. But if she keeps practicing it, then she will find that her game improves. Similarly, mnemonic systems may seem at first to be more trouble than they are worth, but a person who makes the effort to learn them and get used to using them will find that they are well worth the effort.

Second, remember that in memory the number of *chunks* is more important than the number of *items*. You can remember a sentence containing forty letters better than you can remember a series of ten unrelated letters. Thus, the amount of material you must remember is not the main concern. Once you learn the additional material involved in a mnemonic system, you will find that its advantages in terms of organization and meaningfulness far outweigh the disadvantage of having additional material to remember. In the words of two researchers, "Recall seems to be helped rather than hindered by elaboration despite the extra duty it entails. Whatever advantage it confers more than makes up for the extra burdens on memory."[56]

It's a Crutch

A criticism made by some people who hear a mnemonic technique or system described for the first time is that a person may become dependent upon it, and use it as a memory crutch. Then he will not be able to remember the material without the crutch. For example, how many people can remember how many days are in November without going through the rhyme, "Thirty days. . ."? The critic asks, "What happens when you forget the crutch?"

There are at least three ways to respond to this question. First the "crutches" are frequently not forgotten as easily as the items would be without the crutch.[57] For example, you may remember some mnemonics long after you have forgotten the material they represent (such as, "On Old Olympus. . ."). But remembering the mnemonic is not responsible for your forgetting the material.

The second response to the crutch criticism is that such dependency frequently does not happen. It may be possible that this may occur with some material that you do not learn very thoroughly and/or use very often. However, if the material is something that you use regularly, you will soon find that you no longer need to recall the mnemonic association in order to recall the material. Soon the material comes automatically. I can recall material that I learned several years ago using a mnemonic system, but cannot remember some of the associations I originally used to learn the material.

A third response to the crutch criticism is that even if a person did become dependent on a mnemonic to remember certain material, is that necessarily bad? Is it undesirable for a person with poor eyesight to become dependent on eyeglasses to help him see better? Is it more undesirable for you to be dependent on a twelve-digit number for remembering a year's calendar than to not remember the calendar, or to depend on mnemonic techniques to remember the names of everyone you meet than to forget everyone's name? I think not. Even if the crutch criticism were true, it is usually better to remember material with a mnemonic than to not remember the material.

An irony of the crutch criticism is that it serves as the basis for two conflicting criticisms. On one hand, the critic says that you cannot remember the material without the crutch (meaning that you are lost if you forget the crutch). On the other hand, the critic says that you become too dependent on the crutch to remember the material (meaning that you cannot forget the crutch).

It's a Trick

Isaac Asimov described an experience that illustrates a view of intelligence similar to some people's view of memory. When Asimov buys several objects at a store, he watches the clerk write the numbers on a slip of paper — say, $1.55, $1.45, $2.39, and $2.49 — and automatically mutters the total — $7.88. When the clerk finishes his addition and gets $7.88, he looks up in awe and says, "That's amazing. You must be very smart to be able to do a thing like that." Then Asimov explains how to do it: "You don't add $1.45 and $1.55. You take five cents from one and add it to the other so you have $1.50 and $1.50, which comes to $3 at once. Then instead of adding $2.39 and $2.49 you add a penny to each and add $2.40 and $2.50, which comes to $4.90, remembering that you will have to remove the pennies you added. The $3 and the $4.90 are $7.90 and when you take off the two pennies, you have $7.88 and that's your answer. If you practice that sort of thing, you can..."

About this point, Asimov has to stop because he cannot ignore the clerk's cold stare as he says, "Oh it's just a trick." Asimov observes, "Not only am I no longer intelligent, I am nothing but a faker. To the average person, in other words, understanding the properties of numbers and using those properties is *not* intelligent. Performing mechanical operations *is* intelligent."[58]

Some people have a similar view of memory. Understanding the principles of memory and applying them via mnemonic techniques is *not* memorizing. Rote repetition and drill *is* memorizing. Such a view results in the claim that the use of mnemonics is unfair. Since a mnemonic is a trick or gimmick, it is unfair to use a mnemonic system because you are not really remembering.

This criticism seems to be saying that you are cheating if you do not do things the hard way. You are cheating to use an aid. Actually, the "unfairness" to the critics probably lies in the fact that you can remember so much more than they can. It is no less "fair" to use aids to train the memory than it is to use special training techniques to train long-distance runners, or keyboard-learning aids to teach piano lessons, or a mathematical formula for finding the circumference of a circular field given the diameter (is it somehow more "fair" to walk around the field and measure it with a tape measure than to use πd?).

It's Not Practical

Frequently people will come up to me after a lecture and demonstration, in which I have memorized a list of twenty-five words called out by the audience or been tested on a magazine I memorized, and say that they do not have much use for remembering a long list of unrelated nouns, or for knowing where everything can be found in a magazine. After all, they are not planning to give lectures and demonstrations. I anticipate these questions and emphasize in my lecture that mnemonic systems are not just for show. One memory performer and teacher, F. Stephen Hamilton, reported similar experiences and noted:

> I cannot say too often that memory training is not merely the perfection of a number of memory feats which, though startling in effect, have no applicability other than that of diversion. Those who have not taken courses in memory education seem to have some difficulty appreciating this. Many people who attend my lectures applaud the demonstrations as if they were witnessing a conjurer's performance instead of an exhibition of applied psychology.[59]

The mnemonic systems do have practical uses, and many such uses will be suggested and described in subsequent chapters. At this point, let us merely note some possible uses of mnemonics in education. Laird Cermak predicted that mnemonic methods of organization will some day be taught as a high school subject. Gordon Bower suggested a number of educational uses of mnemonics, primarily in rote learning situations, and gave examples of how different mnemonics can be used. Ernest Hilgard and Gordon Bower suggested that teaching pupils techniques of mnemonics and imagery is "likely to maximize the amount of learning obtained within the least time, and with the least repetitive drill and difficulty." Allan Paivio suggested that "probably the most important practical outcome of research on imagery and verbal process will be in relation to problems of education."[60]

There are at least two ways in which imagery has implications for school instruction: (1) It has implications for the way in which instructional materials can best present information to students to help learning and retention (for example, concrete vs. abstract, pictorial vs. verbal, interacting vs. separate); (2) it has implications for the kinds of activities students should be taught to increase their power of learning (for example, verbal and visual elaboration).[61]

The feasibility of using mnemonic training in education is further supported by findings that visual imagery helped in learning reading material like that found in textbooks, for third-, fourth-, fifth-, and sixth-graders and for high-school students;[62] and by the findings noted earlier in this chapter that educationally disadvantaged children and retarded children can be taught to use mnemonic elaboration.

MNEMONIC SYSTEMS

The mnemonic systems discussed in following chapters are based on the principles discussed in this chapter. Allan Paivio noted that there are at least three critical assumptions underlying the use of mnemonic systems: (1) Concrete objects are easier to remember than words; (2) concrete objects are particularly effective as retrieval cues for associated material; and (3) visual images of the concrete objects can serve as effective mediators for verbal material.[63] We have seen evidence in this chapter, and in previous chapters, that supports each of these assumptions.

The next four chapters discuss four kinds of mnemonic systems: the Link system, the Loci system, the Peg system, and the Phonetic system. Each of these systems has some advantages over the previous systems. Each of the following four chapters is organized into three major sections. The first section describes the mnemonic system. The second section discusses research evidence concerning how well the system works (the reader who has no interest in such research evidence can skip this section without a loss of continuity). The third section suggests ways in which the system might be used in practical memory tasks.

After you have studied the mnemonic systems in Chapters 6 to 9, read this chapter again. Many of the points discussed in this chapter will be even more meaningful when you are familiar with these systems.

SUMMARY

Although most people do not especially *want* to do the kinds of memory demonstrations done by memory performers, most people *can* do them. Mnemonic techniques and systems can be used to accomplish memory tasks that seem like miracles to the person who is unfamiliar with mnemonics.

Mnemonics refers generally to memory aids, and more specifically to rather unusual, artifical memory aids. Examples of mnemonics include specific-purpose techniques such as rhymes, patterns, acrostics, acronyms, and special techniques for remembering months and dates, and more general-purpose systems, such as the Link, Loci, Peg, and Phonetic systems.

Mnemonic systems may be viewed quite literally as mental filing systems. They help you store information in your memory in such a way that you will be able to make a systematic search of memory to find the information and get it back out when you want it.

Mnemonic techniques and systems seem like somewhat mysterious oddities to many people, but mnemonics do not replace the basic principles of effective learning. Rather, they are based on the principles of learning. Mnemonics use the principles of meaningfulness, association, organization, visualization, attention, and interest. They also help reduce interference. In addition, the strategies for effective learning may be used along with mnemonics.

Because visualization plays a central role in most mnemonic systems, and is the most unique feature, it helps to know some techniques for forming effective visual associations. The items being associated should be pictured as interacting in some way, rather than pictured separately. The visual images should be as vivid as possible. Motion, substitution, and exaggeration may help make pictures vivid. Contrary to what most popular memory training books advise, it is not necessary that the images be bizarre, although bizarre images can be used if desired. To use visual imagery to remember abstract information, concrete substitute words must be found to represent the abstract terms, and visual associations then formed using the substitute words.

Mnemonic techniques and systems are not all-powerful answers to every learning task; they have some limitations, many of which result from using visual imagery. (1) It takes some time to form visual images, and if material is presented too fast, you may not be able to use visual imagery to remember it. This limitation also applies somewhat to other ways of coding information. (2) Visual associations do not work as well with abstract material as they do with concrete material. (3) Although the evidence is quite consistent that mnemonics help one to learn certain kinds of material faster, there is some disagreement as to how much they help to remember the material longer. (4) People differ in their ability to use visual association; although most people can be trained to use visual imagery, the person who has a difficult time with it will not find the mnemonic systems as powerful. (5) The mnemonic systems are not especially appropriate for word-for-word memorization. (6) When decoding pictures that could represent more than one word, some interference may occur in trying to determine which word the picture represents.

In addition to the limitations, there are also some pseudo-limitations of mnemonics—criticisms that are not really valid. (1) What about understanding? Mnemonic systems are not designed to help so much in learning tasks involving reasoning and understanding. But enough memory tasks involve rote memory to justify learning the systems. (2) You have more to remember. This is generally true, but the advantages in terms of meaningfulness and organization outweigh the additional material to be learned. (3) It's a crutch. It is not necessarily true that learners will always be dependent on the mnemonic used to learn material, or that if they forget the mnemonic they will forget the material. (4) It's a trick. The use of mnemonics is claimed to be a trick or gimmick that is not really using the memory. Of course, the use of aids to help the memory is no less reasonable than the use of aids to help anything else. (5) It's not practical. This is the response of people who see memory demonstrations, and do not realize that the same principles apply to other more practical information. Mnemonic systems do have practical uses, and several researchers have suggested their implications for educational settings.

CHAPTER 6

Using Mnemonics — The Link System

The Link system is the most elementary of the mnemonic systems. In fact, it may really be too simple to be called a "system." It is the system I usually describe when I give a one-hour lecture on mnemonics, because, although it is simple, it is adequate to illustrate the principles on which mnemonic systems are based, and to illustrate how powerful they can be for appropriate kinds of material. The Link system is appropriate for serial learning tasks, where you have a series of items to remember. The Link helps you remember all the items in order.

WHAT IS THE LINK SYSTEM?

The Link system, which could also be called the Chain system, consists of two steps. First, form a visual image for each item in the list to be learned. Second, associate the image for each item with the image for the next item. Thus, you form a visual association between the first two items, then between the second and third items, then between the third and fourth items, and so on. You do not try to associate every item with every other item in one big picture, but rather associate them two at a time. The reason for the name of this system should be obvious — you are linking the items together to form a chain of associations.

As an example, suppose that a person were given a list that begins with the following five items: paper, tire, doctor, rose, ball.* To use the Link system in remembering these five items, you first form a visual association relating *paper* and *tire*. You might picture a car driving on paper tires, or yourself using a tire to erase writing from a paper. Next, associate *tire* and *doctor*. You might picture a tire running over a doctor, or a tire performing an operation. To associate *doctor* and *rose*, you might picture a doctor operating on a rose, or a doctor giving roses to a patient. To associate *rose* and *ball*, you might picture two people playing catch with a rose, or balls growing on a rose brush.

The visual associations I have suggested vary—some are bizarre and some are plausible. If you like bizarreness, you can use bizarre images. If not, you can use plausible ones, as long as they are vivid and interacting. Generally, you should use the first association that comes to your mind, because it will likely also be the first one to come to your mind when you want to recall the items. Whatever your association is, use the guides and principles discussed in Chapter 5 to form an effective visual association.

The associations I have suggested for these five items are some possibilities that come to my mind; they may not be the most memorable ones for you. Several research studies have shown that both visual and verbal mediators are more effective if you think them up yourself than if they are given to you by someone else, probably because other people suggest different associations than you would make up yourself.[1] However, people who may not be able to construct good mediators may benefit by having associations suggested to them—such as young children and mental retardates.[2]

When I am giving a list of words orally so an audience can try using the Link system, I emphasize two points: First, I tell them to make sure they actually *see* each of their associations, even if it is only for a brief second. Second, I tell them that after I have given them about eight or ten words of the list they are going to worry about forgetting the first few words, and will want to go back and review those words. I tell them, "Do not go back and review, or you will miss the new associations. Just concentrate on making a good association with each item as it comes, and trust your memory that you will be able to get the items back when you want them."

To recall a list learned by the Link system, you begin with the first item, and proceed in order as each item leads to the next one. For our example, think of paper; see the image that involves paper and it reminds you of tire; tire leads you to doctor; doctor leads to rose; and rose leads to ball.

*With only five items to remember, it may be just as easy for some people to remember the items without using a system. However, the procedure is the same whether you have five items or fifty items.

Using the Link system, you have a word to cue you for each following word, except for the first word. How can you cue yourself to remember the first word? One strategy is to associate the first word with the source of the list. For example, if a person is giving you the list, associate the first item on the list with that person.

The Story System

A method that is a variant of the Link system is the Story system, in which you weave the items into a connected story. The Story system is an extension of the use of sentences as mediators in a paired-associate task; you just continue with additional sentences to form a story based on the items you want to remember. For example, you might use something like the following for the previous five-item list: The *paper* boy rolled a *tire* down the sidewalk, and it hit the *doctor* coming to make a house call (now that's a bizarre idea!). It knocked him into a *rose* bush, and he picked up a *ball* and threw it at the boy.

The Story system is very similar to the Link system. However, there are at least four differences. First, in the Link system you link each pair of items independent of the previous links, while in the Story system you link the items in a continuous, integrated, sequence. This logical sequence is an advantage of the Story system over the Link system for some people, who find it easier to recall a story than a series of unrelated associations. Second, the Story system may require a little more time to make each association than the Link system does, because you must think of an association that fits the narrative of the story, rather than using the first association that comes to your mind. A third difference is that the longer the list, the harder it is to work each succeeding item into an integrated story. Most people find it very hard to put together a story to remember a list of twenty items.[3] However, it is not much harder to use the Link system on a list of twenty items than on a list of ten items. Fourth, items learned by the Link system can be recalled in backward order almost as well as forward; but items weaved into a story may be harder to recall backward.

The procedure for recalling the items with the Story system is essentially the same as with the Link system. Begin with the first item and proceed through the story, picking the key words out as you come to them.

The Story system can be used effectively without visual imagery, but it is probably more powerful if you actually picture the events happening as you think of them. In fact, the Link system can also be used with verbal mediators, for a person who cannot use visual imagery (verbal associations may also be effectively used in the mnemonic systems discussed in subsequent chapters).[4] If you use verbal mediators for the Link or Story systems, then you may be able to apply them more directly to abstract material without having to use concrete substitute words.

HOW WELL DOES
THE LINK SYSTEM WORK?

Research Evidence

One study found that when people were given the task of remembering a series of words, three-fourths of them reported that they sometimes grouped words in "strings," by creating mental pictures or formulating stories. For example to remember *citizen, magnet, Bible,* and *trouble,* one person reported using the sentence: "There was a citizen who was drawn like a magnet to a Bible when he was in trouble."[5] When people were asked what aids they might use in learning a list of words, only 6 percent of them reported that they would use a story, but when people were actually given a list of words to learn, 22 percent used a story.[6]

P.S. Delin has conducted several studies on the Link System, instructing college students to learn lists of words by linking the items together with bizarre imagery.[7] The Link system helped people learn the lists faster and make fewer errors in recall. In addition, Delin found that emphasizing that the pictures should be vivid and active helped make the Link system even more effective, but emphasizing bizarreness did not help. In another study, college students and eighth-graders were read a twenty-word list once. The college students who used the Link system recalled an average of three times as many words in order as did the students who did not use a system (fifteen vs. five); for the eighth-grade students the ratio was about two to one (eleven vs. six). In addition, 15 to 25 percent of the Link students recalled all twenty words in order after hearing them only once.[8] Other studies have also found that linking items together using visual imagery aids memory.[9]

Demonstrations

I frequently use the Link system to help an audience demonstrate to themselves the power of visual association, because I can explain the system to them in about 5 minutes and let them try it. First I read to them a list of twenty words to remember, and have them write as many as they can recall in order. Then I explain the Link system. Finally, I read to them a second list of twenty words to remember using the Link system, and have them recall as many as they can in order. Very few people recall all twenty words from the first list (those who do generally use some kind of mnemonic technique). However, after learning the Link system, about half the audience generally recalls all twenty words from the second list. Many of them are astounded at their own performance.

For example, I conducted this demonstration in a psychology class when we were discussing learning and memory. On the first twenty-word list, the class recalled an average of about twelve words (only eight of forty-one students recalled at least eighteen of the twenty words, and only two recalled all twenty words). Using the Link system, the class recalled an average of about eighteen words on the second list (thirty students recalled at least eighteen words, and twenty recalled all twenty words).

When I conducted the demonstration in my most recent memory class, the twenty-two students recalled an average of ten and a half words on the first list; the highest score was eighteen words recalled by one student. Using the Link system, the class recalled an average of about eighteen words on the second list; ten of the twenty-two students recalled all twenty words. These results are more striking than those found in some research studies because of several procedural differences (for example, I give my audiences about 10 seconds per word, a little slower presentation rate than is used in most research studies; and it is the same people learning both sets of words rather than some people using the Link compared with others not using it).

Evidence on The Story System

Although I have not used the Story system in my demonstrations, studies that have used it have reported equally striking results. Some people were given sixteen lists of ten items each. One group was instructed to make up a story to remember each list, and the other group was not told how to remember the lists. They were tested for recall of each list immediately after hearing each list, and again after hearing all sixteen lists, by being given the first word in each list and recalling the other words in order. They were also tested for recall after one week, two weeks, and four weeks. There was no difference between the Story group and the other group when tested immediately after each list. However, at the end of the session when they were tested on all sixteen lists, the Story group recalled an average of 72 percent of the words and the other group recalled an average of 33 percent of the words. The recall of the Story group was also better at one week. However, there was no difference at two or four weeks, suggesting that if you want to remember material for a long time using the Story system, or any other system, you may need to review the material occasionally.[10]

Another study found even more striking results for the Story system. People were given twelve different lists of ten words each during a period of

30 to 40 minutes. Some used the Story system and others were left to their own resources. After all twelve lists had been presented to them, recall was tested—the people were given the first word of each list and told to recall the other items in order. The Story group recalled about seven times as much as the other students—93 percent vs. 13 percent.[11]

A study that compared the Story system with the use of acronyms showed that the Story can help memory for abstract words. People learned a list of sixteen concrete words or sixteen abstract words. Recall was tested the next day. The Story was extremely effective for concrete words, resulting in almost perfect recall of all sixteen words. For abstract words, the Story still yielded an average recall of over fourteen words—significantly higher than the recall of people who learned the abstract words without any mnemonic method. The acronym was slightly less effective than the Story for concrete words, and slightly more effective for abstract words.[12]

Further evidence for the efficacy of the Story system is the finding that it aided recall of a list of nineteen nouns as long as eight weeks after learning, and the finding that sentences are also remembered better when they are presented as a connected story than when they are presented as unrelated sentences.[13]

Thus, there is considerable evidence that the Link and Story systems really can make a difference in memory. It is important to note also that these research studies were with people who were using the systems for the first time; with practice, you could expect to become more effective in using them. (This consideration also applies to the research on the Loci, Peg, and Phonetic systems discussed in the next three chapters.) Lists of concrete and abstract words that you can use to practice the Link and Story systems are provided in Appendix A.

HOW CAN YOU USE THE LINK SYSTEM?

After hearing the Link system described to this point, some people wonder what use it is. After all, how often does someone come up to you and ask you to memorize a list of twenty unrelated nouns? Of course, if this were the only application, then the system would probably not be worth the effort of using (except perhaps to amaze your friends). What are some practical situations in which the Link system could be used?

Learning Lists

The Link system can be used in virtually any situation where you want to remember lists of things. This may seem to be rather restrictive, but actually there are many kinds of everyday memory tasks that involve serial learning (or even free-recall, where the order is not important — the Link just orders the items to help recall them). One category would include lists such as shopping lists, lists of things to do, etc. The use for shopping lists is fairly straightforward — just link the items on the list. One woman who attended one of my lectures reported later that since she had started using the Link system, she hardly ever wrote her shopping lists down any more. Not only did the Link enable her to remember them, but she had more fun doing it.

The use of the Link for lists of things to do may not be quite as straightforward as for shopping lists, but the procedure is the same. Suppose that you need to do the following tasks tomorrow: Call the newspaper office about your subscription, get the flat tire on your car fixed, go to the doctor's office, have some roses sent to a friend, and pick up the tickets for the upcoming ball game. To help you remember these items, you might pick a key word to represent each of these tasks: paper, tire, doctor, rose, and ball (do these words look familiar?). Then link the words together or weave them into a story, as described at the beginning of the chapter.

Another situation in which the Link system may be used is to learn material that consists of separate, ordered parts, such as the amendments to the Constitution, the Ten Commandments, or the names of the presidents. The procedure for such a task is to pick a key word representing each item then link the words together or form a story with them. For example, to remember the Ten Commandments, you might link the following: One god, graven image, swearing, Sabbath, parents, kill, adultery, steal, lie, covet. As discussed in Chapter 5, you could use concrete pictures to represent the terms that are not too concrete (thus, you might picture a church meeting to represent *Sabbath*, or a person whose face is green with envy and who has dollar signs in his eyes to represent *covet*).

The procedure for remembering a series of names would be similar, and can be illustrated by the experience of another woman who attended one of my lectures. She reported that she had used the Link system to learn the twelve apostles named in the New Testament, for a Sunday School lesson she was giving. She made up a substitute word to represent each of the names (mat for Matthew, beater for Peter, etc.) and linked them together. Then she surprised her class (and herself) by being able to name all twelve men in order.

Remember that items to be remembered by the Link or Story do not necessarily *have* to have a natural order to them. A wife may think of things that she wants her husband to do when he comes home, link the first task to him, and link each succeeding task in the order they come to her mind (take out the garbage, mow the lawn, replace the hall light bulb, etc.). Similarly, she may use the same procedure to remember things that happened during the day to tell him (a letter came from his folks, their son got an "A" on his homework, the dog had puppies, etc.).

Using The Story System

The Story system, using substitute words, can be used to remember the names of the cranial nerves (an alternative to the acronym we learned in Chapter 3—"On Old Olympus'...):

> At the oil factory (olfactory nerve) the optician (optic) looked for the occupant (oculomotor) of the truck (trochlear). He was searching because three gems (trigeminal) had been abducted (abducents) by a man who was hiding his face (facial) and ears (acoustic). A glossy photograph (glossopharyngeal) had been taken of him, but it was too vague (vagus) to use. He appeared to be spineless (spinal accessory) and hypocritical (hypoglossal).[14]

A similar example of a use of the Story system is the following story used to remember the names of the thirteen original states in the order they entered the Union:

> A lady from *Delaware* bought a ticket on the *Pennsylvania* railroad. She packed a *new jersey* sweater in her suitcase, and went to visit her friend *Georgia* in *Connecticut*. The next morning she and her friend attended *mass* in a church on *Mary's land*. Then they took the *South car line* home, and dined on a *new ham*, which had been roasted by *Virginia* (the cook from *New York*). After dinner they took the *North car line* and *rode to the island*.[15]

One of the students in my memory class, who was a second-grade teacher, tried this story with her students and was so impressed with how fast they learned the states that she called the principal in to see what the children had accomplished in such a short time. Two weeks later, with some intermittant review, twenty-six of the thirty-three children could recall at least twelve of the thirteen states.

The Story method may even be used to learn equations, in this case the equation for changing Fahrenheit (F) temperature to Centigrade (C): $F = 9/5C + 32$. The sentence is: "Friday (F) is the same (=) 9 to 5 (9/5) drag in College (C); but I've only got 32 minutes (32) to go!"[16]

Other Uses

Another possible use of the Link or Story is for remembering speeches. Suppose you want to make the following points in a speech to your local PTA group: A traffic light should be installed at the intersection by the school; a fence should be constructed along the side of the playground by the street;

funds need to be raised to buy more musical instruments for the school; classrooms are too crowded; some changes should be made in the route of the school bus; and the audiovisual media section of the library needs expanding. The first step in using the Link or Story to remember your points is to pick a concrete key word to represent each point — traffic light, fence, musical instruments, crowded classroom, bus, audiovisual supplies. (You may want to be more specific and use trombones for musical instruments, and movie projector for audiovisual supplies.) Once you pick your key words, then you link them in the order you want to talk about them.

The procedure for learning your speech could be applied also to remembering speeches other people give, or remembering lectures in school. You can link the points together in order as the speaker covers them. Of course, this requires skill at forming associations rapidly, and also requires you to concentrate on the speech to be able to select the key points. With practice, you may even be able to apply the same procedure to remembering what you read.[17]

An example described by Chesley Young suggests a use of the Link system in learning foreign languages. Jacques Romano, who died in 1962 at the age of 98, was known for his remarkable memory. He was especially noted for his ability to speak many foreign languages. Romano found that he needed only about 125 basic words to communicate in a new language. He could acquire this basic vocabulary in about two weeks by learning ten words a day. (This time could probably be shortened by using the key word method described in Chapter 10.) He then built interlocking chains of new words by linking them to the 125 basic words and increased his vocabulary until he became fluent in the language.[18]

Some tasks may involve a combined Link and paired-associate approach. For example, being able to give the capital city of each state when someone tells you the state name, or the vice-president when someone tells you each president's name, are paired-associate tasks. But how about being able to recall each state name *and* its capital? You could use the Link system to link the state names together, and associate the capital to each state.

A student in my memory class used the Link system to complete a self-paced physics course. The course employed a twenty-four-chapter textbook, a six-unit study guide, a series of films on the major units, and optional filmed lectures. The student linked the information under each unit to acquire a chain of information relating to each unit, then associated each chain to the appropriate film. Thus, he could use the films to cue himself as to which chain of information he needed, and the chain to get the information. Using this filing system, he completed the one-semester course in two weeks — and obtained A's on all four exams! He said, "The class was a first of its kind for me, so I was a little leary of how I would perform," and he reported (rather surprised) that "the results were quite amazing."

Of course, these examples of possible uses of the Link and Story systems do not exhaust all the possibilities. They are given to show that mnemonic systems really do have practical value, and to suggest ideas that may stir up your imagination as to applications that might better fill your own needs. In addition, popular memory-training books contain numerous examples of how to put the mnemonic systems to practical use; some of the examples in this chapter, as well as following chapters, are adapted from these books.[19]

SUMMARY

The Link system is a very elementary mnemonic method, but is adequate to illustrate the principles on which mnemonic systems are based, and how powerful they can be for appropriate kinds of material. The Link system is appropriate for serial learning tasks in which you have a series of items to remember. It helps you remember all the items in order.

The Link system consists of forming associations (preferably visual) between each pair of items in the list. A similar method, the Story system, consists of weaving the items in the list into a narrative story. To recall the items, you begin with the first item and proceed through the associations, or the story, to retrieve the items. Both methods can be used with visual imagery or with verbal mediation. College students who are given lists of words to learn without any instructions do not report spontaneously using the Link system, but do frequently report using the Story system.

There is a considerable amount of evidence that the Link and Story systems can make a significant contribution to memory in serial learning tasks. The improvement in memory from using these systems has ranged from 50 percent improvement on a single list of twenty items to as much as 700 percent improvement in recall for twelve lists of ten items each. All of this research is with people who have not had practice in using the systems, and we would expect people who practice them to become even more proficient at using them.

The practical applications of the Link system lie in tasks involving a series of items. This includes such things as shopping lists and lists of things to do; such material as amendments to the Constitution Ten Commandments, or groups of names; and speeches or lectures.

CHAPTER 7

Using Mnemonics —
The Loci System

One limitation of the Link system discussed in the previous chapter stems from the fact that each item is associated with the previous item — forgetting one item thus affects memory for subsequent items. The Loci system does not have that limitation. In the Loci system you build up a mental file of previously memorized images with which you can associate new information to be learned. These images exist independently of the information to be learned. Thus, the Loci system fits our previous analogy of a mental filing system better than does the Link system.

WHAT IS THE LOCI SYSTEM?

The Loci system, which is also called the Topical system, is the most ancient mnemonic system, dating back to about 500 B.C. It was *the* mnemonic system until about the middle of the seventeenth century, when other systems such as the Peg and Phonetic systems, discussed in the next two chapters, began to evolve. Frances Yates has traced the history of the Loci system in detail from 500 B.C. through the seventeenth century; her book is recommended for anyone who is interested in the history of mnemonics.[1] This chapter will note just a few interesting facts about the origin and ancient uses of the Loci system, as described by Yates.

Origin

The origin of the Loci system is generally attributed to the following story told by Cicero. A poet named Simonides was speaking at a banquet, when a message was brought to him that someone was outside to see him. While Simonides was outside, the roof of the banquet hall collapsed, crushing the occupants beyond recognition. Simonides was able to identify the bodies by remembering the places at which the guests had been sitting. This experience suggested to Simonides a system for memorizing. Noting that it was his memory of the places where the guests were sitting that had enabled him to identify them, he inferred that a person could improve memory by associating mental images of the items to be remembered with mental images of locations for the items. This observation reportedly gave rise to the Loci system.

The word *loci* is the plural of *locus,* which means "place or location"; this is also the meaning of the Greek *topo.* Thus, the Loci, or Topical, system is the system that uses places or locations. The Loci system was used by Greek and Roman orators to remember long speeches without notes. Orators visualized objects that represented the topics to be covered in their speeches, then mentally placed the objects in different locations—usually parts of a building. Then, they moved through this building mentally while delivering the speech, retrieving the object images from the locations as they came to them. The important role of this use of places to remember speeches may be the origin of the expression, "in the first place," and of the reference to "topics" in speeches.

How to Use It

The Loci system consists basically of two steps. First, memorize (overlearn) a series of mental images of familiar locations in some natural or logical order. Second, associate a visual image of each item to be remembered with a location in the series; do this by placing the items, in the order they are to be remembered, in the locations as you take an imaginary walk past the locations. Locations have an advantage of being concrete (thus easy to visualize), and of being learned in a natural serial order.

This series of locations is your mental filing system, which you use over again for each new list of items. This is an important feature, because the system would hardly be worth the effort if you had to memorize a new set of locations every time you wanted to memorize a new list of items; you would just have twice as much to remember.

Let us consider an example. Picture in your mind each of the following locations in a house with which you are very familiar. The first location is the front walk that leads up to the house. The second location is the front porch. The third location is the front door. The fourth is the coat closet where you hang your coat after entering the house (or the corner where you throw it).

The fifth location is the next logical place—the refrigerator. Picture yourself taking a walk up the front walk, onto the porch, through the door, to the closet, then to the refrigerator. Make sure you see each of these locations in your mind as clearly as possible while taking your mental walk.

Now, suppose you want to use these locations to remember the same five items we discussed in Chapter 6: paper, tire, doctor, rose, and ball. (As was noted in Chapter 6, it may not be worth the effort to learn a system for only five items, but the procedure is the same for fifty items.) You might proceed as follows: Associate *paper* with your front walk; you might see it made of paper (which you can hear crinkling under your feet as you walk on it), or see your newspaper coming down the walk to meet you. Associate *tire* with porch; you might see tires rolling off your porch or see your porch made of tires. Associate *doctor* with door; you might see a doctor hanging on the doorknob, or stuck in the doorway. Associate *rose* with front closet; you might see the closet completely empty except for a rose bush growing from the shelf, or see a large red rose hanging from a coat hanger. Finally, associate *ball* with refrigerator; you might see your refrigerator in the shape of a giant ball, or hundreds of balls rolling out of the refrigerator when you open the door.

Now take a mental walk through these five locations and try retrieving the five items. You will probably find this task to be quite easy. The Loci system enables you to take what is essentially a free-recall task and change it in several ways to make recall easier. First, the task is changed to an aided-recall task, because you can use the locations as aids to cue yourself. Second, the task incorporates paired-associate learning, with the location serving as the first word in each pair and the item serving as the second word. Third, the task incorporates serial learning, because the locations are organized in a natural serial order.

It is not difficult to construct several extensive mental files of locations. In the house example, you could continue to the living room, then the bedroom, and so on to each room in your house; then you could go downstairs, then out into the yard, etc. You could increase the number of loci in your series by visualizing two or three distinctive locations in each room (for example, the refrigerator, table, and sink in the kitchen; the couch, window, and TV in the living room; and the bed, dresser, and clothes closet in the bedroom). Other buildings could also be used, such as a familiar school building, office building, or store. Nor are you limited to buildings. You could take a walk through your neighborhood, or downtown, and construct a file of mental locations. A familiar golf course has at least thirty-six ready-made locations (eighteen tees and eighteen greens). You could also use different parts of your own body, or of your automobile, for loci.

Other Features

In ancient times it was recommended that the locations be widely spaced. However, it appears to be more important for the loci to be *distinct* than it is for them to be *distant,* at least with respect to how fast items can be retrieved. Glenn Lea had college students learn a list of twelve concrete words using twelve campus buildings as loci. He then named different locations, one at a time, and measured the time required to find a location that was either one, two, or three positions away from the named location. The search time was not related to the actual physical distances between the loci, but *was* related to the number of loci covered. It took twice as long to find a location two positions away as a location one position away, and three times as long for a location three positions away. This finding indicates that people do not skip over loci to get directly to the desired one, but process the intervening loci one at a time, step by step (the same way in which you go through your chain of associations using the Link system).[2]

The characteristics of the Loci system have been analyzed in considerable detail by Gordon Bower.[3] In addition to some of the points we have discussed, two further points made by Bower are worth noting here:

1. It is important to form a good, strong association between each item and its corresponding location. If a person learns a series of locations but is not told how and when to use them, he shows no memory improvement whatever. The locations are effective retrieval cues only if you consciously associate them with the list items when the items are presented. (Remember the same emphasis on forming good, strong associations between each pair of items in the Link system.)

2. It is not necessary that only one item be associated with each location. You could associate more than one item with each location if you picture a grand scene showing interactions among all the items and the location. The important point is that the several items must be *simultaneously* in mind. Thus, for example, you could learn a list of forty items using only ten loci by associating four items with each location. However, you may lose the order of the four items that are associated with each location. (A way to overcome this limitation will be discussed later in this chapter.)

It was noted at the beginning of this chapter that the Link system has the disadvantage that forgetting one item affects memory for following items; when a person does not recall a word, it is common that the next word in the sequence is also missing.[4] We can see why the Loci system has an advantage over the Link system in this respect. Forgetting one item does not affect recall of subsequent items in the Loci system, because the items to be remembered are associated with an independent series of locations rather than with each other.

Like the Link system, the Loci system enables you to remember all the items, and to remember them in order. Of course, both systems can also be used to remember items where the order is not important. One limitation of both the Link and Loci systems is that they do not enable you to directly retrieve an item at a particular position on the list. For example, to find the twelfth item in the Link system, you must proceed through your links until you reach the twelfth item. Likewise, as we saw earlier in this section, a mental walk through a series of loci is also a step-by-step process, in which the loci are identified one at a time. Thus, for the Loci system you must walk through your mental locations until you reach the twelfth location, then retrieve the item from that location.* An ancient technique to help remember the order of the locations will also help alleviate this limitation of the Loci system: Give some distinguishing mark to, say, every fifth location. For example, you might always picture a hand (with five fingers) in the fifth location, and a ten-dollar bill in the tenth location. Then, when you want to recall, say, the twelfth item, you can find the tenth location quickly and have to count only two more locations from there.

HOW WELL DOES
THE LOCI SYSTEM WORK?

In Chapter 2 some of the amazing memory feats performed by the Russian newspaper reporter, S, were described. The following is Luria's description of one of the methods S used to perform such feats:

> When S read through a long series of words, each word would elicit a graphic image. And since the series was fairly long, he had to find some way of distributing these images in a mental row or sequence. Most often (and this habit persisted throughout his life), he would "distribute" them along some roadway or street he visualized in his mind. . . .Frequently he would take a mental walk along that street. . .and slowly make his way down, "distributing" his images at houses, gates, and in store windows. . . .This technique of converting a series of words into a series of graphic images explains why S could so readily reproduce a series from start to finish or in reverse order; how he could rapidly name the word that preceded or followed one I'd selected from the series. To do this

*Of course, the same limitation applies to any serially ordered information, even information that we have learned very thoroughly. For example, can you name the twelfth letter of the alphabet without having to count through the letters? or the eighth letter? or the nineteenth letter? If you are like most people, you cannot retrieve a letter directly in this manner.

he would simply begin his walk, either from the beginning or end of the street, find the image of the object I had named, and "take a look at" whatever happened to be situated on either side of it.[5]

Does that procedure sound familiar? Of course, it is essentially the Loci system. Anyone who becomes skilled at using the Loci system can perform memory feats that are almost as amazing as those performed by S. We will examine some of the feats that people have accomplished with the Loci system in controlled experiments, after examining some related research findings on memory for locations and on using locations to aid memory. (The use of the Loci system is based on the assumptions that people can remember locations easily, and that memory for locations will help memory for the events associated with those locations.)

Memory for Locations

Have you ever had the experience of not being able to remember specific information, but being able to remember where you saw it? You might remember that it was on the left-hand page, in the upper right-hand corner of the page. You may even remember what part of the book it was in (for example, toward the end of the book). This experience illustrates what is meant by memory for location. A similar experience may occur when we see a person we have met before; we may be able to remember where we met her without remembering her name. Sometimes when I see former students of mine on campus, I can place which classroom they were in and even where they sat in class before I can recall their names.

Research on memory for location is relevant to the Loci system, because the basis of the Loci system lies in associating events with distinctive locations. Several studies on memory for location have suggested that, even when the location of an experience might seem irrelevant to the experience, remembering the location may aid memory for the experience.[6] In these studies, people read a passage of textbook material. They were told to remember the information, but nothing was said about remembering the location. They later were able to recall where specific bits of information were located on the page (upper left-hand corner, etc.), and within the text sequence (first part of the passage, etc.). In fact, these people recalled the location of information as well as did other people who were told to remember the location. The studies also found a positive relationship between memory for location and memory for content (people who recalled the location tended also to recall the information better). One possible explanation of this finding is that recall of location may help recall of content.

Similar results were found in a study in which people saw slides with one word in each of the four quadrants of each slide, and in a study in which people saw cards with one object pictured in each of the four quadrants of each card; in these two studies, memory for location was positively related to memory for the word or object.[7]

A list of words representing objects that are spatially organized (such as *chimney, roof, ceiling, wall, carpet, floor,* etc.) is easier to learn than a list that is not so organized. Placing words in a pattern on different parts of a page helps one learn them better than if they are just listed under each other in a vertical column, because the person can use the locations on the page as cues to retrieve the words in an orderly way. Similarly, memory for the location of objects in pictures is better when the pictures are organized than when they are not.[8]

Most studies on remembering locations have used college students. However, even young children can associate a spatial location with an event. Young children went on walks through a variety of environments, were exposed to an event, and were later asked to recall where the event had occurred. Even 3-year-olds showed the ability to remember the location of the event.[9]

Using Locations to Aid Memory

Placing people in the location where we met them frequently helps us remember them. We have noted the story of how Simonides used the location of the people to recall the people themselves. Similarly, locations may provide us with a systematic way of searching memory for people. As Allan Paivio reported, "Occasionally, when I have to list the names of my colleagues from memory, I have found myself visualizing the hallways in which their offices are located, systematically moving past these offices, then picturing and naming the occupants."[10] I have used a similar approach to recall the names of all the students in a particular class; I proceed mentally down each row, picturing and naming the occupant of each seat.

When people were given a list of names and were asked to recall what the named people look like, they generally recalled a recent personal interaction, movie, photograph, or television show in which the person appeared; in other words, they tried to locate where they had seen the person, and they used that location to help them recall the person. Similarly, when people were shown other people's faces and asked to recall the names, their memory for where they had seen the people before helped them recall the names.[11]

Several studies have used techniques very close to the Loci system to show that associating information with location can aid memory for the information. People were given a description of a map (a small village of about a dozen locations). The setting description was presented either as a picture or as a verbal description of that picture. The people studied the setting, then read a passage relating several episodes that had taken place in the village. Other people read the passage without any knowledge of the setting. The people who had been given the setting recalled more of the gist of the passage than did those who had not; this was especially true of those who had been told to keep in mind a mental picture of the setting as they read the passage. This finding suggests that a knowledge in visual form of locations helps us remember a related message.[12]

In a study that approximates the Loci system even more closely, college students learned a list of twenty-four words by associating each word with a picture of a location in the school cafeteria. Students were tested for recall by being shown the pictures and asked to recall the words. After one presentation, they recalled an average of almost twenty words, and after two presentations, twenty of twenty-two students recalled all twenty-four words. In contrast, a group of students who learned the same words without the pictured locations recalled about fifteen words after one presentation, and after two presentations only one student recalled all twenty-four words.[13]

Can children use locations to help memory? Two studies indicate that they can. In the first study, second- and fourth-grade children used three locations (a house, a garden, and a street, representing stages in a doll's journey to school) to remember the order of twenty-four items, with eight items in each location. Other children learned the items without the help of the locations. The items were then presented in pairs to the children, and they were asked to recall which item was more recent on the list. The use of the locations helped the fourth-graders significantly in remembering which items were more recent. After training, the second-graders also improved their recall by using the location cues.[14]

In the second study with children, sixth-graders were shown pictures of twenty-four items, and eight pictures of locations where the items might be found in groups of three. For example, a monkey, camel, and bear were associated with a picture of three empty zoo cages; and a table, lamp, and couch were associated with a picture of a room. Other children were shown the twenty-four items without the eight location cues. Children who associated the items with the location cues were shown the cue pictures when recalling the twenty-four items. They recalled about 25 percent more items than did the children who did not have the advantage of the location cues.[15]

Research Evidence

We have seen that people can remember locations, and that they can use locations to remember events. Let us now look at the evidence that these two factors can be combined to make the Loci system an effective memory system.

Four lists of forty items each (one list each day for four days) were presented to college students who had memorized a series of loci on a walk around their campus. Students determined their own rates in viewing the items, taking an average of about 14 seconds per item. Recall was tested immediately after each list had been presented once, again one day later, and again after all four lists had been presented at the end of the four days. The average immediate recall of words, in the same order they were presented, was about thirty-seven words; the average recall a day later was about thirty-four words; and the average recall at the end of all four lists was about twenty-nine words. The average recall when the words did not have to be recalled in correct order was even higher—about thirty-five items per list at the end of the four days. Although there was some interference from previous lists (at the end of the four days the students recalled an average of thirty-nine words in order from list 4, thirty-two words from list 3, twenty-five words from list 2, and twenty words from list 1), this performance using the Loci system is still way above what we could expect from people not using any system.[16]

Some people studied five successive lists with twenty unrelated words on each list, for 5 seconds per word. After learning the lists, students who used the Loci system or slight variations of it recalled an average of seventy-two items out of one hundred, whereas students left to their own resources in learning the lists recalled an average of only twenty-eight items. In addition, items recalled by the Loci system were usually assigned to the right position on the right list, a feat the other students hardly ever accomplished.[17]

In another study, some people learned a list of twenty-five concrete words using the Loci system, and others were left to their own resources to learn the words. All of these people took as much time as they desired to learn the list thoroughly. The Loci group took less time to learn the list (about 14 minutes vs. 17 minutes) and recalled more words in correct order: The Loci group recalled an average of six more words after one week, and ten more words after five weeks (twenty words for the Loci group vs. ten words for the other group). Both groups were able to recognize almost all the words from a list of fifty words, indicating that the words were *available* to both groups but that the Loci system made them more *accessible* for recall. The Loci system gave the people a systematic means of searching memory to recall the items. A later study using the same procedure, on both concrete and abstract words, found that the people who used the Loci system to learn abstract words took the longest to learn the words, and that the people who used the Loci system to learn high-imagery words showed the most efficient retrieval after six weeks.[18]

Three studies by Herbert Crovitz have shed light on some of the factors involved in making the Loci system work. Crovitz found that it is not necessary that the locations be memorized by the person. He drew a map with the names of twenty stores and buildings along a street (electric company, gas station, etc.), then read a list of forty concrete and abstract items to twelve people. This procedure required the people to put two items in each location (one item in each location up to twenty, then start over with item 21 in the first location, etc.). They recalled an average of thirty-four out of forty items; ten of the twelve people had recall scores over 35, but the other two did not follow instructions and had poor recall scores.[19]

Crovitz found that not only is it unnecessary for the locations to be memorized, but it is also apparently unnecessary that the associations be constructed by the learner.[20] A list of twenty nouns was read to fifty college students, along with a suggested association for each noun with each of the twenty locations. The average number of words recalled with only one presentation of the list was seventeen—58 percent of the students recalled at least eighteen of the twenty words, and 34 percent recalled all twenty words.*

The third study by Crovitz shows that a list of loci does not help if you are not trained in making effective visual associations. People were given the list of stores and buildings, then listened to a series of twenty words which were read and related to the locations (for example, "electric company. The word is 'plow'"). Others followed the same procedure, but were previously given a few minutes of mnemonic training in making visual associations between the items and the locations (for example, to relate *roller derby* and *mice*, "picture thousands of mice skating madly around the ring, pushing each other down . . ."). The trained group recalled more words than the untrained group, averaging about fifteen words recalled when the words were presented once.[22]

Whereas most studies of the Loci system have compared one group of people who used the system with another group who did not use it, one study compared the same people both before and after learning the Loci system. College students and high school students were given a list of thirty moderately concrete words to learn. The same students were then taught the Loci system, and learned a second list of words using the Loci system. They showed a significant increase in number of words recalled on the second list over the first list. There was no significant difference in recall between people who were good visualizers and those who were not (as measured by an

---

*These two studies by Crovitz suggest that it is not necessary that people make up their own loci or associations. However, the findings are not consistent on this point. There is some evidence that learners should make up their own loci in order for them to be effective,[21] and we saw in Chapter 6 that mediators made up by the learners themselves tend to be more effective than those provided by someone else. It would probably be safest to construct your own loci and associations.

imagery test), suggesting that the Loci system can help even people who previously report poor imagery ability.[23]

HOW CAN YOU USE
THE LOCI SYSTEM?

All of the uses of the Link system discussed in Chapter 6 are also possible uses of the Loci system—shopping lists, things to do, naturally ordered material such as the Ten Commandments, names, speeches, etc. The only difference is that you associate each item to a location rather than to the previous item. In addition to all of these uses, there are some further uses for the Loci system.

A Mental Filing System

The Loci system can be used literally as a mental filing system. For example, do you ever think of an idea at a time when it is inconvenient to write it down? Maybe you think of something you need to do tomorrow, or an idea for a speech you are preparing, just as you are falling asleep at night; but you do not want to get up and turn on the light to hunt for paper and pencil to write the idea down. Or an idea might come to you when you are in a movie theater where it is too dark to write, or while driving down the street (where your passengers might get a little nervous if you let go of the steering wheel to write), or in the middle of doing dishes or mowing the lawn, or any other situation in which you cannot immediately write an idea down when it comes to you. The next morning, or after the movie, or at the next stoplight, or when the dishes or lawn are done, you have lost the idea. You might remember that you had an idea, but you cannot remember what it was. One solution to this problem is to associate the idea to one of your locations as soon as the idea comes to you. Later you can retrieve it, and write it down for more permanent storage if you wish.

Suppose, for example, that you use a series of loci around your house. You recall as you are drifting off to sleep that you must give your children lunch money for school tomorrow morning. You might picture nickels, dimes, and quarters rolling down your front sidewalk. Then, when you wake up in the morning and remember that there was something you needed to remember, you can search your loci for it. Or suppose that while you are sitting in a dark movie theater you remember that you need to put a note out for the milkman when you get home. You might picture milk bottles cluttering up your front sidewalk. Then, when you get home and think, "Now what was it I needed to do before I go to bed?" you can search your loci and recall the task.

If you write things down in a notebook, or put things in a filing cabinet for more permanent storage, you must still remember to look at your notebook or filing cabinet occasionally if they are going to do you any good. Likewise, the use of the Loci system as a filing system in which you can record items for future use requires that you remember to search the loci. Often, this is not a problem; you can remember that you wanted to remember something—you just cannot remember what it is. However, if you cannot even remember that you wanted to remember something, or if you use the Loci system regularly, then you should get into the habit of having a set time (or times) each day to search your loci. If you develop the habit of taking a few minutes to review your loci say, before breakfast, during lunch, and before going to bed, then you will not need to make a special effort to remember to search your loci.

Using the Same Loci Over and Over

We have noted that the same loci can be used over for new lists. This presents a potential problem in practical uses of the Loci system—learning several lists attached to the same loci might lead to unwanted interference. For example, suppose you have a series of twenty loci, and you want to learn three different lists of about twenty items each. If all items are associated with the same set of loci, you might get interference and confuse which item is on which list. This problem is not as serious in situations in which you only want to remember a list for a short time, or where there is enough time (say, a day or two) between learning the two lists to allow forgetting of the first list, because when you put the new list in the locations it will weaken the old list.

There are at least two ways to overcome such interference. First, you can construct multiple sets of locations so that you do not have to use the same set so many times in close succession. A student could select a set of loci in one part of campus to use in memorizing material for one class, and loci in a different part of campus for another class. People could similarly have one set of loci around the house, another around the office, another on a familiar neighborhood street. This way, if you have three lists to learn close together, you could use your home loci for one list, your office loci for the second list, and your neighborhood loci for the third list. You might even use each set of loci for specific kinds of memory storage—for example, your home loci to remember things that concern your home and family, your office loci to remember things connected with work, and your school loci to remember things connected with school. If you use the Loci system every day, it might be worth your time to construct seven sets of loci so you can use a different set every day.

A second suggested way to reduce interference among several lists learned with the same loci is "progressive elaboration"—adding each subsequent word at a particular location to a progressive picture. Re-imagine each earlier item in its location when you associate the new item by elaborating a grand scene of interacting objects. For example, if the second location in your set were your front porch, and the second word in each of three lists were *swing, hat,* and *fish,* then the scenes might be: list 1—a swing hanging from your porch; list 2—a hat swinging on the swing on your porch; list 3—a fish wearing a hat while swinging on the porch.

Does progressive elaboration really help reduce interference among different lists? People using progressive elaboration were given one presentation of each of five twenty-item lists, and tested for recall immediately after each list, again after learning all five lists, and again after one week. Average recall of words, in the order they were presented and on the correct list, was about 88 percent of the twenty words after each list, about 70 percent of the hundred words after all five lists, and about 54 percent of the words after a week. Recall after all five lists, and after one week, was superior to that of people who had learned the items by associating each item separately without using progressive elaboration.[24] Other research has also found that progressive elaboration helps reduce interference among different lists, and thus increase retention, not only for college students but also for grade-school children and for preschool children.[25]

Which of these two methods of reducing interlist interference—multiple sets of loci and progressive elaboration—is preferable? This will depend on the person who is using them, but my recommendation for the person who may make frequent use of the Loci system is to learn several different sets of loci and use the multiple-sets method. I think that the benefits of having several sets of loci are worth the effort it takes to learn them.

You may recognize that the method of progressive elaboration is sort of a combination of the Loci system and the Story or Link systems. The loci are used to start each story or link, and a story or link serves to retrieve the items in order at each location. Notice that the item order would be lost if the items at each location were just pictured in a single photographic image, rather than ordered sequentially using the Link or Story systems.

Other Uses

There is another way in which the Loci system can be combined with the Link or Story systems. A set of ten loci could easily be used to remember 100 items. Place the first item in the first location, then use the Link or Story systems to associate the next 9 items in order; then place the 11th item in the second location, and link the next 9 items onto it; and so on until you place the 91st item in the tenth location and link items 92 to 100 onto it. In recall, you then use your loci to cue you for the first item in each group of ten, and your inter-item associations to recall the next nine. You can thus recall 100 items with no single chain of associations longer than 10 items.

The experience of one person who used forty loci to memorize a forty-digit number may suggest additional ways in which you could use the Loci system (though a more efficient way to learn numbers will be described in Chapter 9). He associated something representing each number with each location. For example, to associate the digit "1" with the location "ice cream store" — "I am a rather fat little boy so I only can have *one* ice cream cone"; to associate "6" with "fire station" — "They tell me there is a *six*-alarm fire. It must be very unusually exciting, for I had never heard of as many as six alarms for a fire before"; to associate "2" with "the market" — "I have been sent to the market to get *two* bags of potatoes."[26]

As with the Link system, these suggested uses of the Loci system do not exhaust all the possibilities. They are intended to suggest the variety in kinds of possible applications of the system. You might adapt some of these suggestions to your own needs, or even be stimulated to think up some additional uses for the Loci system.

SUMMARY

The Loci system is the most ancient mnemonic system, dating back to about 500 B.C. It was developed and used by Greek and Roman orators to deliver long speeches without using notes. The word *loci* means locations; thus, the Loci system is the system using locations. It consists basically of two steps: First, memorize a series of mental images of familiar locations in some natural or logical order. Second, associate a visual image of each item to be remembered with a location in the series. In recalling the material, you take an imaginary walk past the locations and retrieve the items. The same set of locations is used over again for learning new material. It is important that the associations between items and locations be strong, but is not necessary that only one item be pictured in each location.

The Loci system has an advantage over the Link system in that the items to be remembered are associated with an independent series of locations rather than with each other — thus, forgetting one item does not affect recall of subsequent items. Both the Link and Loci systems have the limitation that it is difficult to go directly to a certain numbered item (for example, the twelfth item); recall is sequential. However, this limitation can be alleviated somewhat for the Loci system by marking every fifth location with some distinctive mark.

Research on memory for locations, and on using locations of information to help remember the information itself, is relevant for the Loci system. There is considerable evidence that people can remember where they saw an event, even when they cannot remember the exact nature of the event itself. In addition, memory for the location of the event may be an aid in remembering the content of the event. There is also a considerable amount of research evidence that shows that the Loci system itself can make a significant difference in people's memory ability. The evidence consistently indicates that people using the Loci system can remember more than people not using it.

The Loci system can be used for any of the uses of the Link system. It can help remember such information as shopping lists, things to do, naturally ordered material such as the Ten Commandments, names, and speeches. In addition, it can be used as you might literally use a portable filing system. When a thought comes to your mind, you can associate it with a location before you forget it. Then, in reviewing your locations later, you will be able to retrieve the thought. This is especially handy when you remember something at a time when it is not convenient to write it down.

Using the same loci over again for several different lists can sometimes result in interference among the lists, especially if they are learned in close succession. There are at least two ways to alleviate this problem. First, you can construct multiple sets of loci and alternate among them so that you do not use the same set to memorize different material in close succession. Second, you can use the technique of progressive elaboration; rather than associating each item in each list independently with a location, add each subsequent word to a progressive picture by re-imagining each earlier item in the location when you associate the new item. In this way you progressively elaborate a grand scene of interacting objects at each location.

Progressive elaboration involves a combined use of the Loci system and the Link or Story systems. There are also other possible combinations among the Loci and Link systems which increase their power over using them independently.

CHAPTER 8

Using Mnemonics —
The Peg System

As was noted in Chapter 7, direct retrieval of an item at a certain position in a memorized list (for example, the twelfth item) is difficult for both the Link and Loci systems. They are both dependent on sequential retrieval. The Loci system associates items to be learned with pre-memorized information. To use the same approach in such a way that you can retrieve an item directly, you might associate items to information that you already have memorized, and know very well — the number sequence. If you could associate the first item with number 1, the second item with number 2, and so on, then for recall, you could just recall what item was associated with each number. If you wanted to retrieve the twelfth item directly, you would just think of number 12 and see what item was associated with it. The main problem with this strategy is that numbers are abstract, and thus are hard to associate with items. But the strategy would be feasible if a way could be found to make the numbers concrete, or to substitute something concrete for the numbers. This is what the Peg system does.

WHAT IS THE PEG SYSTEM?

The Peg system is a mental filing system consisting of a series of pre-memorized concrete nouns. The concrete nouns are not randomly selected, but are selected to correspond with numbers.

Origin

The Peg system can be traced back to the mid-seventeenth century, when Henry Herdson developed an extension of the Loci system; he dispensed with the spatial locations of the objects, and merely used the objects themselves. Each digit was represented by any one of several objects that resemble the numbers (for example, 1 = candle; 3 = trident; 8 = spectacles; 0 = orange).

A system that used rhyming syllables and words to represent the numbers was introduced in England around 1879 by John Sambrook.[1] The nouns rhyme with the numbers they represent so that it will be easy to remember what noun represents each number. The following is a widely used version of the Peg system based on rhymes, indicating the word which represents each number:

one-bun	five-hive	eight-gate
two-shoe	six-sticks	nine-wine
three-tree	seven-heaven	ten-hen
four-door		

How to Use It

Most people can learn these pegwords with little effort. In fact, you may already know half of them from the nursery rhyme. "One two buckle my shoe, three four shut the door," etc. Each of the pegword objects should be pictured as vividly as possible. The bun should be a specific kind of bun, such as a breakfast bun, a dinner roll, or a hamburger bun. The shoe could be a man's dress shoe, a woman's high-heeled shoe, a gym shoe, or a boot. The tree could be a pine tree in the forest, a Christmas tree, or a palm tree.

The Peg system gets its name from the fact that the pegwords serve as mental pegs, or hooks on which the person "hangs" the items to be remembered. To use the Peg system to learn new material, you associate the new material with each of the pegwords in order. For example, the first five pegwords could be used to learn the list we have used in the last two chapters—paper, tire, doctor, rose, ball—as follows: Associate *paper* with bun; perhaps see yourself eating a bun made of paper, or reading the evening newsbun. Associate *tire* with shoe; perhaps see yourself wearing tires on your feet, or see a car that has four shoes in the place of tires. Associate *doctor* with tree; see a doctor operating on a tree, or a doctor climbing a tree. Associate *rose* with door; see a rose in the place of the doorknob, or a rosebush growing from the middle of the door. Associate *ball* with hive; see a round beehive in the shape of a ball, or balls rather than bees flying out of the hive. Of course, all the considerations involving effective visual associations that were discussed in Chapter 5 are relevant in making these associations.

To recall the items in order, you recall the pegwords and retrieve the items associated with them. Recall of items out of order proceeds in the same manner. For example, which item was number 4? Think of "door" and retrieve the item associated with it. What was the third item? Retrieve the item associated with "tree."

Other Pegs

The Peg system that I have described is one that is commonly used and the one on which most research has been done, but actually there are a number of Peg systems. They all have in common the characteristic of using a concrete object to represent each number, but there are various ways to choose the object to represent each number. The system discussed thus far uses pegwords that rhyme with the numbers. Other rhymes have been used: one-gun, two-glue, three-bee, four-core, five-knives, six-picks, seven-oven, eight-plate, nine-line, ten-pen. Pegwords that represent objects that look like the numbers can also be selected—for example, 1-pencil, 2-swan (the curve of the neck resembling a two), 8-hourglass, and 10-knife and plate. Pegwords can be selected on the basis of meaning also—for example, one-me (there's only one me), three-pitchfork (three prongs), five-hand (five fingers), nine-baseball (nine players on a team). Peg systems often do not include a pegword for "0" (zero), but on the basis of rhyme, you could use "Nero," on the basis of look-alikes you could use "donut," and on the basis of meaning you could use an empty "box."

One limitation of the Peg system is that it is difficult to find good pegwords to represent numbers beyond ten. It is hard to find words, for example, that rhyme with (or look like) the numbers twenty-four or thirty-seven. One research study used the following pegwords to represent the numbers from eleven to twenty; they did aid memory, but are not as satisfactory as the pegwords for one to ten: eleven is "penny-one," hotdog bun; twelve is "penny-two," airplane glue; thirteen is "penny-three," bumblebee; fourteen is "penny-four," grocery store; fifteen is "penny-five," big beehive; sixteen is "penny-six," magic tricks; seventeen is "penny-seven," go to heaven; eighteen is "penny-eight," golden gate; nineteen is "penny-nine," ball of twine; twenty is "penny-ten," ball point pen.[2]

Rhyming words have been suggested for the numbers from eleven to twenty. Most of them are verbs representing an action that can be visualized. The following are some examples: eleven-leaven, or a football eleven; twelve-shelve, or elf; thirteen-hurting, or thirsting; fourteen-courting, or fording; fifteen-lifting, or fitting; sixteen-licking, or Sistine; seventeen-leavening, or deafening; eighteen-waiting, or painting; nineteen-pining, or dining; twenty-horn of plenty, or penny.[3]

Another possible approach to generate pegwords for the numbers from eleven to twenty is to use rhyming pegwords for one to ten, then pegwords based on look-alikes or meaning to represent the second digit of the numbers from eleven to twenty. For example, 11 = pencil, 12 = swan, 13 = pitch-fork, etc.

Alphabet Pegs

It was suggested at the beginning of this chapter that numbers would make a good series of pegs if they were not so abstract, because they are naturally ordered, and you know them very well. There is another possible source of pegs that also consists of information that is naturally ordered and that you know very well — the alphabet. The alphabet provides a ready-made series of twenty-six pre-memorized pegs. However, the letters have somewhat the same problem that numbers do — they are not very concrete and meaningful. If we could make them concrete, then we could use the alphabet as a Peg system. One way to do this is to associate a concrete word with each letter in such a way that the words are easy to learn.

Each of the following alphabet pegwords either rhymes with the letter of the alphabet it represents or has the letter as the initial sound of the word. Words that are not concrete can be visualized by using substitute words (for example, effort — a person working; age — an old person).

A-hay	J-jay	S-ass
B-bee	K-key	T-tea
C-sea	L-el	U-ewe
D-deed	M-hem	V-veal
E-eve	N-hen	W-waterloo
F-effigy	O-hoe	X-ax
G-jeep	P-pea	Y-wire
H-age	Q-cue	Z-zebra
I-eye	R-oar	

A second alphabet Peg system could be compiled from concrete words that begin with each letter of the alphabet but do not rhyme:

A-ape	J-jack	S-sock
B-boy	K-kite	T-toy
C-cat	L-log	U-umbrella
D-dog	M-man	V-vane
E-egg	N-nut	W-wig
F-fig	O-owl	X-X ray
G-goat	P-pig	Y-yak
H-hat	Q-quilt	Z-zoo
I-ice	R-rock	

Alphabet pegwords would be used in exactly the same way as number pegwords. The only difference is that if you do not know the numerical positions of the letters (which most people do not), the alphabet pegwords are not amenable to direct retrieval of an item at a given numbered position. The alphabet pegwords could also be used in other ways. For example, if you want to learn the alphabet backwards, you could link the words from *zebra* to *hay* or *zoo* to *ape*.

Peg and Loci Compared

There are a number of similarities between the Peg system and the Loci system, and performance has been found to be equivalent for the two systems.[4] The following are four similarities:

1. The Peg system is similar to the Loci system in that items to be learned are associated with previously memorized concrete items. These previously memorized items make up the mental filing system to which new items are attached. The pegwords are used in exactly the same way the locations are used in the Loci system. As with the locations in the Loci system, the pegwords can be used over again to learn new items. The same considerations regarding interference apply as were discussed in connection with the Loci system. Recall is also similar for both systems; you proceed through your locations or pegwords and retrieve the items associated with them.

2. In the Peg system, the mental filing system consists of a series of concrete nouns rather than of locations, but locations are merely objects that are spatially ordered. For example, the five loci used in the example in the previous chapter were a sidewalk, a porch, a door, a closet, and a refrigerator.

3. As with the Loci system, the Peg system changes a free-recall task to aided recall via a paired-associate task, with the pegwords serving as the first word in each pair. Thus, the Peg system and the Loci system are essentially the same as paired-associated learning, except that the learner generates his own cue-words rather than having them given to him by someone else.

4. The Peg system and the Loci system have several advantages over free recall. First, the learners have a definite and consistent learning strategy; they know exactly what to do with each item as they study it (that is, associate it with a location or pegword). Second, they have definite pigeon-holes (pegwords or locations) into which to file the items. Third, they have a systematic retrieval plan telling them where to begin recall, how to proceed systematically from one item to the next, and how to monitor the adequacy of recall (they can tell how many items they have forgotten, and which ones). Thus, the systems overcome one of the major problems in free recall—how to remind yourself of all the things you are supposed to recall.[5]

Although the Peg and Loci systems are similar, they have at least two significant differences. First, as has been noted, the Peg system has the advantage of permitting direct retrieval. If you want to know what the eighth item is without going through the first seven, you merely think of "gate" and see what is associated with it. Second, the Loci system has the advantage of allowing a large number of mental images to make up the mental filing system—there is really no limit on the number of locations you can use; but it is difficult to find a large number of pegwords that rhyme with or look like the numbers larger than ten, and especially larger than twenty.

HOW WELL DOES THE PEG SYSTEM WORK?

Some psychologists described an interesting experience in teaching the Peg system to a sceptical friend. They told him the pegwords and told him how to use them. Then, despite his protestations that it would never work because he was too tired, they gave him a list of ten words to learn.

> The words were read one at a time, and after reading the word, we waited until he announced that he had the association. It took about five seconds on the average to form the connection. After the seventh word he said that he was sure the first six were already forgotten. But we persevered.
>
> After one trial through the list we waited a minute or two so that he could collect himself and ask any questions that came to mind. Then we said, "What is number eight?"
>
> He stared blankly, and then a smile crossed his face, "I'll be damned," he said. "It's a lamp."
>
> "And what number is a cigarette?"
>
> He laughed outright now, and then gave the correct answer.
>
> "And there is no strain," he said, "absolutely no sweat."

They then proceeded to demonstrate, to his amazement, that he could in fact name every word correctly.[6]

Research Evidence

It was noted in the previous section that the Peg system is similar to paired-associate learning, except that the learners provide their own pegwords rather than having them given to them by someone else. This means that the research that shows the effectiveness of visual imagery in paired-associate learning also suggests the effectiveness of the Peg system. As we noted in Chapter 3, there are numerous studies showing that visual imagery aids learning and memory in paired-associate learning.

People using the Peg system typically recall a list of ten words correctly, in order, after hearing them once. People not using the system typically recall about half as many.[7] In general, concrete words are learned slightly better than abstract words with the Peg system, but abstract words are still learned readily by using concrete "substitute words" as discussed in Chapter 5.[8] Let us look at some of the specific research findings.

Ian Hunter read a list of ten numbered words to a group of 32 college students who had been taught the Peg system, and to 32 other students who had not been taught the Peg system. They recalled the words, and wrote them after the appropriate numbers. The students who had not been taught the Peg system recalled an average of less than seven words, with only 2 students (6 percent) recalling all ten words. However, the students who used the Peg system recalled an average of more than nine words, with 17 students (53 percent) recalling all ten words. Hunter reported that he has used the Peg system with more than 800 students, with different lists, and the use of the system never fails to improve the recall of most students—often to the surprise of the students themselves. He noted that when a few students do not benefit from the system, it is usually because either they decide privately not to use it or they cannot resist recalling earlier items while later items are still being presented to them (as we noted in discussing the Link system, one must concentrate on making a good association as each new item is presented and resist the temptation to review earlier associations).[9]

In another study, a list of ten numbered words was read once to people, and they recalled the words in order. Some of the people were then taught the Peg system and given the same task with a new list of ten words. When the words were presented at a rate of 2 seconds each, the Peg system did not help (consistent with our discussion of time limitations in Chapter 5). However, the Peg system made a significant difference when the words were presented at 4 and 8 seconds each. At an 8-second presentation rate, people who used the system on the second list had almost perfect recall (97 percent), as compared with their recall of only about half the words on the first list; people who did not use the system recalled about half the words on both lists.[10]

One program of research tested recall of forty-word lists under a number of different kinds of mnemonic instructions. People who were given pegwords remembered twenty-five to thirty words, compared with fifteen to twenty words for people who were left to their own resources. In addition, the Peg system helped recall more when items were presented at a 5-second rate than at a 2-second rate, and the people who used the pegwords generally showed an improvement with practice while those not given pegwords did not show improvement with practice.[11]

Some people used the Peg system to learn six consecutive lists of ten items each, while others did not use the Peg system. The words were presented only once, at a rate determined by the learner (they averaged about 7 seconds per word). After all six lists had been presented, the average recall for the people who used the Peg system was 63 percent, and for the others was 22 percent. In addition, those using the Peg system recalled words equally well from all six lists, whereas the others recalled most of their words from the last two lists.[12]

One study used alphabet pegwords that started with the first letters of the alphabet (A-apple, B-boy, etc.). To benefit from these pegwords the people did not need to memorize the alphabet list, but simply needed to recognize that the alphabet words constituted the first word in each pair of a paired-associate list of twenty-four items (X and Z were omitted). The people were then given the twenty-four words in a standard paired-associate manner (apple-shoe, boy-stone, cat-grass, etc.), and were tested at random: "What went with cat (c)?" etc. People who were instructed to imagine associations attained astonishing scores compared with those who were asked merely to learn the pairs.[13]

In one study people were given one, two, five, ten, or twenty pegs to use in learning a twenty-item list. The people using less than twenty pegwords thus had to associate more than one list with each peg (twenty items per peg for one peg, ten for two pegs, four for five pegs, and two for ten pegs; having only one or two pegs was essentially the same as using the Link system). The recall measure was free recall; the words did not have to be in order. The people were given one study and recall of each of five lists of twenty concrete nouns, followed by a final recall test for all five lists. All groups recalled 80 to 90 percent of the items immediately after each list, and 66 to 75 percent of the items at the end of the session. In contrast, people who had not been given any pegwords recalled an average of only 52 percent after each list and 28 percent after all five lists. This study suggests that the Peg system can be used effectively with progressive elaboration, as described also for the Loci system in Chapter 7.[14]

Abstract Pegwords

It was noted in the previous section that the pegwords are all concrete. Is this necessary? Could abstract pegwords be used? Paivio's "conceptual peg" hypothesis, which says that in paired-associate lists it is more important to have a concrete word as the first word in each pair than as the second word, suggests that abstract pegwords would not be effective.[15] However, the evidence on this issue is not consistent. Two studies have found that a variation of the Peg system using abstract pegwords (one-fun, two-true, three-free, four-bore, five-live, six-tricks, seven-given, eight-fate, nine-time, ten-sin) was as effective as a Peg system using concrete pegwords. However, a third study that tried to duplicate this finding found that the concrete peg-words aided recall more than did the abstract pegwords; people who used abstract pegwords did not recall any better than people who did not use any pegwords. The results of this third study indicate that concreteness of peg-words is critical in the Peg system. A fourth study found that whether con-crete or abstract pegwords are more effective depends on the visual imagery ability of the user. Because we know that concrete pegwords work, but do not really know whether abstract pegwords work, it is probably best to use con-crete pegwords.[16]

The research described in this section has used adults. However, the Peg system has also been shown to be effective with children; training in the use of pegwords and visual imagery was found to aid memory in a group of black grade-school children enrolled in a summer urban action program.[17]

HOW CAN YOU USE
THE PEG SYSTEM?

The Peg system can be used for any of the uses of the Link and Loci systems, including lists, naturally ordered material, names, speeches, as a mental filing system for temporary storage when it is inconvenient to write some-thing down, and as a mental filing system for more permanent storage on a regular day-to-day basis.

The Peg system can be used also for tasks for which direct access is desirable. For example, I used the Peg system to teach my two daughters (who had just turned 5 and 7) the Ten Commandments so they could recall them out of order as well as in order. The first step was to teach them the Peg system. Both girls were able to recall all the pegwords after two times through the list. The second step was to teach the children how to use the pegwords. I gave them a list of ten items to memorize, and coached them in forming visual associations between the pegwords and the items. Both girls recalled all ten items after the list was presented, and recalled nine of the ten the following day. They were given additional practice with a second list of ten items, and again recalled all ten items on immediate recall. When tested the next day, they each needed prodding—"What is the pegword?" "What is (pegword) doing?"—on two items.

The final step was to use the pegwords to learn the Ten Command-ments. A concrete item representing each commandment was associated visually with the corresponding pegword. For example, a thief stealing a gate (eight-gate) represented the eighth commandment—Thou shalt not steal. Both girls learned all ten commandments in order and out of order, and were even able to recall them in a surprise test two months later. Not only was the system effective but it was fun for the girls, and they were anxious to apply it to learning new things.

A student in my memory class related a similar experience which shows that the Peg system can work even when the user does not believe it will work. After teaching his wife the Ten Commandments using the procedure described above, he reported, "She was amazed that they could be learned so easily. Previous to this experiment she had told me that she couldn't do it. She also had mentioned that it seemed like more work (having to memorize pegwords), but she doesn't feel that way now."

Remembering Numbers

A use of the Peg system that goes beyond the Loci system is for learning numbers (although the Phonetic system in the next chapter is even more efficient for numbers). You can remember a long number by linking the pegwords together. For example, the ten-digit number, 1639420574, could be remembered by using the Link system to remember bun-sticks-tree-wine, etc. This way your capacity for a string of numbers can be extended way beyond the short-term memory span of seven or so discussed in Chapter 2 — as long as the digits are presented slowly enough for you to make associations.

The Peg system could be used to remember the twelve-digit number representing a calendar year (see Chapter 5); the number for 1977 (266-315-374-264) could be remembered by linking shoe-sticks-sticks-tree, etc. This method has a disadvantage of requiring sequential retrieval (to remember the digit for September, for example, you must remember that September is the ninth month, then run through the number until you reach the ninth digit). A more efficient method would be to make up a pegword for each month, based either on rhyme or meaning (for example, Jan = Jam, Feb = valentine, April = ape, July = jewel, September = sceptre). Then associate the pegword for each digit with the pegword for the corresponding month as paired associates (Jam-shoe, valentine-sticks, ape-tree, jewel-tree, sceptre-door). To find the key digit with this method for, say, September, you do not have to run through the number sequentially until you reach the ninth digit, but can just recall directly September-sceptre-door-four.

The Peg system can be used to count things, in any kind of a monotonous, repetitious task in which you may lose count of how many times you have done it. For example, I use the pegwords to count laps around the track when jogging. The track where I jog is an indoor track that is one-fifth of a mile. This means that to run two miles, for example, I must circle the track ten times. After running for a while, it is easy to lose track (pun intended) of how many laps I have completed. To help me overcome this problem, I picture myself jumping over a bun as I complete my first lap, jumping over a shoe as I complete lap 2, running into a tree at the end of lap 3, etc. Another day I might picture the appropriate item sitting off to the side of the track as I complete each lap, or picture each item damaged in some way (a squashed bun, a broken shoe, a sawed tree, etc.), or picture each item on fire. Varying it from day to day helps reduce interference from the previous day, so that I can tell that I am counting today's laps rather than yesterday's laps. Of course, the procedure could be adapted to count repetitions in any kind of a routine task.

Using the Same Pegwords
Over and Over

In Chapter 7, two possible ways of reducing interference among different lists that are learned in close succession with the Loci system were discussed. First, you can construct several different loci lists so that you will not have to use the same list so often. Second, you can use progressive elaboration. These same two methods can help reduce interference that may come from using the Peg system on several successive lists. You could either construct several lists of pegwords (perhaps one based on rhymes, one on look-alikes, one on meaning, and one on the alphabet), or you could attach more than one item to each pegword by using progressive elaboration (the study on progressive elaboration that was described in Chapter 7 found equivalent results for the Loci and Peg systems).[18]

Other Uses

As with the Link and Loci, the Peg system can be used in school settings also. Gordon Bower has suggested that the Peg system could be used to learn arbitrary lists of things such as the order of presidents of the United States, the fifty states and their capital cities, sequences of historical events, the laws of visual perception, the defining criteria of mammals, etc. He suggested that "it is good for practically any arbitrary list where the items are in some sense already familiar and meaningful to the person and his main problem is one of getting ready and reliable access to what he knows."[19] Bower reported also that the Peg system has, in fact, been validated in several instances with actual school learning materials, like geographic facts about a country.

Like the Loci system, the Peg system can be combined with the Link system to remember as many as 100 items. Associate the first item with "bun" and link the next nine items; associate item 11 with "shoe" and link the next nine items, etc. This way you do not have any link longer than ten words, and you use the pegwords to cue you as to the first word in each link.

Additional practical applications of the Peg system can be found in popular memory-training books such as those referenced at the end of Chapter 6.

SUMMARY

If you could associate items to numbers, you could retrieve a given numbered item directly by thinking of the number and retrieving the item associated with it. The Peg system, which is over 300 years old, enables you to do this. The Peg system consists of concrete nouns that rhyme with the numbers (one-bun, two-shoe, etc.). The nouns are pre-memorized, and serve as mental "pegs" on which to hang items to be remembered. To learn a list of numbered items, you associate the first item with "bun," the second item with "shoe," etc. In recall, you think of the pegwords and retrieve the items associated with them.

There are several ways in which pegwords can be selected to represent numbers. A commonly used system is based on rhymes. Other systems may be based on objects that look like the corresponding numbers, or on objects that are related in meaning to the corresponding numbers. The alphabet provides another potential source of pegwords; each of the twenty-six pegwords could either rhyme with each letter of the alphabet or begin with each letter of the alphabet.

The Peg system and the Loci system are similar in several ways. They are both mental filing systems consisting of a pre-memorized series of concrete items, which are used in the same manner in both systems. The pre-memorized items are either locations or objects; locations are really nothing more than objects ordered spatially. A series of locations or objects can be used over and over for learning new material. Both systems change a free-recall task to aided recall via a paired-associate task.

There are also a couple of differences between the Peg system and the Loci system. The advantage of the Peg system is that it enables direct retrieval; if you want to remember the eighth item, you do not have to proceed sequentially until you reach the eighth location, but can merely see what is associated with "gate." The advantage of the Loci system is that it is easier for most people to construct a lengthy series of locations than a lengthy series of pegwords.

A number of studies have shown that the Peg system does make a significant difference in people's ability to remember. Since the Peg system is essentially a paired-associate task, with the learners providing their own cue words, the voluminous amount of research evidence showing the effectiveness of visual imagery also applies to the Peg system. People using the Peg system typically recall a list of ten words correctly, in order, after hearing them once, whereas those not using the system typically recall about half as many.

The Peg system can be used for any of the uses of the Link or Loci systems. In addition, it can be used in situations for which direct retrieval is desired. For example, it could be used to learn the Ten Commandments so that you could name them out of order as well as in order. The Peg system can also be used to learn numbers, by linking the pegwords representing the digits together. It can also be used to count things and to learn lists of information in school.

CHAPTER 9

Using Mnemonics — The Phonetic System

The Phonetic system is the most sophisticated and most versatile of the mnemonic systems discussed in this book. It is also the most complex, and thus requires the most study and effort to master. However, for use as a mental filing system, the Phonetic system overcomes a limitation of the Peg system by allowing construction of more than ten to twenty pegwords. At the same time, it retains the Peg system's advantage of direct retrieval. In addition, the Phonetic system enables us to make numbers meaningful so they can be better remembered by association.

WHAT IS THE PHONETIC SYSTEM?

The system discussed in this chapter has been referred to by such terms as "figure-alphabet," "digit-letter," "number-alphabet," "Hook," "number-consonant," and "number-to-sound." Of these many labels, the most descriptive is the last one, the "number-to-sound" system. The other labels are more descriptive of older versions of the system. The reason why I have chosen to call the system the "Phonetic system" will become clear as it is described.

In the Phonetic system, each of the digits from 0 to 9 is represented by a consonant sound; these consonant sounds are then combined with vowels to code numbers into words, which are more meaningful and thus easier to remember.

Origin

The origin of the Phonetic system can be traced back over 300 years to 1648, when Winckelman (also spelled "Wenusheim" or "Wennsshein" in some references) introduced a digit-letter system in which the digits were represented by letters of the alphabet. These letters were then used to form words to represent a given number sequence. In 1730 Richard Grey published a refinement of Winckelman's digit-letter system.[1]

In these early systems the digits were represented by both consonants and vowels, and the letters selected to represent each digit were selected arbitrarily. In 1813 Gregor von Feinaigle described a further refinement of the system. In Feinaigle's system the digits were represented by consonants only; vowels had no numerical value. In addition, the consonants representing each digit were not selected arbitrarily, but were selected on the basis of their similarity to, or association with, the digits they represented (for example, "t" = 1 because it resembles a "1," "n" = 2 because it has two downstrokes, "d" = 6 because it resembles a reversed "6"). Words were then formed to represent numbers, by inserting vowels; thus, "6" could be represented by "aid," and "16" could be represented by "tide."[2]

Further modifications of the digit-consonant system were made by mnemonists during the 1800s. In 1844 Francis Fauvel-Gouraud published the *Phreno-mnemonotechnic Dictionary*, which was an attempted classification of all the words in the English language that could represent numbers up to 10,000. By the end of the nineteenth century, the digit-consonant system had evolved into its present form. During the 1890s it was briefly described in Williams James' classic psychology textbook, and more thoroughly described as the system of "analytic substitutions" by A. Loisette.[3] The digits were represented not just by consonants, but by consonant *sounds*. This version of the system has remained essentially unchanged in memory books and commercial courses during the twentieth century.

Description

The following display summarizes the phonetic system:

Digit	Consonant Sound	Memory Aid
1	t, d, th	"t" and "d" each have one downstroke
2	n	two downstrokes
3	m	three downstrokes
4	r	last sound for the word "four" in several languages

5	l	Roman numeral for "50" is "L"
6	j, sh, ch, soft "g"	reversed script "j" resembles "6" (𝓁)
7	k, q, hard "c," hard "g," ng	"7" resembles a skeleton key (⌐); "k" made of two 7's (𝒦)
8	f, v, ph	script "f" resembles "8" (𝑓)
9	b, p	both resemble "9" when inverted
0	z, s, soft "c"	"z" = "zero," "c" = "cipher"

It is important to realize that in the Phonetic system, it is the consonant *sounds* that are important, not the letters themselves. This is why I have chosen to call it the Phonetic system. All of the digits except 2, 3, 4, and 5 are actually represented by families of similar sounds, rather than by a single sound. Say the following words aloud and pay close attention to how similarly the underlined consonants in each group are formed with your mouth and tongue: For "6," Joe, show, chow, and age; for "7," key, quo, cow, and go; for "8," foe, vow, and phase; for "9," bay and pay; for "0," zoo, sue, and ace.

There are several advantages to the way in which the consonant sounds have been selected to represent the digits in the Phonetic system: (1) The sound-digit correspondences are easy to learn (see the memory aids); (2) the sounds are grouped by similar phonetic families; (3) the sounds are mutually exclusive—each digit is represented by one, and only one, sound; (4) the sounds are exhaustive—all the consonant sounds in the English language are included, except for W, H, and Y, which you can easily remember by the word "why" (the letter "H" has value only as it changes the sounds of other consonants—th, ch, ph, sh).

The emphasis on consonant *sounds* is important, because different letters or letter combinations may take on the same sounds. For example, the "sh" sound can be made by all of the following letters: "ci" (gracious), "ti" (ratio), "si" (vision), "sci" (conscience), "s" (pleasure), "z" (azure), and "c" (ocean). Not only can different letters take on the same sound, but the same letter can take on different sounds. For example, sound the "t" in *ratio* vs. *patio;* the "c" in *ace* vs. *act;* the "g" in *age* vs. *ago;* the "gh" in *ghost* vs. *tough;* the "ch" in *church* vs. *chronic;* the "ng" in *sing* vs. *singe;* the "s" in *noose* vs. *nose.* The letter "x" (eks) takes on two consonant sounds as it is pronounced in most words (ox), but may also be sounded as a "z" (xylophone).

When a repeated consonant makes only one sound it counts as only one number ("button" = 912, not 9112, and "account" = 721, not 7721). When a repeated consonant makes two different sounds it counts as two numbers ("accent" = 7021). A silent consonant is disregarded; it has no value if you do not hear it when pronouncing a word: "lamb" = 53, not 539 (but "lumber" = 5394); "bought" = 91, not 971; "knife" = 28, not 728; "could" = 71, not

751; "descend" = 1021, not 10721 (but "escape" = 079). Two different consonants together represent only one digit if they form only one sound ("tack" = 17, not 177; "acquaint" = 721, not 7721).

Most discussions of the Phonetic system have "ng" represent the number "7," when sounded as in "sing." This is how I will treat "ng" in this chapter (although in my personal use of the Phonetic system I always treat "ng" as two different sounds, "n" and "g" representing 27). The important consideration, as with the other examples also, is that you go by what *you* hear and that you be consistent. Whichever you prefer, remember that it is the sound that is important: "sing" = 07, "engage" = 276, "angel" = 265.

Obviously, the Phonetic system is more complex than the other mnemonic systems, and thus takes more effort to learn. However, I believe that its many potential uses justify the effort expended in learning it. The sounds representing each digit should be thoroughly learned. Most of the examples that I have discussed, plus others that will help illustrate the differences between sound and letter, are contained in the following display showing examples of different consonants and combinations that may represent each digit.

Digit	Sound	Examples
1	t	tot (11), wetter (14), patio (91)
	d	did (11), wedding (17), could (71)
	th	the (1), with (1), either (14)
2	n	noon (22), winner (24), gnat (21), knit (21), mnemonic (2327), pneumonia (232)
3	m	mom (33), mummy (33), lamb (53), hymn (3)
4	r	roar (44), barrel (945), wren (42)
5	l	law (5), lilly (55)
6	j	judge (66), gauge (76), angel (265)
	sh	she (6), ratio (46), ocean (62), anxious (angshus = 760), vision (862), azure (64)
	ch	choose (60), witch (6), conscious (7260)
7	k	kite (71), back (97), school (075), talk (16), xerox (zeroks = 0470), jackknife (6728)
	q	quilt (751), acquaint (721)
	hard c	cow (7), circus (0470), accent (7021), account (721)
	hard g	gauge (76), tagged (171), angle (275), ghost (701)
	ng	sing (07), anxious (angshus = 760)
8	f	off (8), food (81), phone (82), cough (78)
	v	oven (82), of (8)

9	b	bob (99), rubber (494)
	p	pop (99), apple (95)
0	z	zoo (0), dazzle (105), toys (10), nose (20), xerox (zeroks = 0470)
	s	seal (05), tossed (101), descend (1021), psychology (0756), noose (20)
	soft c	circus (0470), accent (7021)

How to Use It

After the consonant sounds representing each digit have been thoroughly learned, the Phonetic system can then be used in two general areas: (1) Keywords can be constructed to serve as a mental filing system for use in the same way described for the Loci and Peg systems; (2) any numerical information can be coded into words to make it easier to learn. Let us briefly consider each of these areas.

The Phonetic system can be used to construct keywords to serve as a mental filing system. (To avoid confusion as to whether I am talking about the Peg system or the Phonetic system, I will refer to the Peg system words as "pegwords" and the Phonetic system words as "keywords.") The keywords are constructed by combining vowels with the consonants. For example, there are many words that could represent the number "1": doe, day, die, tie, toe, tea, eat, hat, head, wade, the. For reasons discussed in Chapter 5, a concrete word would be selected; thus, "toe" would be better than "day."

We saw in the last chapter that one problem with the Peg system is that rhyming or look-alike nouns are hard to find for numbers beyond ten, and even harder for numbers beyond twenty. Thus, it is hard to construct pegwords for numbers beyond ten to twenty. The Phonetic system does not have this limitation. Two-digit numbers are represented by a word that begins with a consonant sound representing the first digit and ends with a consonant sound representing the second digit. For example, the number 13 could be represented by "tomb," "dome," or "dime," and the number 25 could be represented by "nail," "Nile," or "kneel." The procedure for three-digit numbers is the same; for 145 you could use "trail," "drill," or "twirl." However, numbers of more than two digits are sometimes difficult to represent by a single word, and may require two words, or a phrase. For example, 889 may be represented by "ivy fob," and 8890 by "five apes."

By combining consonants and vowels, keywords for numbers up to 100 can easily be constructed. Examples of a possible keyword for each of the numbers from 1 to 20 are the following:

1. tie	8. ivy	15. doll
2. inn	9. pie	16. dish
3. ma	10. toes	17. duck
4. hare	11. tot	18. dove
5. hill	12. dune	19. tub
6. shoe	13. tomb	20. nose
7. key	14. tire	

Several possible keywords for each number from 1 to 100 are listed in Appendix B.* You should choose one keyword that you can visualize easily for each number, and use it consistently. The keywords serve as your mental filing system. They are used in the same way as the locations are used in the Loci system and the pegwords are used in the Peg system. Thus, the first item on the list to be learned should always be associated with "tie," the second item with "inn," and the twentieth item with "nose" (or whatever keywords you select). Recall also proceeds the same as with the Peg system. You think first of the number, then the keyword, then the item that was associated with the keyword.

You can increase your basic 100-word list to 1099 by learning only ten more words. The ten words are adjectives that represent the numbers from 1 to 10; examples might be, 1 = wet, 2 = new, 3 = my, 4 = hairy, 5 = oily, 6 = huge, 7 = weak, 8 = heavy, 9 = happy, 10 = dizzy. For numbers from 101 to 999 you would use your basic keyword to represent the last two digits of the number, and the adjective to represent the first digit; for example, 101 = wet suit, 201 = new suit, 462 = hairy chin, 938 = happy movie, and 1099 = dizzy baby.

The second major area in which the Phonetic system is useful is in coding numerical information into words, so that the information will be more meaningful and easier to associate. Numerous examples of this use are presented later in the chapter.

The reason for listing several possible keywords for each number in Appendix B is to provide additional keywords so that you can avoid using the same word too many times in coding a series of numbers. For example, you will have less interference if you code the number 6149234949 by linking "sheet-rope-gnome-rib-robe" than if you linked "sheet-rope-gnome-rope-rope." Also, if you were memorizing several phone numbers, for example, which had a 72 in them, you would likely get less interference among them if you used several different words for 72 than if you used the same one in all your associations.

*Additional phonetic keywords for each number up to 1000 have been listed by Buzan, Hersey, and Furst; and, as has been mentioned, several keywords for most numbers up to 10,000 were listed by Fauvel-Gouraud.⁴

HOW WELL DOES
THE PHONETIC SYSTEM WORK?

Less research has been done on the Phonetic system than on the Link, Loci, and Peg systems, for the obvious reason that it takes more time and effort to master the Phonetic system before it can be used. Thus, it is harder for a researcher to teach a group of people the system and have them use it in an experiment. Nevertheless, a few studies have investigated the effectiveness of the Phonetic system.

Research Evidence

Three studies during the 1960s studied the effect of the Phonetic system on rate of learning. In the first study, people were given a one-hour lecture and demonstration of the Phonetic system, then they practiced the system for four days. They were then divided into three groups, and each group was given a ten-item list (three-letter syllables of either low, medium, or high meaningfulness). Other people learned the lists without mnemonic training. The Phonetic group learned faster than the other group for lists of medium meaningfulness, a little faster for lists of low meaningfulness, and no faster for lists of high meaningfulness.[5] This study does not give very strong support to the contention that the Phonetic system aids learning. However, several procedural factors may have affected this finding: (1) There was no check on whether the people who were taught the Phonetic system actually *used* the system in the experiment; (2) the items were presented at a rate of 4 seconds per item, which may have been too fast to recall the keyword and associate it with the item; and (3) the lists contained only ten words, which may not have been enough to tax the memories of the people who did not use the Phonetic system.

A second study on the rate of learning used longer lists (twenty items rather than ten), and presented each item for a longer time (12 seconds rather than 4 seconds). Otherwise, the procedure was similar to that of the first study. Some people were trained for 30 minutes in the Phonetic system, and practiced it for a week. They were then given the task of learning a list of twenty items (three-letter syllables), containing ten meaningful items and ten meaningless items. Another group of people learned the same list without mnemonic training. Contrary to the findings of the first study, this second study found that the people who used the Phonetic system learned both kinds of items faster than those who did not use it. In fact, the Phonetic group learned the meaningless items as easily as the other group learned the meaningful items.[6]

The third study relating the Phonetic system to rate of learning found results consistent with the second study. One group of people was trained in the Phonetic system for about 30 minutes, and given practice in using the keywords to learn a list of twenty words. A second group received practice in learning the twenty-word list, but no training in the keywords. All the people were then given a list of twenty concrete nouns and allowed to study them until they could recall all words in the correct order. Half the Phonetic group had a printed list of keywords to refer to during learning and recall, while the other half did not. The Phonetic group without the list of keywords learned the list in the least amount of time, the Phonetic group with the list of keywords was next fastest, and the other group was the slowest.[7] Thus, the research indicates that the Phonetic system can make a significant difference in learning.

In a study that investigated the effect of the Phonetic system on retention as well as learning, people learned three consecutive lists of twenty words each. Some people were given a lecture demonstration of the Phonetic system, and practiced using the keywords to learn four lists of nouns. A second group received the lecture demonstration of the Phonetic system but no practice. A third group practiced learning the four lists of nouns, but received no exposure to the Phonetic system. The two Phonetic groups were told to practice the keywords before the testing session, which was the next day. The next day all the people were given one presentation of each of three twenty-word lists at a slow rate—each word was exposed for 30 seconds (other variables were also investigated, but are not of concern here). The people were tested for recall of the words in numerical order immediately after each list had been presented, and again after all three lists had been presented. In immediate recall, the two Phonetic groups recalled an average of about half the words, while the recall of the other group ranged from 20 to 40 percent. In recall at the end of the session, the Phonetic groups averaged about 40 percent recall while the other group averaged about 19 percent.[8]

In a study that used a slightly different procedure from those discussed so far in this section, people were not actually instructed in the Phonetic system, but were given a printed list of twenty-five Phonetic keywords to use in learning two consecutive twenty-five-item lists. They were also trained in making visual associations with the keywords. Other people were not given the keywords or the training (again, other variables were also investigated, but are not of concern here). The Phonetic group showed an average recall of about 60 percent, while the other group showed an average recall of about 19 percent.[9]

Three of the mnemonic systems were investigated in one study. Different groups of people were taught ten pegwords, ten keywords, or ten numbered loci as parts of an automobile. They were then read five lists of ten numbered nouns, and tested for recall. All three mnemonic systems resulted in increased recall of concrete nouns, as compared with results from people who had received no mnemonic training. However, none of the three systems increased recall for abstract nouns. The study found no significant differences among the three systems.[10]

Stefan Slak devised his own letter-number system to learn three-digit numbers. The first and third digits were represented by consonants and the middle digit was represented by a vowel. Slak reported that the system helped him in a memory-span task, in serial learning, and in free learning. He also taught a simplified version of the system to a group of people who used it to learn eight three-digit numbers. The group learned the numbers twice as fast as a group that had not been taught the system; they required an average of about six and a half presentations of the numbers before they could recall all of them once without error, while the other group required an average of fourteen presentations.[11]

Demonstrations

When I give lectures on memory to various groups, I typically begin with a demonstration for which I use the Phonetic system keywords. The numbers from 1 to 25 are written on the chalkboard, and the audience makes up a list of twenty-five words by calling out a number and a word for each number. A volunteer from the audience writes the words on the board as they are called out, while I stand facing the audience, with my back to the board. After the list is completed, I tell the audience that I am going to repeat all the words back to them, and I usually ask, "How do you want them, forward, backward, or odd and even?" This question generally produces looks of disbelief and a low roar of incredulous murmurs; and frequently someone suggests "start in the middle and work both ways," or "every third one." (If there are no suggestions, I usually just recall them in reverse order from 25 to 1.) Of course, the order of recall does not matter with the Phonetic system.

I have done this demonstration several dozen times during the last few years, and almost always recall all twenty-five items, although I once recalled only twenty-two items (for which I apologized profusely to the audience). Of course, this demonstration situation is more taxing than most uses of the Phonetic system; the words frequently come very rapidly, almost on top of one another, and I am sometimes distracted and do not form good, vivid associations. I have also tried this task four times with 100 words, but have not successfully recalled all 100 words; my recall has ranged from 93 to 97 words.

The use of the Phonetic system by students in my memory course provides a different kind of evidence from that provided by the research studies; it involves the same group of people learning with and without the Phonetic system, rather than two different groups of people. On the first night of class, I read to the students a list of twenty numbered nouns in random order, and have them recall as many as they can recall in correct numbered order. Later in the course, after we have discussed the Phonetic system, I give them the same task with another twenty-noun list. The sixty-two students in my three most recent classes recalled an average of about ten words before learning the Phonetic system and about nineteen words after learning it. The following display shows their recall performance before and after they learned the Phonetic system. (The person who recalled only two words before learning the system was among the 56 percent who recalled all twenty words after learning it.)

Number of Words Recalled	Before Phonetic	After Phonetic
20	1	35
19	1	13
18	2	6
17	2	1
16	3	1
15	3	2
14	4	2
13	4	1
12	4	1
11	4	
10	6	
9	5	
8	3	
7	4	
6	5	
5	5	
4	3	
3	2	
2	1	

HOW CAN YOU USE
THE PHONETIC SYSTEM?

The Phonetic system can be used for all of the previous uses described for the Link, Loci, and Peg systems. Its main advantage over the Peg system is that you can use it for long lists. Its main advantage over the Loci system is that you can retrieve numbered items directly. (Of course, the items do not *have* to be numbered.) It has an additional advantage over all previous systems in that you can use it to remember numbers.

A Mental Filing System

The Phonetic system keywords can be used as a literal mental filing system, in a similar way as described for the Loci system in Chapter 7. I use my keywords from 51 to 100 in groups of ten for this purpose: 50 to 59 for miscellaneous things to do; 60 to 69 for home and family; 70 to 79 for church and civic; 80 to 89 for school; and 90 to 99 for miscellaneous ideas (of course, you can use any categories). Suppose that just as I am drifting off to sleep at night I remember several things I have to do tomorrow. I remember that I need to leave my wife some money (home and family), mail a letter on the way to work (miscellaneous things to do), pick up some income tax forms (miscellaneous things to do), grade the exams for a class (school), and order a book for another class (school). I may form associations between: lot (51) and letter, lion (52) and tax, juice (60) and money, vase (80) and exam, and fit (81) and books. Then in the morning before I leave for school, I can take a quick mental search in each category, do the things that need to be done that morning, and write the others down in my notebook if I desire.

Another way you could use at least seventy keywords profitably is similar to suggestions offered concerning use of the Loci and Peg systems every day; to reduce day-to-day interference, it was suggested that you might have a different set of loci or pegwords for each day. Similarly, you could use your Phonetic keywords from 1 to 10 on Sunday, 11 to 20 on Monday, 21 to 30 on Tuesday, and so on; this would eliminate the interference that could result from using the same ten keywords day after day.

In Chapter 2, I described a memory demonstration using a fifty-page magazine. To memorize the magazine I use my keywords to represent the page numbers, and link what is on each page to the keyword. Suppose, for example, that page 36 contained a picture of three people in the upper right-hand corner, a report on how they broke the world's record for trio-flagpole-sitting to the left of the picture, a poem on love in the lower left-hand corner, and two ads in the lower right-hand corner (one for vitamin pills and one for an effortless exerciser). I could remember that information by using the Link system to form the following link: match (36), flagpole, picture of people, heart (for love), pill, and exerciser. This would give me the basic framework of what is on page 36. I could fill in the details by reading the material carefully. Remembering where each item was located on the page usually comes almost without conscious effort (as was discussed in Chapter 7), but may be aided by linking the items in order, say, from upper left to upper right to lower left to lower right. To do this with each page for a fifty-page magazine, to the extent that I can answer almost any question as described in Chapter 2, usually takes me about three hours of study. The same procedure may be adapted to studying other kinds of textual material.

If the material you want to remember is presented orally, rather than in written form, such as in a lecture or speech, you can associate the first main point to "tie," the second point to "inn," etc. Of course this procedure requires active concentration and participation in the listening process.

The Phonetic system may serve as the basis for some amazing memory feats with playing cards. One method involves representing each card by a keyword that begins with the first letter of the suit of the card and ends with the Phonetic sound representing the number of the card. For example, the four of clubs could be "car" or "core," the nine of spades could be "sub" or "soap." Special procedures may be required for the face cards. The card keywords may then be associated to help remember them.

For people who play cards there are a number of card games in which there are obvious advantages to being able to remember what cards have been played. For those who do not play cards, a number of amazing memory feats can be performed. You can look through a shuffled deck of cards once, and use the Link system to link the card keywords together, then name all the cards in order. Or you can associate each card keyword with the Phonetic keywords from 1 to 52 and not only name all the cards in order, but tell what card is in any location (for example, "you'll find the four aces at numbers 3, 17, 37, and 41"). A fast and easy, but impressive, demonstration is the missing-card stunt. Have someone remove one or more cards from the deck. You look through the deck once and tell which cards are missing. This is done by mutilating each card keyword as you come to it (see it broken, burned, etc.). Then after you have gone through the deck, you run through the card keywords in your mind and the ones that are not mutilated are the ones that were missing. This is also a way to keep track of cards that have been played in some card games.

You could learn the numerical order of the letters of the alphabet by associating each alphabet pegword from Chapter 8 with the corresponding Phonetic keyword for 1 to 26; for example, hay-tie (A = 1), jay-toes (J = 10), oar-dove (R = 18). This would enable you to retrieve the letter at any given numbered position without having to count through all the letters until you reached that number. One of my memory class students taught this method to his daughter, who was having a hard time arranging words in alphabetical order. She then had no difficulty alphabetizing words by converting the initial letters to numbers and ordering the words numerically.

Remembering Numbers

The most unique advantage of the Phonetic system over the previous systems is its usefulness in learning numbers. Much of the information we need to remember consists of numbers: phone numbers, street addresses, historical dates, economic data, stock numbers, population figures, ages, identification numbers, social security numbers, license plates, time schedules, prices, style numbers, etc. Unfortunately, numbers are about the most abstract kind of material to remember.

There are at least two approaches in using the Phonetic system to remember numbers. Both of them involve turning the numbers into words, which are more meaningful. When possible, the words should represent something concrete that can be visualized. But even when this is not possible, the words will still be easier to remember than numbers. The first approach is to make up a word or phrase in which each of the digits in the number translates into one of the consonant sounds in order. The second approach is to make up a phrase or sentence in which each digit in the number translates into the first consonant sound in each word. For example, to remember the number 60374 by the first approach, you might use "juice maker;" by the second approach, you might use, "She sews many gowns readily."

The following are a few examples of how selected numbers might be coded: To remember my automobile license plate number (KFK 207) I think of the German psychologist, "Koffka" as a "nice guy." A clothes locker in a gym I visited once was number C12-B (aisle C, booth 12, locker B), which I remembered by cotton ball. The deepest hole drilled by man is a gas well that went down 31,441 feet, which I can picture being measured by a meter rod. The Empire State Building is 1,250 feet tall; and I can see it filled with tunnels. The highest manmade structure in the world is a radio mast in Poland, which rises 2,119 feet—I can see myself on the top. The Carlsbad Caverns reach a depth of 1,320 feet, at which depth I can imagine demons. The highest waterfall in the world is in Venezuela; it falls 3,212 feet, as high as a mountain. I can remember the 1970 population of my hometown, Spokane, Washington, by imagining myself returning home to see a "dogsled show" (170,516). I can see a square mile covered with chairs to remember that it equals 640 acres, or associate a mile with digit to remember that it equals 1.61 kilometers.

If the word or phrase bears some meaningful relationship to the item it represents (such as the Carlsbad Caverns example), then the association will be most memorable, but even if the relationship is arbitrary (such as the Spokane population example), the association will still be more memorable than an abstract number would have been.

You can make modifications for numbers with decimals by using words beginning with "S" only for decimals, and using the "S" as the initial letter to represent a decimal point.[12] If no number precedes the decimal, the S indicates the decimal point (.51 = salt, .94 = sparrow, .734 = skimmer, etc.). If a number precedes the decimal, use two separate words, the decimal word beginning with "S" (945.51 = barley sold, 3.1416 = my store dish, etc.).

People who must remember formulas, equations, and other mathematical expressions may be able to adapt a procedure that one of my memory students suggested to me. The procedure involves several of the systems. Letters are represented by alphabet pegwords. Numbers are represented by Phonetic words. Symbols are represented by objects that remind you of the symbols. Examples might be a "house" for the square-root sign ($\sqrt{}$), a "slide" for the slash representing division (/), a "pie" for pi (π), and a cross for the plus sign (+). Thus, you might remember the formula for finding the volume of a sphere $(4/3\ \pi r^3)$ by linking "sphere-hare-slide-ma-pie-oar-cube."

I used the Phonetic system to memorize the 136 phone numbers of the members of a group to which I belong. The first two digits are the same for all phone numbers in our area, so I made up a word or phrase to represent the last five digits of each number. Then I made up substitute words to represent the names of the people. The association of each name with its number was a paired-associate learning task. The following are a few examples: Evans, 59941 (oven, wallpapered); Wille, 79812 (will, cup of tin); James, 77970 (Jesse James, cookbooks); Taylor, 41319 (tailor, ready-made bow).

Suppose you memorize a four-digit number such as 1478 by associating your keywords (say, *tire* and *cave*) with the person. Later when you recall the number you think of *tire* and *cave*, but are not sure whether the number is 1478 or 7814. One way to avoid this problem is to use your keyword for the last two digits of a four-digit number, and any word other than your keyword for the first two digits. Thus, 1478 might be coded as "door cave" or "dry cave," and 7814 might be coded as "calf tire" or "goofy tire."

A useful application for remembering numbers is remembering the twelve-digit number we discussed earlier for memorizing a year's calendar. For example, the number for 1977 (266-315-374-264) could be represented by: new choo-choo, motel, mugger, injury. These terms could be linked together in order by the Link or Story systems. (I can picture a new choo-choo crashing into a motel, running over a mugger, and causing serious injury — a rather violent association, but memorable.) This procedure requires sequential retrieval. To allow direct retrieval of a given month's digit, associate each digit directly with the month's pegword similar to the manner described for the Peg system (associate hen with Jam, shoe with Valentine, shoe with March, ma with Ape, etc.)

Using the Phonetic system to learn a twelve-digit number and a key digit for each year, methods have been devised by which you could remember the day of the week for every date in the twentieth century.[13] The mental arithmetic is a little more complex than that required for the use of a different twelve-digit number each year, but this feat can be accomplished by a person with a normal memory using the appropriate system—it is not limited to mental wizards, lightning calculators, or idiot savants.

You could also use the Phonetic system to remember dates such as birthdays and anniversaries. Suppose, for example, that a friend's birthday is on January 23, and your parents' anniversary is on June 16. One method for remembering these dates is to form associations among the person, the month pegword, and the date—"friend-Jam-gnome," and "parents-Spoon-dish." Another method is to use a number such that the first digit represents the month and the last digit represents the date, then turn that number into a word to associate with the person—"friend-denim," and "parents-huge ditch."

If you made up a pegword for each day of the week (for example, Monday = money, Wednesday = windy), you could construct a mental filing system for keeping track of daily appointments. Thus, if you need to go to the dentist at 10:00 on Monday, and take your car in for an oil change at 3:00 Wednesday, you could associate "dentist-money-toes" and "oil-windy-ma."

The keywords could also be used in the same manner as the pegwords to count things, and keep track of your count. Thus, in keeping count of my laps around the track as described for the Peg system, I can vary the monotony, and reduce interference, by using the pegwords one day and the keywords another day. In addition, with the Phonetic keywords I would not be limited to counting only 10 laps, but could easily count up to 100 (not that I will ever be running that many laps, but I do run more than 10 sometimes; also, there may be other things that one would want to count that *do* go up to 100).

Other Uses

At the end of Chapter 5 on mnemonics it was suggested that you might get more out of that chapter after you have read about the mnemonic systems. Now that you have read about the mnemonic systems, you might find it interesting and beneficial to re-read Chapter 5. Some of the points in that chapter might be more meaningful now.

As was the case with the other mnemonic systems, there are many more possible uses for the Phonetic system besides those mentioned here. Memory-training books suggest additional uses, plus more detail on some of the possible uses suggested here (such as the mental filing system for remembering daily appointments, and the methods for remembering dates and playing cards), and give examples of how the system can be applied in various occupations.[14]

SUMMARY

The Phonetic system is the most sophisticated and most versatile of the mnemonic systems discussed in this book. It is also the most complex, and thus the most difficult to learn. However, it overcomes the Peg system's limitation of having a limited number of pegwords, while retaining the advantage of direct retrieval. The most unique characteristic of the Phonetic system is its usefulness in remembering numbers.

The history of the Phonetic system can be traced back to the mid-1600s. The system underwent numerous refinements and modifications until the end of the nineteenth century; as now used it is essentially the same as it was at the beginning of the twentieth century. The Phonetic system is based on consonant sounds; hence its name. Each of the digits from 0 to 9 is represented by a consonant sound, or a group of similar sounds. The correspondences between the digits and sounds must be thoroughly learned. These sounds are then used to represent numbers with words, when the consonants are combined with vowels. The vowels have no numerical value, but merely serve to make words.

This system can be used in two ways. First, one can construct a list of keywords for the numbers 1 to 100, and beyond if desired. These keywords are used in the same manner as the Peg system pegwords, both for learning and for retrieval. The items to be learned are associated with the keywords. In retrieval, the keywords are recalled and the items associated with them are retrieved. Second, one can change any material involving numbers into meaningful words to aid in remembering the numbers.

Less research has been done on the Phonetic system than on the other three mnemonic systems, because the system is too complex to have people learn and use in one experimental session. However, a few studies have been done. The studies have shown that the Phonetic system can make a significant difference in learning and remembering verbal material. Evidence from students enrolled in memory courses provides additional evidence that the system really can help.

The Phonetic system can be used for all of the previous uses described for the Link, Loci, and Peg systems, and can also be used for remembering numbers. It can be used as a literal mental filing system. It can be used to remember material in magazines and books, when the keywords are made to represent each page and the contents of the page are linked to the keywords. It can serve as the basis for some amazing memory feats with playing cards; in this case, card keywords are used which begin with the first letter of the suit of the card and end with the Phonetic sound representing the number of the card. It can be used to remember numbers (phone numbers, addresses, dates, identification numbers, prices, style numbers, etc.) when the numbers are converted into words or phrases so they can be associated.

CHAPTER 10

More Miracles
with Mnemonics

Chapter 5 discussed mnemonics in general, some specific mnemonic techniques, and the principles underlying mnemonics. Chapters 6 to 9 discussed mnemonic systems that use the principles discussed in Chapter 5. This chapter will discuss some additional practical applications that do not actually use mnemonic systems, but do use the mnemonic techniques and principles. These applications include remembering names and faces, learning foreign languages, and overcoming absent-mindedness.

REMEMBERING NAMES AND FACES

Just because people learn how to remember speeches, numbers, cards, or lists, does not necessarily mean they will be able to remember names. Memory for names must be trained just like any other kind of memory. One must learn the techniques and practice using them. The following two examples show this fact, as well as illustrating the importance of interest.

In the section on "photographic memory" in Chapter 2, a man (VP) with an amazing verbal memory was discussed. Despite his impressive memory for verbal material, VP has commented that his ability to remember faces is not unusually good. He failed to recognize the wife of one of the researchers on meeting her at the store where he works, although he had met her socially on two or three occasions. He commented, "It's really applications of memory that are of importance in the learning process. That politician, Mr. Nixon, would certainly remember your wife by name and face, no matter what the circumstances in which he met her."[1]

Similarly, Bob Barker, the host of a TV show, meets many people on each show and remembers their names. When he was asked what his secret was for remembering people's names he replied, "It's all concentration. People on the show are my tools. I MUST know their names. It's my job. But introduce me to people at a cocktail party, and I can't remember who they are two minutes later."[2]

When we forget a person's name, then we may be subject to embarrassing moments such as one incident that reportedly happened to Clare Boothe Luce, former ambassador to Italy. At a gathering, she was introduced to David Burpee, flower and vegetable seed distributor. A short time later she could not remember his name, but did not say anything. Sensing her embarrassment, he said quietly, "I'm Burpee." Mrs. Luce replied, "That's quite all right. I'm sometimes troubled that way myself."[3]

Remembering names and faces is a paired-associate task—in most situations we see the face and recall the name; the face serves as the cue and the name serves as the response. We will look at some research on memory for names and faces, then at some strategies for remembering names and faces.

Recognition memory for faces is usually quite good. One study found a 96 percent recognition accuracy, while another found a 90 percent recognition accuracy for as many as sixty faces.[4] One study found that people in their fifties and sixties still recognized 75 percent of their high school classmates' faces, and that memory for faces declined slower than memory for names.[5]

Remembering faces is generally easier than remembering names, for at least three reasons: (1) We generally see the face, but only hear the name. (2) As noted in Chapter 2, face memory is a recognition task, whereas name memory is a recall task. (3) Even if we saw both the face and the name, and if both kinds of memory were recognition tasks, we noted in Chapter 2 that pictures (faces) are easier to remember than words (names).

Let us look at some studies that are relevant to the distinction between recognition and recall in remembering people. One study tried measuring both names and faces by both recognition and recall. For the recognition measure, people were shown a series of either names or faces, then shown a larger set of names or faces and asked to pick the ones they had just seen. They were then tested for recall of names by being shown the faces and asked to recall the names. They were tested for recall of faces by being shown the names and reporting whether they could recall the faces. Recognition yielded higher accuracy scores than recall both for names (97 percent vs. 36 percent) and for faces (91 percent vs. 54 percent).[6] In another similar study, people were given the names of some famous people, and were asked to imagine the faces. They were given the faces of other people and were asked to recall the names. Reported recall of the face given the name was more frequent than recall of the name given the face. However, accuracy of recall was not measured.[7]

The strength of recognition in measuring memory for names is shown by the finding that fifteen years after graduation from high school, people can recall only about 15 percent of their classmates' names, but can recognize 90 percent of the names from a list of names.[8] Recognition of names has also been found to be faster than recognition of faces.[9]

One problem in studying recall of faces is the difficulty of checking the accuracy of recall. Recently developed methods may help in overcoming this problem. The Photo-Fit Kit consists of a number of separate features that a person puts together to construct a face. It was designed to enable witnesses to reconstruct the faces of people wanted for police questioning. However, people using the kit have difficulty reconstructing a face even when the original face is present, and it is even harder when the face has to be recalled from memory.[10] This poor recall of faces contrasts with the typically high scores for recognition measures of face memory.

All this evidence points to the fact that one of the main reasons name memory is more of a problem than face memory is because name memory is a recall task and face memory is a recognition task.

As was noted in Chapter 7 on Loci, one strategy that may help in recalling a name is to try to recall anything else about the person you can (such as where you met him). In trying to remember a famous person's name when shown his picture, people first try to locate the person's profession, then the place where they may have seen him, then when they last saw the person. The more you know about a person the more paths you have to try to retrieve the name.[11] When people tried to recall the name of an object given its definition, they frequently could recall a visual image of the object before (or even instead of) recalling the name.[12] Similarly, thinking of what a person looks like when trying to recall his or her name may help bring the name to you.

One of the most common reasons for enrolling in memory-training courses is to improve one's memory for names and faces. Many popular memory-training books devote at least one chapter to discussions of memory for names and faces, and an entire book has recently been devoted to the subject.[13] Further details on each of the following strategies for remembering names and faces may be found in memory-training books, and you can read those books if you want more explanation and examples of these strategies.[14] However, the primary determinant of your memory for names is your awareness of these strategies, then your *practice* of them. These are the steps used by people who remember hundreds of people's names after meeting them just once: (1) Make sure you get the name; (2) focus on a distinctive feature of the person's appearance; (3) make the name meaningful; (4) associate the name with the distinctive feature; (5) review the association. Let us now consider these strategies, along with some relevant research findings.

Get the Name

As was noted in Chapter 3, failure to pay attention may be the single most common reason why we "forget" the names of people we are introduced to; we never really *got* the name in the first place. Memory for names can be improved significantly (some say as much as 50 percent) without any particular mnemonic technique, but merely by concentrating on the name and paying attention to it.

Even when you are paying attention, you may not get a person's name if it is spoken too fast, or too quietly. If this happens, stop the introducer and ask him to repeat the name. Why do people not do that more often? One reason may be that they do not want to be rude by interrupting the conversation. Another may be that they are somewhat embarrassed that they did not get the name; but they are likely to be even more embarrassed later to not be able to remember the name. So, make sure you get the name.

Use the name in the conversation, repeat it, spell it aloud, work it over, ask about it. These activities help you make sure you get the name. They force you to concentrate on it. Repeating the name and using it involves applying the principles of repetition and recitation discussed in Chapter 4. Of course this can be overdone, but at the very least you could use the name at least three times without appearing too obvious; once when you first meet the person, once during the conversation, and once when parting. For example, "I'm happy to meet you Mr. Jones," then later, "What do you think about that, Mr. Jones?", and finally, "It was nice talking with you, Mr. Jones."

Focus on the Face

The next step is to note distinctive features of the person's face or appearance, features that would likely first draw your attention the next time you meet him. The purpose of focusing on the face is to find something distinctive that will help you recognize it.

There has been a considerable amount of research on people's ability to recognize faces and to distinguish among them. The procedure in most such research is to show faces to people, then have the people pick the faces they have seen from a larger number of faces. We will discuss some of the findings concerning recognition memory for faces.

There is a considerable amount of difference among people in their ability to accurately remember faces, and also considerable differences in how memorable different faces are.[15]

Several studies have found differences between males and females in their memory for faces, the most consistent difference being that females tend to remember faces better than do males.[16] A possible reason for this is that females are more interested in facial features, and also more trained in noting them, because of their experiences with cosmetics.

Carefully looking at a face helps memory for it. People in one study looked at seventy-two faces and were told to indicate either which sex they were, or how honest they were. Assuming that a person would study the pictures more thoroughly to make a judgment of honesty than of sex, people rating honesty should be better able to recognize the faces later. This is what was found. When people were judging for honesty, they scored 80 percent in the recognition tests, whereas when they were judging for sex they scored only 56 percent. The researchers concluded that "if you want to remember a person's face, try to make a number of difficult personal judgments about his face when you are first meeting him."[17] Of course, this is just one means of making you concentrate on the features of the person.

We tend to remember faces that are distinctive and distinguishable better than ones that are not. For example, we remember very attractive and very unattractive faces better than moderately attractive faces; we remember faces of members of our own race better than those of another race. Even an expression on a face, such as a smile, can help make it distinctive enough to aid memory for it.[18] However, a feature as changeable as a smile would not be a good feature to base your recognition on, because the person may not smile the next time you see her; the same suggestion holds for other nonpermanent features, such as whether or not the person is wearing glasses.

Many people who are not used to studying faces have a hard time at first finding something really distinctive about every face. To many people, all faces include two eyes, a nose, and a mouth. How can you make that distinctive? Actually, there are many distinguishing features in a face; but you must train yourself to look for them. Once you do, you will see much more in a face, just as a botanist on a walk through the forest sees many differences in plants that look the same to most people, or a geologist sees many differences in rocks that are indistinguishable to the untrained eye.

For example, one study used at least twenty-one different aspects of facial features to teach a computer to distinguish among faces.[19] These facial features include characteristics of the hair (coverage, length, texture, shade), mouth (upper lip thickness, lower lip thickness, lip overlap, width), eyes (width of opening, distance apart, shade), nose (length, tip, shape), ears (length, protrusion), eyebrows (bushiness, distance apart), chin (shape), forehead (slant), and cheeks (fullness). In addition, you may note features that are unique to one person such as dimples, a cleft in the chin, striking teeth, or lines in the forehead.

Which features are the most helpful in distinguishing among faces? The eyes? The mouth? Research findings are not consistent. There is some evidence that the eyes may be the most helpful, while other studies have not found a clear superiority of any one facial feature.[20] It may be that most people's eyes reveal more about them than any other facial feature, but it may not be wise to try to distinguish a person on the basis of his eyes if he has a bulbous nose, protruding ears, curly red hair, or some other definite distinguishing feature.

Make the Name Meaningful

The next step requires that the names be made meaningful and concrete. This is not hard for names that already have meaning. Many names have meaning in themselves or through association with something that is meaningful. Look through a phone book and you may be surprised at how many names already have meaning to you. There are names of cities or countries (London, Holland), colors (White, Green), occupations (Barber, Cook), adjectives (Strong, Short), famous people (Lincoln, Ford), metals (Silver, Steel), plants (Rose, Oaks), animals (Wolf, Lamb), things (Hammer, Ball), and commercial products (Dodge, Hershey).

For names that do not have any readily apparent meaning, you can use the principle of substitute words discussed in Chapter 5 to give meaning to the name. For example, *hug bee* may represent "Higbee," *wood taker* may represent "Whittaker," *paw low ski* may represent "Pawlowski," *fresh neck* may represent "Frischknecht," *hunt singer* may represent "Huntzinger," *magnet mare* may represent "McNamara," *saw press key* may represent "Zabriskie," *mule stein* may represent "Muhlestein," *lamb or row* may represent "Lamoreaux," *awl storm* may represent "Ahlstrom." I picked these examples randomly from the local telephone directory. A good way to acquire the skill of making substitute words is to practice with the names in a phone directory.

Even if there is an occasional name that you cannot make meaningful, merely trying to do so will force you to concentrate on the name and work it over, and thus increase the likelihood that you will remember it.

Associate the Face with the Name

Once you have made something meaningful of the person's name, then you form a conscious, visual association between the name and the distinctive feature of that individual's appearance. For example, if Mr. Ball has red hair, you could picture hundreds of red balls coming out of his hair; if Miss Cook has long eyelashes, you could picture her eyelashes cooking; if Mr. Whittaker has large ears, you could picture him carrying wood (*wood taker*) with his ears; if Mrs. McNamara has a round mouth, you could picture a *magnet* riding a *mare* out of her mouth; if Miss Huntzinger has dimples, you could picture a *hunter* sitting in her dimple *singing*.

Of course, the common criticism of this method, especially by people who have not tried it, is that you might think of the substitute word but not the name. That is true. It is one of the hazards of using substitute words in visual associations. This procedure does not necessarily make memory perfect, but it does improve memory, and the more you practice it the more you can improve. Even if you did fail to recall a few names, would you be any worse off than you are now?

Nowhere is the misconception that was discussed in Chapter 1 concerning the search for a simple "key" to memory more applicable than in remembering names. I have known a number of people who want to know the secret of remembering names, but when they are told the secret (as described in these steps), they dismiss it as too much work.

Review the Association

Review was discussed as part of SQ3R in Chapter 4. If you really want to remember a name for a long time you should review it as soon as possible after meeting the person, then occasionally afterwards. For example, if you meet several people at a party one night, immediately after the party you should review in your mind the names and faces of the people you met.

Since it takes some time to form associations, when possible you would want to arrange to meet people with a little break between introductions, rather than having a whole bunch of names thrown at you one after another. This would not only allow you time to review the ones you have met so far,[21] but would also allow you time to make a strong association for each person.

Proactive interference (see Chapter 2) has been found for faces as well as for verbal material, suggesting that interference can affect memory for faces as well as for names.[22] To reduce the negative effects of such interference when you meet several people in succession, you might try to apply some of the principles for reducing interference in Chapter 4 (meet the people in different rooms, or different parts of the room; space the introductions, etc.).

When you get a chance, write the name down. People who hear and see words remember them better than people who only hear (or only see) the words. Also, children and adults have been found to remember spelling words better when they see them than when they hear them. Similarly, looking at a name in addition to hearing it should help fix it more firmly in your memory.[23]

Do These Strategies Work?

A textbook on memory suggested that there are two fundamental factors that cause the forgetting of names.[24] The first is interference. Storage takes time, and anything that interferes before the name is stored in long-term memory may prevent storage. Therefore, do not let your mind wander before you have stored the name. The second factor is inefficient association. The five suggestions above help to overcome both of these problems.

A student in my memory class, a man in his middle fifties, told the class how he had been a member of a club of about 150 men for ten years, and he knew the names of only about thirty or forty of them. On their next dinner meeting after we had discussed names and faces in our class, he made it a point to sit at a table at which he did not know any of the men. When they introduced themselves he made a special effort to make sure he got each of the eight names. He then made a visual or verbal association of each name with each person, used the names during the night, and reviewed the associations. He reported to the class that, somewhat to his surprise, he knew every man's name at the end of the evening, and that he is going to continue the same strategy until he knows the names of all 150 men in the club.

At the end of a class period in which we discussed names and faces, I had each of the twenty-six class members introduce himself or herself and stand for about 15 seconds, to give the class members a chance to try some of these strategies. After all the students had introduced themselves, then each student stood again for a few seconds while the others tried to recall his name. Even though this was the first time most of them had tried any of the techniques, more than half the class members were able to remember at least two-thirds of the names. (The student with the best recall—twenty-five out of twenty-six—was a telephone operator who remembered the people by their voices.)

Perhaps the most striking proof that the strategies work is provided by people who can remember the names of hundreds of people after meeting them once. For example, one memory performer, Harry Lorayne, has met several hundred people in one night and been able to call them all by name.[25] Likewise, people remember thousands of names over periods of months or years using these strategies.

LEARNING A FOREIGN LANGUAGE

As was noted in Chapter 3, learning a foreign language vocabulary is a paired-associate task (in fact, people who do well in standard paired-associate learning also tend to do well in learning a foreign language[26]). Because visual associations help in paired-associate learning, they might also help in language learning. However, foreign-language words are abstract and meaningless to many people. Because visual imagery is not as powerful with abstract words as with concrete words, how can imagery be used for a foreign language? Most approaches have used the principle of concrete substitute words discussed in Chapter 5. Does this work? Research shows that visual associations can make a significant difference in learning Spanish, Russian, German, and possibly even Chinese. The research has been concerned with learning the vocabulary more than the grammar, pronunciation, etc. Let us look at the evidence.

The Keyword Method

Richard Atkinson and Michael Raugh have conducted several experiments evaluating the effectiveness of visual associations in learning Spanish and Russian vocabulary.[27] The following discussion of Spanish and Russian is based on their research. Their method, which they call the "keyword" method, consists of two steps. The first step is to associate the spoken foreign word with an English word or phrase that sounds approximately like the foreign word (such as "charcoal" for *Charco* or "see you, dad" for *ciudad*), or that sounds like only a part of the foreign word (such as "pot" for *pato*, "tree" for *trigo*, "cheese" for *chispa*, or "log" for *lagartija*). The second step in the keyword method is to associate the keyword with the English word, using interacting visual imagery. For example, the English word *pot* (for *pato* = duck) could be associated with *duck* by seeing a duck hiding under an overturned flower pot with its feet and tail sticking out. You may recognize the keyword method as being equivalent to the use of substitute words for abstract terms, as discussed in Chapter 5.

The following criteria appear to be important in selecting each key word: (1) The keyword should sound as much as possible like part (not necessarily all) of the foreign word; (2) it should be easy to form a memorable imagery link between the keyword and the English word; (3) the keyword should be unique (different from the other keywords used in the test vocabulary).

Using Keywords for Spanish and Russian

People in one study learned a Spanish vocabulary of 60 to 120 words using different methods. The keyword method was the most effective technique in all cases. In one study, people using visual imagery to associate the keywords scored 88 percent in a test of translating Spanish to English, while others using the keywords without imagery scored about 30 percent. In another study, members of one group who learned the keywords at the same time as learning the vocabulary words, and used visual associations, scored 59 percent in Spanish to English, while people with keywords (who used rehearsal to learn) scored 30 percent. When people were left to their own resources in learning Spanish, they used keywords almost as often as those in the keyword conditions; in fact, people who were instructed to use another method still used keywords for nearly half the items. This suggests that the use of keywords appears to be a natural technique for many people.

The keyword method has also been used to teach Russian, which is a non-Romance language, is more difficult to learn than Spanish, and involves phonemes that do not occur in English. Examples of keywords are "Jell-O" for *Délo** (affair), "zap it" for *zapad* (west), "rut" for *rot* (mouth), "cravat" for *króvát* (bed), and "garage" for *gorá* (mountain). People learned 40 new words each day for three days, for a total of 120 words. Recall was tested by hearing the Russian words and writing the English words. The keyword group performed much better than did people who were left to their own resources on all three days, averaging 72 percent vs. 46 percent recall across the three days. The keyword group also performed better on an unexpected recall test about six weeks later (43 percent vs. 28 percent). Thus, the keyword group remembered about 50 percent more words both in the immediate tests and the delayed tests.

Keywords can be used to form verbal associations as well as visual associations. People have used the keywords to form sentences connecting each foreign word with its English equivalent. These verbal mediators were helpful, but not quite as much as the imagery instructions (64 percent recall for sentences vs. 73 percent for imagery). The most effective strategy for learning appears to be to try and form an image, but relate the two words with a phrase or sentence if an image does not come quickly to mind.

The research described thus far shows that visual associations help to recall the English word given the foreign word. How effective is the keyword method when the person is given the English word and asked to recall the foreign word? Atkinson had some people learn Spanish-English associations using keywords and images, while others used rote rehearsal. All of the people learned the associations equally well (which, of course, took less time for the keyword group than for the rote-rehearsal group). They were then given the English words and recalled the Spanish equivalents. Even though both groups had learned the Spanish-English associations equally well, the keyword group recalled 19 percent more than the other group in English-to-Spanish translations.

*For clarity, the English alphabet has been used instead of the Cyrillic alphabet.

Conclusions about Keywords

Atkinson and Raugh have suggested several conclusions from their research: (1) It is better for the teacher to construct and provide keywords than to have the learners generate their own, especially for beginners. (2) However, it is better for the learners to generate their own associative images between the keyword and the English word than for the teacher to provide them. (3) The keywords do not need to approximate the full sound of the foreign word. In fact, when keywords spanned the full sound of the foreign word (for example, "race-free-auto" for *resfriado*), people did not do as well as when only one-syllable keywords were used, perhaps because they had too much to remember. (4) The keyword method may prove useful only in the early stages of learning a language, for some kinds of words more than for others, and for some languages more than others. The research is still in the early stages.

Does the keyword method interfere with correct pronunciation? Atkinson and Raugh reported that the keyword method does not interfere with pronunciation, and, in fact, may even help pronunciation. What about becoming dependent on the keywords? Will the person always have to retrieve the keyword and the image in order to make the translation? They reported that once an item has been thoroughly learned, it comes to mind immediately and the learner is rarely aware of the related keyword unless he makes a conscious effort to recall it. (This point is related to the crutch criticism discussed in Chapter 5.) What about the amount of time it takes to recall words using the keyword method? Does the keyword method take more time for recall, since one must retrieve the keyword then the association? The evidence indicates that retrieval time is not affected by the method; it takes no longer to recall a word via a keyword mediator than to recall a word learned without a keyword.

Atkinson has developed a vocabulary-learning program under computer control to supplement the second-year course in Russian at Stanford, using a total of about 750 words (nouns, adjectives, and verbs). He reports that there has been no difficulty in selecting keywords, the students are enthusiastic about the procedure and say it is helpful, and the program has been well-received by the Slavic Languages Department.

Learning German

When people were given the task of learning one-syllable German words, 57 percent of them used some kind of elaborative devices to learn the words, suggesting that elaboration strategies are used extensively by people in language memorization without instructions to do so.[28]

In a study in which the learners had had no experience with learning foreign languages, some people (group 1) received pictures showing interactions between the German and English words (for example, for the word "Ei," meaning an egg, the picture showed an eye peering out of an egg). Group 2 members were instructed to generate their own pictures. Group 3 was instructed to use repetition. People in group 4 were instructed to use their own resources.

The four groups learned twenty-four one-syllable German nouns and adjectives. Concrete substitute words were selected to represent the abstract foreign words in a manner similar to the keyword method described previously. Groups 1 and 2 learned faster and showed greater retention than groups 3 and 4 immediately after learning, and two weeks later. However, the most striking results are those comparing people who used elaboration with those who used repetition. As noted previously, people frequently use elaboration techniques even when not instructed to do so. Thus, about two-thirds of the people in groups 3 and 4 used some kind of visual or verbal elaboration. All the people in all four groups who had used elaboration were compared with the people in all four groups who had not used elaboration. People using elaboration scored 78 percent vs. 11 percent for those using repetition, on immediate recall, and 87 percent vs. 7 percent on recall two weeks later. The researchers concluded that the use of elaboration appears to be a natural and effective way to learn languages.[29]

Learning French

This section on language learning has been concerned with the use of visual associations in learning a foreign language vocabulary. Constance Knop described a variety of nonimagery mnemonics used in teaching grammar, pronunciation, and other aspects of French. Most of the techniques are acronyms, such as MRS. VANDERTAMP discussed in Chapter 5, and rhymes such as the following one that teaches the adjectives that precede the nouns they modify:

> Petit, grand, gros,
> Vilain, joli, beau,
> Autre, long,
> Mauvais, bon,
> Jeune, vieux, nouveau.

Knop reports that the devices have worked well in teaching French in high school and in college. The students find many of the devices corny, but those are the devices they remember best. Knop warns, however, that mnemonic devices, like rules of grammar, can be glibly recited by students without being applied to their speaking or writing of French, and that mnemonic devices are no substitutes for drill and practice in the language: "Mnemonic devices are best used after pattern practices and rule eliciting, as another means of clarifying the concept or pattern. Students should consider them a forerunner to more oral and written work which will apply the concept that mnemonic devices try to describe, clarify, and reinforce."[30]

Learning Chinese

Chinese is different from all the other languages described in this section, because it does not even use the same alphabet. Can mnemonic elaboration techniques be used to help one learn Chinese characters? There is limited evidence from two studies that mnemonics might help.[31] In the first study, twelve pairs of English-Chinese words were presented to high school and college students. Half of the students were told to learn the pairs by repeating them over and over, while the other half were told to form a picture in their minds that would help them remember the English meaning and the Chinese character. The students were later given a recall test and a recognition test. In all the tests, mnemonic elaboration groups scored slightly better than rote repetition groups, but the difference was large enough to be significant only in the recognition test for the high school students. One possible reason why the difference was not larger for the college students is that the college students in the repetition group reported using a considerable amount of spontaneous elaboration.

In the second study, the same twelve pairs were presented to high school students. Half the students were told to study the pairs by noting the geometrical features of the Chinese characters. The other half were told to ask themselves what each Chinese character reminded them of, and how the picture in their minds reminded them of the English word. Memory was measured by recall and recognition. The people instructed to use mental pictures scored slightly better than the other people, but the difference was again significant only on the recognition measure. Characters that had been rated as high in imagery value were remembered better than those rated as low.

These two studies do not prove that visual associations make a significant contribution to learning Chinese vocabulary, but they do suggest the possibility.

CONQUERING ABSENT-MINDEDNESS

There are several kinds of experiences that are called "absent-mindedness." One of the major kinds of absent-mindedness is forgetting to do something that we intended to do. Another kind involves forgetting where we put things. A third kind involves forgetting what we are doing. Some of the mnemonic principles can be applied to help overcome each of these problems.

Remembering Intended Actions

Almost all of this book is concerned with remembering the past. Another kind of memory involves memory for performing future actions. In fact, when many people complain about their memory lapses, they are more concerned with their failure to remember to perform an intended action than with their failure to retrieve information they have learned in the past.

It has been observed that when a person forgets something he has learned in the past, we say that his *memory* is unreliable, but when he forgets to do something he said he would do then we say that *he* is unreliable.[32] Memory for intended actions is what makes an efficient, well-organized person.

A distinction may be drawn between two kinds of remembering the future. Habitual remembering involves things that we do on a regular basis, such as brushing our teeth; episodic remembering involves things we do only occasionally, such as picking up a loaf of bread, mailing a letter, or making a phone call. It is with episodic remembering that we generally have the most problems. The wife may forget to tell her husband about an important phone call he needs to return, or an appointment with the doctor; the husband may forget to mail a letter or forget an anniversary; the student may forget to take a certain book to school or to take lunch money.

One way to remember intended actions is to make a list of what you need to do, either written in a notebook or filed mentally as described for the Loci and Phonetic systems. This method requires you to remember to look at the list frequently and regularly. Another way to help remember episodic intentions is to visualize some act or object that is associated with the intended action, and associate it with the intended action. The wife may picture her husband coming home that night with a phone hanging around his neck; the husband may picture himself sitting on top of the mailbox that is next to the bus stop where he waits for the bus; the student may picture herself eating her breakfast out of her book. Then, when the wife sees the husband come in the door, the husband sees the mailbox by the bus stop, and the student sees her breakfast, they are likely to remember the intended actions.

A simple example of my own use of this technique occurred when I was jogging around the track and suddenly remembered I needed to make a phone call concerning a piano. I couldn't very well make the call then, nor write a note to remind me to do it, so I pictured a piano sitting in my office.

When I finished running and returned to my office, I thought of the piano as soon as I opened the door, and I made the phone call.

One woman reported that she imagines a Dr. Seuss kind of household pet, a nine-foot Gleech, with bathmat ears and multicolored mink tail. When she must remember to do something, she pictures him doing it. For example, he may be at the telephone calling the rug cleaner. Later, when she calls him to mind, she sees him there, and that reminds her that she should be doing that also.[33]

Physical Reminders

Another technique that helps some people remember to perform intended actions is to make a physical change in their environment to cue them to remember the action. This is an external memory aid rather than an internal memory aid, and may be necessary if you are very busy, if you become engrossed in something else, or if you may be distracted by unexpected events. A rather straightforward example is to put a book by the door so you will remember to take it back to the library the next time you go out, or hang your coat on the knob of the door so you will remember to take it to the cleaners. A related method is to do something else to cue yourself. The well-known example of the string around the finger illustrates this strategy. The string is intended to remind you that there is something you need to remember, and unless you normally wear a string around your finger, the novelty of the string will usually serve that purpose. If you want to be less conspicuous than having a string around your finger, you might move your watch to the other wrist, or move a ring to a different finger, or turn a ring around so the stone faces the palm, or put your keys in a different pocket. All of these serve to cue you that you need to remember something.

A similar strategy may be used for the times when you remember at night (as you are trying to get to sleep) something you need to do in the morning—then in the morning you cannot remember what it was, or maybe cannot even remember that you needed to remember something. A useful technique is to turn your alarm clock on end, throw a book on the floor, or turn the radio around—something that you will notice in the morning. Then when you get up you will see that there is something you need to remember.

There is one limitation of these physical reminders. They help you remember that you wanted to remember something, and thus start the search for retrieval, but they do not help you directly remember what it was you wanted to remember. Is the string around your finger to remind you to buy some string? Is the book lying in the middle of the floor to remind you to take it back to the library?

The additional step that will make these techniques more effective is to associate the physical change with the intended activity. If the string on your finger is to remind you to mail a letter, you might picture yourself dropping string in the mailbox. If the book on the floor is to remind you to leave a note for the milkman, you might picture yourself stuffing the book into a milk bottle. If the watch on the wrong wrist is to remind you to make a phone call, you might picture yourself calling the person on your watch.

In a study of the effectiveness of external cues in remembering to perform intended actions, people were given a set of addressed postcards to mail on specified dates. Some of the people were given a tag to attach to their keychains; the tag was the external cue to remind them to mail the postcards. People with tags returned more cards than people without tags—81 percent vs. 70 percent. However, 70 percent is still a pretty good return rate. The reason for this is that almost all of the people (88 percent) used some kind of memory aid in addition to the tags—for example, one-third of them relied on the calendar to indicate the dates on which to mail the cards; and half of them put the cards in a place that was frequently looked at, such as a bulletin board or dresser top; this is much like placing a library book by the back door to remember to return it.[34]

Other Absent-Mindedness

The discussion of absent-mindedness thus far has been concerned with remembering to perform future actions. Another kind of absent-mindedness is forgetting where you put something—where you laid your umbrella, where you parked the car, or where you put your car keys. Still another example of absent-mindedness is going into another room to get something or to do something, then forgetting why you are there.

A likely cause of both of these kinds of problems is inattention. It was noted in Chapter 3 that if you were not paying attention to what you were doing when you laid your umbrella down or when you parked the car, you are likely to "forget" where they are. However, this kind of absent-mindedness may be more a problem of attention than of memory. You were not consciously paying attention to what you were doing at the time. Your mind was probably on something else (in a very real sense, your mind was absent). Similarly, you may just have a passing thought of something you need to do or get in the other room, and you start moving into the other room as your mind moves on to other things.

Thus, one way to overcome these two kinds of absent-mindedness is to pay attention to what you are doing. Tell yourself as you put the umbrella on the counter, "I am putting the umbrella on the counter," or as you park the car, "I am parking the car in the far northeast corner of the lot," or as you lay the keys on the refrigerator, "I am laying the keys on the refrigerator." In addition, it may help to actually form a mental picture of the umbrella on the counter or the car keys on the refrigerator. Similarly, when you think of something you need to do in the other room, stop and concentrate for just a second on the thought and tell yourself why you are going into the other room before you go, and you are more likely to remember why you are there when you get there. Again, it may be of additional help to picture yourself doing what you intend to do when you get there.

If your problem is more along the line of worrying about whether you locked the door, or unplugged the iron, or turned off the stove when you are away from the house, you would also likely be helped if you consciously concentrate on what you are doing as you lock the door, unplug the iron, or turn off the stove. This will increase the likelihood that you will later be able to remember whether you have done these things.

SUMMARY

Mnemonic techniques can be applied in at least three areas in addition to those discussed thus far in the book: remembering names and faces, learning foreign languages, and overcoming absent-mindedness.

Unclear or "lost" memory for names and faces is one of the most common memory complaints, and one of the most common reasons people have for enrolling in memory courses. Memory for faces is usually easier than memory for names, so the problem becomes one of remembering the name and pairing it with the right face. Some specific steps can be suggested to improve memory for names and faces. First, make sure you get the name in the first place. Use it, repeat it, work it over, ask about it. Second, focus on the appearance of the person, and find something distinctive about his face or appearance that will help you remember him. Even if you cannot find a distinctive feature, merely having tried will help you remember the face because you have had to study it. Third, make something meaningful of the name. Some names already have meaning; others must be made meaningful by the use of substitute words. Even for those names for which you cannot think of a meaningful substitute word, merely having tried will help you remember the name because you have been forced to concentrate on the name and work it over. Fourth, associate the name with the face. Form a conscious, visual association between the meaningful name and the distinctive feature. Fifth, review the association.

The method for learning a foreign language vocabulary is similar to that for learning names. It involves using meaningful, substitute words for the foreign words, and forming visual associations between each foreign word and its English equivalent. Recent research has found this method to be helpful in learning Spanish, Russian, German, and possibly even Chinese. Other verbal mnemonics can also be used, and some examples were suggested for French.

What many people have in mind when they speak of memory lapses is their failure to do something they intended to do, or their failure to remember where they put something. These kinds of memory problems fall under the heading of absent-mindedness. One technique to remember intended actions is to form a visual association between the intended action and some act or object that is related to the intended action. Then when the time comes that you engage in the act or see the object, you will likely be reminded of the intended action. Another technique is to make some physical change in your environment, such as tying a string around your finger, or wearing your watch on the wrong wrist, to remind you of the intended action. Noticing this physical change later reminds you that you need to do something. To help you remember what you need to do, you should form a visual association between the physical change and the intended action.

The problem of remembering where you left something is primarily a problem of inattention—your mind is literally absent. It can be helped if you consciously concentrate on what you are doing at the time you put the object down. It may help, in addition, to actually picture yourself putting the object down at the time you are doing it.

Practice Words
for Visual Associations

The following lists of nouns can be used to practice visual associations with any of the mnemonic systems. These nouns have been rated for their concreteness and frequency of use by A. Paivio, J. C. Yuille, and S. Madigan, "Concreteness, Imagery, and Meaningfulness Values for 925 Nouns," *Journal of Experimental Psychology Monograph Supplement,* 76 (1968), 1-25. (The concrete words have a scale value of at least 6.75 on a 7-point scale, and the abstract words have a scale value of 2.00 or lower.) Of course you could practice with any list of words made up by you or by a friend. However, these words have an advantage over words that a person might generate randomly because you know exactly what kind of words you are working with. You can practice with concrete or abstract nouns, and with common (high-frequency) or rare (low-frequency) nouns.

	Abstract Nouns		
Common		Rare	
anger	confidence	animosity	hankering
moral	brain	insolence	greed
virtue	glory	misconception	discretion
theory	truth	ego	fallacy
shame	pride	unreality	competence
freedom	memory	obsession	boredom
happiness	passion	ingratitude	clemency
chance	honor	afterlife	exactitude
attitude	necessity	concept	forethought

Abstract Nouns

Common		Rare	
love	thought	essence	gist
knowledge	spirit	betrayal	figment
hope	soul	aptitude	deceit
fate		prestige	criterion
		wistfulness	bravery

Concrete Nouns

Common		Rare	
flower	sugar	goblet	glacier
grass	water	bungalow	headlight
child	table	icebox	brassiere
arm	garden	poster	kerchief
building	cotton	spinach	kerosene
skin	board	skillet	scorpion
stone	iron	mosquito	stagecoach
ocean	rock	whale	microscope
house	shoes	yacht	lobster
baby	meat	timepiece	tomahawk
dress	paper	nutmeg	whalebone
window	sea	revolver	hairpin
tree	ship	shotgun	daffodil
door	lake	missile	cowhide
bird	book	locker	leggings
girl	cat	keg	macaroni
chair	boy	lemonade	sheepskin
horse	letter	bagpipe	leopard
plant	butter	corpse	tripod
lip	car	basement	wigwam
mountain		flask	tweezers

APPENDIX B

Keywords
for the Phonetic System

The following list consists of several keywords for each number from 00 to 09 and from 0 to 100. These keywords are based on the Phonetic system and can be used in at least two ways. First, you can select a keyword for each number from 1 to 100 that will be meaningful and memorable to you, constructing a mental filing system for memorizing 100 items. Second, you can reduce forgetting caused by interference among different numbers that have the same pairs of digits in them by using a different keyword each time a pair of digits is repeated. For example, there will be less interference among the phone numbers 3905, 0542, and 4239 if they are remembered by *mop-sail, seal-rain,* and *horn-map* than if they are remembered by *mop-sail, sail-rain,* and *rain-mop.*

00. sauce zoos hoses seas seesaw oasis icehouse Zeus Seuss
01. suit seed sod seat soot waste waist city soda stew acid
02. sun scene zone sin snow swine swan
03. sum zoom Siam swim seam asthma
04. sore soar seer sewer sower hosiery czar
05. sail seal sale sly slow sleigh soil soul
06. sash sage switch siege
07. sack sock sick hassock ski sky whisky squaw
08. safe sieve sofa housewife
09. soap sub spy wasp asp soup subway

0. hose sew sow saw house zoo sea ace ice
1. tie tee tea hat head doe toe toy wheat dye hood auto weed
2. hen Noah hone inn honey gnu wine hyena
3. ma ham hem hymn aim home mow
4. rye ray hair hare row oar arrow ore wire
5. hole law hill hall heel owl eel ale whale awl halo hell wheel
6. shoe hash hedge ash witch show jaw jay wash Jew
7. cow hog key hood cue echo hawk egg hockey oak wig
8. ivy hoof hive wave wife waif
9. bee pie hub hoop ape pea boy bay buoy oboe whip
10. toes dice heads woods toys daisy
11 tot date dot diet toad tide tattoo teeth
12. tin dune dean heathen dawn down twine
13. tomb dome team tummy dam atom autumn dime thumb
14. tire door tray tree deer tar tower dairy heater water waiter
15 towel doll tool dial hotel tail tile duel huddle Italy idol outlaw
16 dish dash tissue
17. tack dock deck duck dog toga twig dike attic
18. dove dive taffy TV thief
19. tub tape dope deb tube depot
20. nose news henhouse noose knees
21. net nut knot honeydew hunt window wand wind knight nude
    ant aunt
22. nun noon onion noun
23. gnome name enemy
24. Nero winner Henry wiener snare snore winery
25. nail kneel Nellie Nile
26. notch Nash winch hinge niche wench
27. hanky nag neck nick wink ink Inca
28. knave knife Navy nephew envoy
29. knob honeybee nap
30. mice mouse moose moss maze hams Messiah mass
31. mat mit meat mate mud moth mouth maid meadow moat

32. moon man mane money mine woman human
33. Miami mom mummy mama mime
34. mayor mower moor hammer myrrh
35. mail mule male meal mole mill mall
36. match mooch mush mesh image
37. mug mike hammock
38. muff movie Mafia
39. mop map mob amoeba imp
40. rose rice horse rays ears race hearse warehouse iris
41. rot road heart wart rod reed yard radio rut art earth herd wreath
42. rain ruin heron horn Rhine iron urn
43. ram room harem worm rum arm army Rome
44. rower roar rear error harrier warrior aurora
45. roll rail reel role rule railway
46. roach rouge rash ridge rich rajah Russia arch
47. rock rake rag rack rug arc ark
48. roof reef wharf
49. harp rope rib robe rabbi herb ruby
50. hails hills lace louse lice lassoe walls halls
51. lot lead loot hailed light wallet lady eyelid lid
52. line loon lion lane lawn
53. loom lime helm lamb llama limb elm
54. lyre lair lure leer lawyer
55. lily lolly Lulu
56. ledge leech latch lodge
57. log lake lock leak leg elk
58. loaf elf lava leaf wolf
59. lip lab lap loop lobby alp elbow
60. hedges cheese juice shoes Jews chaise chess ashes
61. sheet chute jet washed jade shade shadow shed
62. chin gin jean gene chain ocean China
63. gem gym jam chum chime

64. shore jar cheer chair jury shower sherry usher washer
65. jewel jail Jell-O shale chili shawl jelly
66. hashish judge choo-choo Jewish
67. jack jug shock jock chalk check sheik jockey chick
68. chef chief shave shove java Chevy chaff
69. ship shop chop job jab sheep jeep chip
70. case gas hogs wigs wicks wax ox goose cows ax kiss gauze
71. cat coat goat cod kid gate cot kite caddie act
72. Cain cane can coin gown gun wagon coon queen canoe
73. comb game gum cam comma
74. car core gear cry choir crow
75. coal coil goal gill gale keel quail eagle ghoul glue
76. cage cash gauge couch coach
77. cake cook gag cog keg cock
78. calf gaff cuff cave coffee cove
79. cab hiccup cup cap cape cob gob coop cube cub
80. face fez fuse hoofs waves hives wives vase office
81. feed food feet foot vote photo
82. vein fin fan vane van oven heaven phone vine fawn
83. foam fame fume
84. fire weaver wafer fry heifer fur fairy fir ivory
85. veil fly filly veal foal fowl foil flue flea valley
86. fudge fish voyage effigy
87. fig fog fake havoc
88. fife five
89. fob fib fop VIP
90. pies bees bows boys peas base bus pizza abyss
91. beat pot pad bead pit boot boat path bat poet bed body
92. pin bean bun bone pan pine pane pony piano pen penny pawn weapon
93. bomb boom beam bum poem puma opium
94. boar pear pray beer pier bar berry opera
95. bill bowl bell pile pill plow apple pail ball pillow bull eyeball

96. peach patch beach pitch bush page badge
97. bag bug peg pig back pack pick puck book beak bouquet
98. pave puff beef beehive buff
99. baby pipe pop Pope puppy papa
100. disease thesis doses diocese daisies

Reference Notes

Chapter 1

[1] Wayne H. Bartz, *Memory* (Dubuque, Iowa: William C. Brown Company, Publishers, 1968), p. 29.

[2] Ian M. L. Hunter, *Memory*, rev. (Middlesex, England: Penguin Books, Ltd., 1964), pp. 282-83.

[3] E. L. Thorndike, "Mental Discipline in High School Studies," *Journal of Educational Psychology*, 15 (1924), 83-98.

[4] William James, *Principles of Psychology*, Vol. I (New York: Henry Holt & Co., 1890), pp. 666-68.

[5] Sarnoff A. Mednick, Howard R. Pollio, and Elizabeth F. Loftus, *Learning*, 2nd ed. (Englewood Cliffs, N.J.: Prentice-Hall, Inc., 1973), p. 131.

[6] H. Woodrow, "The Effect of Type of Training Upon Transference," *Journal of Educational Psychology*, 18 (1927), 159-72.

[7] Bartz, *Memory*, p. 29.

[8] Harry Lorayne, *How to Develop a Super-power Memory* (New York: Frederick Fell, Inc., 1957), p. 168.

[9] M. Gregor von Feinaigle, *The New Art of Memory*, 2nd ed. (London: Sherwood, Neely, and Jones, 1813); Morris N. Young, *Bibliography of Memory* (New York: Chilton Book Company, 1961); L. Standing, B. Bond, J. Hall, and J. Weller, "A Bibliography of Picture-Memory Studies," *Psychonomic Science*, 29 (1972), 406-16.

Chapter 2

[1]John Gaito, "A Biochemical Approach to Learning and Memory: Fourteen Years Later," in *Advances in Psychobiology*, eds. Grant Newton and Austin H. Rieser (New York: John Wiley & Sons, Inc., 1974), 2, 225-37.

[2]Ian M. L. Hunter, *Memory*, rev. (Middlesex, England: Penguin Books, Ltd., 1964), p. 14.

[3]For example, see Jack A. Adams, *Learning and Memory: An Introduction* (Homewood, Ill.: Dorsey Press, 1976); Charles N. Cofer, ed., *The Structure of Human Memory* (San Francisco: W. H. Freeman and Co., Publisher, 1976); Ernest L. Hilgard and Gordon H. Bower, *Theories of Learning*, 4th ed. (Englewood Cliffs, N.J.: Prentice-Hall, Inc., 1975); David L. Horton and Thomas W. Turnage, *Human Learning* (Englewood Cliffs, N.J.: Prentice-Hall, Inc., 1975); and Roberta L. Klatzky, *Human Memory: Structures and Processes* (San Francisco: W. H. Freeman and Co., Publishers, 1975).

[4]See E. Tulving and D. M. Thomson, "Encoding Specificity and Retrieval Processes in Episodic Memory," *Psychological Review*, 80 (1973), 352-73.

[5]For more information on short-term and long-term memory, see Diana Deutsch and J. Anthony Deutsch, eds., *Short-term Memory* (New York: Academic Press, 1975); and Alan Kennedy and Alan Wilkes, eds., *Studies in Long Term Memory* (London: John Wiley & Sons, 1975).

[6]G. A. Miller, "The Magical Number Seven Plus or Minus Two: Some Limits on Our Capacity for Processing Information," *Psychological Review*, 63 (1956), 81-97; D. E. Broadbent, "The Magic Number Seven after 15 Years," in *Studies in Long Term Memory*, eds. Alan Kennedy and Alan Wilkes (New York: John Wiley & Sons, Inc., 1975), pp. 3-18.

[7]Herbert A. Simon, "How Big is a Chunk?" *Science*, 183 (1974), 482-88.

[8]M. W. Matlin, "The Relationship Between English Word Length and Short-term Memory," *Journal of General Psychology*, 94 (1976), 47-57.

[9]William G. Chase and Herbert A. Simon, "The Mind's Eye in Chess," in *Visual Information Processing*, ed. William G. Chase (New York: Academic Press, 1973), pp. 215-81; Peter W. Frey and Peter Adesman, "Recall Memory for Visually-presented Chess Positions (paper presented at the meeting of the Psychonomic Society, Denver, November 1975).

[10]H. Buschke, "Spontaneous Remembering After Recall Failure," *Science*, 184 (1974), 579-81.

[11]Wilder Penfield, "Consciousness, Memory, and Man's Conditioned Reflexes," in *On the Biology of Learning*, ed. Karl H. Pribram (New York: Harcourt Brace Jovanovich, 1969), pp. 129-68.

[12]T. Shallice and E. K. Warrington, "Independent Functioning of Verbal Memory Stores: A Neuropsychological Study," *Quarterly Journal of Experimental Psychology*, 22 (1970), 261-73.

[13]Brenda Milner, "Amnesia Following Operation on the Temporal Lobes," in *Amnesia*, eds. Charles W. M. Whitty and Oliver L. Zangwill (London: Butterworth & Co., 1966), pp. 109-33.

[14]L. Postman, E. Kruesi, and J. Regan, "Recognition and Recall as Measures of Long-term Retention," *Quarterly Journal of Experimental Psychology*, 27 (1975), 411-18.

[15]H. M. Clarke, "Recall and Recognition for Names and Faces," *Journal of Applied Psychology*, 18 (1934), 757-63.

[16]R. N. Shepard, "Recognition Memory for Words, Sentences and Pictures," *Journal of Verbal Learning and Verbal Behavior*, 6 (1967), 156-63.

[17]H. E. Burtt, "An Experimental Study of Early Childhood Memory: Final Report," *Journal of Genetic Psychology*, 58 (1941), 435-39.

[18]Allan Paivio, *Imagery and Verbal Processes* (New York: Holt, Rinehart and Winston, Inc., 1971).

[19]G. E. Atwood, "An Experimental Study of Visual Imagination and Memory," *Cognitive Psychology*, 2 (1971), 290-99.

[20]D. Kimura, "The Asymmetry of the Human Brain," *Scientific American*, 228 (1973), 70-78; Robert E. Ornstein, *The Psychology of Consciousness* (San Francisco: W. H. Freeman and Company, 1972).

[21]C. G. Penney, "Modality Effects in Short-term Verbal Memory," *Psychological Bulletin*, 82 (1975), 68-84.

[22]For different speeds, see, for example, W. J. Lutz and C. J. Scheirer, "Coding Processes for Pictures and Words," *Journal of Verbal Learning and Verbal Behavior*, 13 (1974), 316-20. For 26 letters, see R. J. Weber and J. Castleman, "The Time It Takes to Imagine," *Perception and Psychophysics*, 8 (1970), 165-68. For naming vs. reading see P. Fraisse, "Motor and Verbal Reaction Times to Words and Drawings," *Psychonomic Science*, 12 (1968), 235-36.

[23]L. Standing, J. Conezio, and R. N. Haber, "Perception and Memory for Pictures: Single-trial Learning of 2500 Visual Stimuli," *Psychonomic Science*, 19 (1970), 73-74; L. Standing, "Learning 10,000 Pictures," *Quarterly Journal of Experimental Psychology*, 25 (1973), 207-22.

[24]For pictures vs. descriptions, see M. Denis, "Comparative Stability of Learning Pictorial and Verbal Material," *Psychologie Francaise*, 18 (1973), 47-59. For pictures vs. names see, for example, W. Bevan and J. A. Steger, "Free Recall and Abstractness of Stimuli," *Science*, 172 (1971), 597-99; S. M. Keitz and B. R. Gounard, "Age Differences in Adults' Free Recall of Pictorial and Word Stimuli," *Educational Gerontology*, in press; W. H. Levie and D. Levie, "Pictorial Memory Processes," *AV Communication Review*, 23 (1975), 81-97; and A. Paivio, R. Philipchalk, and E. J. Rowe, "Free and Serial Recall of Pictures, Sounds, and Words," *Memory and Cognition*, 3 (1975), 586-90.

[25]A. Paivio and K. Csapo, "Picture Superiority in Free Recall: Imagery or Dual Coding," *Cognitive Psychology*, 5 (1973), 176-206.

[26]See Allan Paivio, "Imagery in Recall and Recognition," in *Recall and Recognition*, ed. J. Brown (New York: John Wiley & Sons, Inc., 1975), pp. 103-29; and Allan Paivio, "Imagery and Long-term Memory," in *Studies in Long Term Memory*, eds. Alan Kennedy and Alan Wilkes (New York: John Wiley & Sons, Inc., 1975), pp. 57-88.

[27]T. O. Nelson and C. C. Hill, "Multiple Retrieval Paths and Long-term Retention," *Journal of Experimental Psychology*, 103 (1974), 185-87.

[28]Paivio and Csapo, "Picture."

[29]E. A. Kirkpatrick, "An Experimental Study of Memory," *Psychological Review*, 1 (1894), 602-9 (p. 605).

[30]R. N. Haber, "How We Remember What We See," *Scientific American*, 222 (1970), 104-15 (p. 105).

[31]William Epstein, "Mechanisms of Directed Forgetting," in *The Psychology of Learning and Motivation*, ed. Gordon H. Bower (New York: Academic Press, 1972), 6, 147-91.

[32]J. Deese, "On the Prediction of Occurrence of Particular Verbal Intrusions in Immediate Recall," *Journal of Experimental Psychology*, 58(1959), 17-22.

[33]Hunter, *Memory*.

[34]For leading questions, see, for example, E. F. Loftus, "Leading Questions and the Eyewitness Report," *Cognitive Psychology*, 7 (1975), 560-72. For implied conclusions see R. J. Harris, R. R. Teske, and M. J. Ginns, "Memory for Pragmatic Implications from Courtroom Testimony," *Bulletin of the Psychonomic Society*, 6 (1975), 494-96.

[35]A. Layerson, ed., *Psychology Today: An Introduction*, 3rd ed. (New York: Random House, Inc., 1975), p. 111.

[36]For example, see E. Tulving, "Cue-dependent Forgetting," *American Scientist*, 62 (1974), 74-82.

[37]B. J. Underwood, "Forgetting," *Scientific American*, 210 (1964), 91-99.

[38]This has been found both for short-term and long-term memory: T. J. Shuell and J. Giglio, "Learning Ability and Short-term Memory," *Journal of Educational Psychology*, 64 (1973), 261-66; T. J. Shuell and G. Keppel, "Learning Ability and Retention," *Journal of Educational Psychology*, 61 (1970), 59-65.

[39]For example, see T. R. Barrett, W. Maier, B. R. Ekstrand, and J. W. Pellegrino, "Effects of Experimenter-imposed Organization on Long-term Forgetting," *Journal of Experimental Psychology: Human Learning and Memory*, 1 (1975), 480-90; L. Hasher, B. Reibman, and F. Wren, "Imagery and the Retention of Free-recall Learning," *Journal of Experimental Psychology: Human Learning and Memory*, 2 (1976), 172-81; and P. M. Wortman, "Long-term Retention of Information as a Function of its Organization," *Journal of Experimental Psychology: Human Learning and Memory*, 1 (1975), 576-83.

[40]For questions, see J. T. Hart, "Second-try Recall, Recognition, and the Memory-monitoring Process," *Journal of Educational Psychology*, 58 (1967), 193-97;

J. L. Freedman and T. K. Landauer, "Retrieval of Long-term Memory: 'Tip-of-the-Tongue' Phenomenon," *Psychonomic Science*, 4 (1966), 309-10. For definitions, see R. Brown and D. McNeill, "The 'Tip of the Tongue' Phenomenon," *Journal of Verbal Learning and Verbal Behavior*, 5 (1966), 325-37.

⁴¹For recent studies, see, for example, M. Blake, "Prediction of Recognition When Recall Fails: Exploring the Feeling-of-Knowing Phenomenon," *Journal of Verbal Learning and Verbal Behavior*, 12 (1973), 311-19; A. Koriat, "Phonetic Symbolism and Feeling of Knowing," *Memory and Cognition*, 3 (1975), 545-48; M. M. Gruneberg and J. Monks, "'Feeling of Knowing' and Cued Recall," *Acta Psychologica*, 38 (1974), 257-65; and D. C. Rubin, "Within Word Structure in the Tip-of-the-Tongue Phenomenon," *Journal of Verbal Learning and Verbal Behavior*, 14 (1975), 392-97. For names, see J. E. May and K. N. Clayton, "Imaginal Processes During the Attempt to Recall Names," *Journal of Verbal Learning and Verbal Behavior*, 12 (1973), 683-88; J. D. Read and R. G. Wilbur II, "Availability of Faces and Names in Recall," *Perceptual and Motor Skills*, 41 (1975), 263-70; and A. D. Yarmey, "I Recognize Your Face But I Can't Remember Your Name: Further Evidence on the Tip-of-the-Tongue Phenomenon," *Memory and Cognition*, 3 (1973), 287-90.

⁴²C. R. Gray and K. Gummerman, "The Enigmatic Eidetic Image: A Critical Examination of Methods, Data, and Theories," *Psychological Bulletin*, 82 (1975), 383-407; R. N. Haber, "Eidetic Images," *Scientific American*, 220 (1969), 36-55.

⁴³Charles F. Stromeyer III, "Eidetikers," *Psychology Today*, 4, no. 6 (November 1970), 46-50.

⁴⁴Alexandr R. Luria, *The Mind of a Mnemonist* (New York: Basic Books, Inc., Publishers, 1968), p. 12.

⁴⁵For VP, see Earl Hunt and Tom Love, "How Good Can Memory Be?" in *Coding Processes in Human Memory*, eds. Arthur W. Melton and Edwin Martin (Washington, D.C.: V.H. Winston & Sons, 1972), pp. 237-60. For 19th-century prodigies, see Paivio, *Verbal Processes*.

⁴⁶Jeanie Kasindorf, "Set Your Dial for Sleeplearning," *McCalls*, (September 1974), p. 50.

⁴⁷L. Aarons, "Sleep-assisted Instruction," *Psychological Bulletin*, 83 (1976), 1-40; Frederick Rubin, *Learning and Sleep* (Bristol, England: John Wright & Sons, 1971).

⁴⁸First study was C. W. Simon and W. H. Emmons, "Responses to Material Presented During Various Levels of Sleep," *Journal of Experimental Psychology*, 51 (1956), 89-97. Second study was W. H. Emmons and C. W. Simon, "The Non-recall of Material Presented During Sleep," *American Journal of Psychology*, 69 (1956), 76-81.

⁴⁹D. J. Bruce, C. R. Evans, P. B. C. Fenwick, and V. Spencer, "Effect of Presenting Novel Verbal Material During Slow-wave Sleep," *Nature*, 225 (1970), 873-74.

⁵⁰"Sleeping Students Don't Learn English," *Consumer Reports*, 35, no. 5 (May 1970), 313.

[51]F. J. Evans and W. Orchard, "Sleep Learning: The Successful Waking Recall of Material Presented During Sleep," *Psychophysiology*, 6 (1969), 269.

[52]For example, see K. Benson and I. Feinberg, "Sleep and Memory: Retention 8 and 24 Hours After Initial Learning," *Psychophysiology*, 12 (1975), 192-95; and Bruce R. Ekstrand, "To Sleep, Perchance to Dream (About Why We Forget)," *Human Memory: Festschrift in Honor of Benton J. Underwood*, eds. Carl P. Duncan, Lee Sechrest, and Arthur W. Melton (New York: Appleton-Century-Crofts, 1972), pp. 59-82.

[53]D. Byrne, "The Effect of a Subliminal Food Stimulus on Verbal Responses," *Journal of Applied Psychology*, 43 (1959), 249; J. V. McConnell, R. L. Cutler, and E. B. McNeil, "Subliminal Stimulation: An Overview," *American Psychologist*, 13 (1958), 229-42.

Chapter 3

[1]William E. Montague, "Elaborative Strategies in Verbal Learning and Memory," in *The Psychology of Learning and Motivation*, ed. Gordon H. Bower (New York: Academic Press, 1972), 6, 225-302.

[2]Frank Restle, *Learning: Animal Behavior and Human Cognition* (New York: McGraw-Hill Book Company, 1975).

[3]D. O. Lyon, "The Relation of Length of Material to Time Taken for Learning and the Optimum Distribution of Time," *Journal of Educational Psychology*, 5 (1914), 1-9, 85-91, 155-63.

[4]L. S. Prytulak, "Natural Language Mediation," *Cognitive Psychology*, 2 (1971), 1-56.

[5]B. Earhard, "Perception and Retention of Familiar and Unfamiliar Material," *Journal of Experimental Psychology*, 76 (1968), 584-95; R. C. Oldfield and A. Wingfield, "Response Latencies in Naming Objects," *Quarterly Journal of Experimental Psychology*, 17 (1965), 273-81.

[6]Joyce Brothers and Edward P. F. Eagan, *Ten Days to a Successful Memory* (Englewood Cliffs, N. J.: Prentice-Hall, Inc., 1957).

[7]Stewart H. Hulse, James Deese, and Howard Egeth, *The Psychology of Learning*, 4th ed. (New York: McGraw-Hill Book Company, 1975).

[8]Jerome Kagan and Ernest Havemann, *Psychology: An Introduction*, 3rd ed. (New York: Harcourt Brace Jovanovich, 1976), p. 102.

[9]D. L. Nelson and D. H. Brooks, "Relative Effectiveness of Rhymes and Synonyms as Retrieval Cues," *Journal of Experimental Psychology*, 102 (1974), 503-7; D. L. Nelson and D. H. Brooks, "Retroactive Inhibition of Rhyme Categories in Free Recall: Inaccessibility and Unavailability of Information," *Journal of Experimental Psychology*, 102 (1974), 277-83.

[10]Arden N. Frandsen, *Educational Psychology*, 2nd ed. (New York: McGraw-Hill Book Company, 1967), p. 388.

[11]T. R. Barrett and B. R. Ekstrand, "Second-order Associations and Single-list Retention," *Journal of Experimental Psychology: Human Learning and Memory*, 104 (1975), 41-49.

[12]George Katona, *Organizing and Memorizing: Studies in the Psychology of Learning and Teaching* (New York: Columbia University Press, 1940).

[13]Eric Pugh, *A Dictionary of Acronyms and Abbreviations* (London: Clive Bingley Ltd. and Hamden, Ct.: Archon Books, 1970); Donald R. White, *A Glossary of Acronyms, Abbreviations, and Symbols* (Germantown, Md.: Don White Consultants, 1971).

[14]B. A. Manning and R. H. Bruning, "Interactive Effects of Mnemonic Techniques and Word-list Characteristics," *Psychological Reports*, 36 (1975), 727-36; D. L. Nelson, and C. S. Archer, "The First Letter Mnemonic,"*Journal of Educational Psychology*, 63 (1972), 482-86; J. R. Pash, and K. A. Blick, "The Effect of a Mnemonic Device on Retention of Verbal Material," *Psychonomic Science*, 19 (1970), 203-4.

[15]For young children, see G. Marchbanks and H. Levin, "Cues by Which Children Recognize Words," *Journal of Educational Psychology*, 56 (1965), 57-61. For adults, see M. Earhard, "The Facilitation of Memorization by Alphabetical Instructions," *Canadian Journal of Psychology*, 21 (1967), 15-24; and N. M. Mercer, "Cues to Retrieval From Long-term Verbal Memory," *Psychological Reports*, 35 (1974), 1234.

[16]G. H. Bower, M. C. Clark, A. M. Lesgold, and D. Winzenz, "Hierarchical Retrieval Schemes in Recall of Categorized Word Lists,"*Journal of Verbal Learning and Verbal Behavior*, 8 (1969), 323-43.

[17]R. W. Kulhavy, C. R. Haynes, and J. W. Dyer, "Coding Efficiency and Mnemonic Transformations in Free Recall," *Psychological Reports*, 36 (1975), 365-68; B. Z. Strand, "Effects of Instructions for Category Organization on Long-term Retention," *Journal of Experimental Psychology: Human Learning and Memory*, 1 (1975), 780-86.

[18]For people imposing their own organization, see George Mandler, "Organization and Recognition," in *Organization of Memory*, eds. Endel Tulving and Wayne Donaldson (New York: Academic Press, 1972), pp. 146-66. For children, see B. E. Moely and W. E. Jeffrey, "The Effect of Organization Training on Children's Free Recall of Category Items," *Child Development*, 45 (1974), 135-43.

[19]For instructions to organize, see P. A. Ornstein, T. Trabasso, and P. N. Johnson-Laird, "To Organize is to Remember: The Effects of Instructions to Organize and to Recall,"*Journal of Experimental Psychology*, 103 (1974), 1014-18. For paragraphs, see J. L. Myers, K. Peydek, and D. Coulson, "Effect of Prose Organization Upon Free Recall," *Journal of Educational Psychology*, 65 (1973), 313-20. For pictures, see, for example, I. Biederman, "Perceiving Real-world Scenes," *Science*, 177 (1972), 77-80; S. E. Palmer, "The Effects of Contextual Scenes on the Identification of Objects," *Memory and Cognition*, 3 (1975), 519-26; and J. M. von Wright, P.

Gebhard, and M. A. Karttunen, "A Developmental Study of the Recall of Spatial Location," *Journal of Experimental Child Psychology*, 20 (1975), 181-90.

[20]For groups of 2 or 3, see J. G. Miscik and K. A. Deffenbacher, "Short-term Retention of Visual Sequence as a Function of Stimulus Duration and Encoding Technique," *Journal of Experimental Psychology*, 103 (1974), 188-90. For time, see J. Kleinberg and H. Kaufman, "Constancy in Short-term Memory: Bits and Chunks," *Journal of Experimental Psychology*, 90 (1971), 326-33.

[21]William James, *Principles of Psychology*, vol. I (New York: Henry Holt & Co., 1890), 662.

[22]R. P. Stratton, K. A. Jacobus, and B. Brinley, "Age-of-Acquisition, Imagery, Familiarity, and Meaningfulness Norms for 543 Words," *Behavior Research Methods and Instrumentation*, 7 (1975), 1-6.

[23]E. A. Kirkpatrick, "An Experimental Study of Memory," *Psychological Review*, 1 (1894), 602-9.

[24]B. R. Bugelski, "Words and Things and Images," *American Psychologist*, 25 (1970), 1002-12; R. R. Holt, "Imagery: The Return of the Ostracized," *American Psychologist*, 19 (1964), 254-64.

[25]John A. McGeoch and Arthur L. Irion, *The Psychology of Human Learning*, 2nd ed. (New York: Longmans, Green & Co., 1952).

[26]Allan Paivio, *Imagery and Verbal Processes* (New York: Holt, Rinehart and Winston, Inc., 1971); Sydney J. Segal, ed., *The Adaptive Functions of Imagery* (New York: Academic Press, 1971); Peter W. Sheehan, ed., *The Function and Nature of Imagery* (New York: Academic Press, 1972).

[27]For discussions of other theories, see John R. Anderson, and Gordon H. Bower, *Human Associative Memory* (Washington, D. C.: V. H. Winston & Sons, 1973); and Allan Paivio, "Imagery and Long-term Memory," in *Studies in Long Term Memory*, eds. Alan Kennedy and Alan Wilkes (New York: John Wiley & Sons, Inc., 1975), pp. 57-88.

[28]Anderson and Bower, *Human;* and D. F. Marks, "Visual Imagery Differences in the Recall of Pictures," *British Journal of Psychology*, 64 (1973), 17-24.

[29]The five studies are, in order, W. H. Wallace, S. H. Turner, and C. C. Perkins, "Preliminary Studies of Human Information Storage," reported in *Plans and the Structure of Behavior*, eds. George A. Miller, Eugene Galanter, and Karl H. Pribram (New York: Henry Holt & Co., 1960); Gordon H. Bower, "Mental Imagery and Associative Learning," in *Cognition in Learning and Memory*, ed. Lee W. Gregg (New York: John Wiley & Sons, 1972), pp. 51-88; B. R. Bugelski, "Images as Mediators in One-trial Paired-associate Learning. II: Self-timing in Successive Lists," *Journal of Experimental Psychology*, 77 (1968), 328-34; J. A. Schnorr and R. C. Atkinson, "Repetition Versus Imagery Instructions in the Short- and Long-term Retention of Paired Associates," *Psychonomic Science*, 5 (1969), 183-84; D. G. Kemler and P. W. Jusczyk, "A Developmental Study of Facilitation by Mnemonic Instruction," *Journal of Experimental Child Psychology*, 20 (1975), 400-10.

[30]For example, see I. Begg and R. Robertson, "Imagery and Long-term Retention," *Journal of Verbal Learning and Verbal Behavior*, 12 (1973), 689-700; and L. D. Groninger, "Imagery and Subjective Categorization Effects on Long-term Recognition and Retrieval," *Bulletin of the Psychonomic Society*, 3 (1974), 261-63.

[31]M. R. Raugh and R. C. Atkinson, "A Mnemonic Method for the Learning of a Second-language Vocabulary," *Journal of Educational Psychology*, 67 (1975), 1-16.

[32]For verbs, see J. L. Pate, P. Ward, and K. B. Harlan, "Effects of Word Order and Imagery on Learning Verbs and Adverbs as Paired Associates," *Journal of Experimental Psychology*, 103 (1974), 792-95. For sentences, see, for example, R. C. Anderson, and J. L. Hidde, "Imagery and Sentence Learning," *Journal of Educational Psychology*, 62 (1971), 526-30.; and J. C. Yuille and K. Holyoak, "Verb Imagery and Noun Phrase Concreteness in the Recognition and Recall of Sentences," *Canadian Journal of Psychology*, 28 (1974), 359-70. For prose, see, for example, R. W. Kulhavy and I. Swenson, "Imagery Instructions and the Comprehension of Text," *British Journal of Educational Psychology*, 45 (1975), 47-51; and A. M. Lesgold, C. McCormick, and R. M. Golinkoff, "Imagery Training and Children's Prose Learning," *Journal of Educational Psychology*, 67 (1975), 663-67. For concepts, see A. N. Katz and A. Paivio, "Imagery Variables in Concept Identification," *Journal of Verbal Learning and Verbal Behavior*, 14 (1975), 284-93.

[33]Harry Lorayne, *How to Develop a Super-power Memory* (New York: Frederick Fell, Inc., 1957), published in paperback by The New American Library Inc., 1974, p. 36.

[34]Hulse, Deese, and Egeth, *Learning*.

[35]Brothers and Eagan, *Ten Days*, p. 24.

[36]Hunter, *Memory*, p. 122.

[37]J. M. Sassenrath, "Theory and Results on Feedback and Retention," *Journal of Educational Psychology*, 67 (1975), 894-99.

[38]R. E. LaPorte and J. F. Voss, "Retention of Prose Materials as a Function of Postacquisition Testing," *Journal of Educational Psychology*, 67 (1975), 259-66.

Chapter 4

[1]Stewart H. Hulse, James Deese, and Howard Egeth, *The Psychology of Learning*, 4th ed. (New York: McGraw-Hill Book Company, 1975), p. 330.

[2]Francis P. Robinson, *Effective Study*, 4th ed. (New York: Harper & Row, Publishers, 1970).

[3]John F. Hall, *Verbal Learning and Retention* (Philadelphia: J. B. Lippincott Company, 1971).

[4]For example, see G. H. Bower, "Selective Facilitation and Interference in Retention of Prose," *Journal of Educational Psychology*, 66 (1974), 1-8.

[5]For example, see Bower, "Selective."; and Hall, *Verbal Learning*.

[6]K. Dallett and S. G. Wilcox, "Contextual Stimuli and Proactive Inhibition," *Journal of Experimental Psychology*, 78 (1968), 475-80; D. McNicol and J. J. Gosbell, "Effects of Context and Imagery on Original and Interpolated Learning: Confusion of List Markers or Reduction of Interference?," *Journal of Experimental Psychology*, 103 (1974), 1006-13.

[7]I. M. Bilodeau and H. Schlosberg, "Similarity in Stimulus Conditions as a Variable in Retroactive Inhibition," *Journal of Experimental Psychology*, 41 (1951), 199-204; J. Greenspoon and R. Ranyard, "Stimulus Conditions and Retroactive Inhibition," *Journal of Experimental Psychology*, 53 (1957), 55-59; B. Z. Strand, "Change of Context and Retroactive Inhibition," *Journal of Verbal Learning and Verbal Behavior*, 9 (1970), 202-6.

[8]B. J. Underwood and J. S. Freund, "Effect of Temporal Separation of Two Tasks on Proactive Inhibition," *Journal of Educational Psychology*, 78 (1968), 50-54.

[9]G. Keppel, "Facilitation in Short- and Long-term Retention of Paired Associates Following Distributed Practice in Learning," *Journal of Verbal Learning and Verbal Behavior*, 3 (1964), 91-111. Similar results were obtained by B. J. Underwood and B. R. Ekstrand, "Studies of Distributed Practice: XXIV. Differentiation and Proactive Inhibition," *Journal of Experimental Psychology*, 74 (1967), 574-80.

[10]Strand, "Change."

[11]For example, see Robert G. Crowder, *Principles of Learning and Memory* (Hillsdale, N. J.: Lawrence Erlbaum Associates, 1976); D. S. Hintzman, "Theoretical Implications of the Spacing Effect," in *Theories in Cognitive Psychology: The Loyola Symposium*, ed. R. L. Solso (Hillsdale, N. J.: Lawrence Erlbaum Associates, 1974); and Robinson, *Effective Study*.

[12]D. P. Ausubel and M. Youssef, "The Effect of Spaced Repetition on Meaningful Retention," *Journal of General Psychology*, 73 (1965), 147-50; J H. Reynolds and R. Glaser, "Effects of Repetition and Spaced Review Upon Retention of a Complex Learning Task," *Journal of Educational Psychology*, 55 (1964), 297-308.

[13]H. L. Roediger, III and R. G. Crowder, "The Spacing of Lists in Free Recall," *Journal of Verbal Learning and Verbal Behavior*, 14 (1975), 590-602.

[14]Richard M. Gorman, *Psychology of Classroom Learning* (Columbus, Ohio: Charles E. Merrill Publishing Co., 1974); Ian M. L. Hunter, *Memory*, rev. (Middlesex England: Penguin Books, Ltd., 1964).

[15]E. J. Fishman, L. Keller, and R. H. Atkinson, "Massed Versus Distributed Practice in Computerized Spelling Drills," *Journal of Educational Psychology*, 59 (1968), 290-96.

[16]H. P. Bahrick, P. O. Bahrick, and R. P. Wittlinger, "Fifty Years of Memory for Names and Faces: A Cross-sectional Approach," *Journal of Experimental Psychology: General*, 104 (1975), 54-75.

[17]See Douglas K. Candland, *Psychology: The Experimental Approach* (New York: McGraw-Hill Book Company, 1968); Hunter, *Memory.*; James M. Sawrey and Charles M. Telford, eds., *Educational Psychology*, 4th ed. (Boston: Allyn & Bacon, Inc., 1973).

[18]J. D. Bransford and M. K. Johnson, "Contextual Prerequisites for Understanding: Some Investigations of Comprehension and Recall,"*Journal of Verbal Learning and Verbal Behavior*, 11 (1972), 717-26; D. J. Dooling and R. Lachman, "Effects of Comprehension on Retention of Prose," *Journal of Experimental Psychology*, 88 (1971), 216-22.

[19]M. J. Breen and J. M. Jurek, "Serial Learning as a Function of Age and Part Versus Whole Learning Procedures,"*Psychological Reports*, 36 (1975), 767-73.

[20]Hunter, *Memory*, p. 133.

[21]L. A. Pechstein, "Whole vs. Part Methods in Learning Nonsensical Syllables," *Journal of Educational Psychology*, 9 (1918), 379-87.

[22]Gorman, *Psychology*.

[23]For the value of repetition, see, for example, L. Brosgole and A. Neylon, "Further Studies on the Role of Repetition in Associative Learning," *Psychological Reports*, 37 (1975), 1132-34; P. L. Derks and J. E. Dunman, "The Effect of Repetition of Objects and Object Names on Free Recall," *Bulletin of the Psychonomic Society*, 3 (1974), 289-92; and D. J. King, "The Influence of Repetition vs. No Repetition Given Equal Presentation Time on the Learning of Connected Discourse," *Bulletin of the Psychonomic Society*, 5 (1975), 501-3. For the inadequacy of repetition alone, see, for example, D. L. Roenker, "Role of Rehearsal in Long-term Retention," *Journal of Experimental Psychology*, 103 (1974), 368-71; E. Tulving, "Subjective Organization and Effects of Repetition in Multi-trial Free-recall Learning," *Journal of Verbal Learning and Verbal Behavior*, 5 (1966), 193-97; and P. H. Winne, W. E. Hauck, and J. W. Moore, "The Efficiency of Implicit Repetition and Cognitive Restructuring,"*Journal of Educational Psychology*, 67 (1975), 770-75.

[24]Joyce Brothers and Edward P. F. Eagan, *Ten Days to a Successful Memory* (Englewood Cliffs, N. J.: Prentice-Hall, Inc., 1957), p. 61.

[25]The study described is W. C. F. Krueger, "The Effect of Overlearning on Retention," *Journal of Experimental Psychology*, 12 (1929), 71-78. Other studies include L. Postman, "Retention as a Function of Degree of Overlearning," *Science*, 135 (1962), 666-67; L. Postman, "Transfer of Training as a Function of Experimental Paradigm and Degree of First-list Learning,"*Journal of Verbal Learning and Verbal Behavior*, 1 (1962), 109-18; and M. Wasim, "Effect of Repeated Learning and Overlearning on Recall," *Pakistan Journal of Psychology*, (June 1974), pp. 59-61.

[26]Bahrick, Bahrick, and Wittlinger, "Fifty Years."

[27]First study was A. I. Gates, "Recitation as a Factor in Memorizing," *Archives of Psychology*, no. 40 (1917). Second study was H. F. Spitzer, "Studies in Retention," *Journal of Educational Psychology*, 30 (1939), 641-56. Third study was Hunter, *Memory*, pp. 103-4.

[28]First quote is from Jerome Kagan and Ernest Havemann, *Psychology: An Introduction*, 3rd ed. (New York: Harcourt Brace Jovanovich, 1976), p. 110. Second quote is from Robinson, *Effective Study*, p. 28. Third quote is from Clifford T. Morgan and James Deese, *How to Study*, 2nd ed. (New York: McGraw-Hill Book Company, 1969), p. 58.

[29]R. E. LaPorte and J. F. Voss, "Retention of Prose Materials as a Function of Postacquisition Testing,"*Journal of Educational Psychology*, 67 (1975), 259-66.

[30]Hunter, *Memory*, p. 108.

[31]E. G. Aiken, G. S. Thomas, and W. A. Shennum, "Memory for a Lecture: Effects of Notes, Lecture Rate, and Information Density," *Journal of Educational Psychology*, 67 (1975), 439-44; J. F. Carter and N. H. Van Matre, "Note Taking Versus Note Having,"*Journal of Educational Psychology*, 67 (1975) 900-904.

[32]L. T. Frase and B. J. Schwartz, "Effect of Question Production and Answering on Prose Recall,"*Journal of Educational Psychology*, 67, (1975), 628-35.

[33]Morgan and Deese, *How to Study;* Robinson, *Effective Study.*

[34]Dooling and Lachman, "Effects."

[35]F. Goldberg, "Effects of Imagery on Learning Incidental Material in the Classroom," *Journal of Educational Psychology*, 66 (1974), 233-37; A. M. Lesgold, J. R. Levin, J. Shimron, and J. Gottman, "Pictures and Young Children's Learning From Oral Prose,"*Journal of Educational Psychology*, 67 (1975), 636-42; J. Peeck, "Retention of Pictorial and Verbal Content of the Text With Illustrations,"*Journal of Educational Psychology*, 66 (1974), 880-88; W. D. Rohwer, Jr. and R. D. Matz, "Improving Aural Comprehension in White and Black Children: Pictures Versus Print," *Journal of Experimental Child Psychology*, 19 (1975), 23-26.

[36]On the value of inserting questions, see, for example, R. C. Anderson and W. B. Biddle, "On Asking People Questions About What They are Reading," in *Psychology of Learning and Motivation*, ed. Gordon H. Bower (New York: Academic Press, 1975), 9, 90-132; and J. Snowman and D. J. Cunningham, "A Comparison of Pictorial and Written Adjunct Aids in Learning From Text,"*Journal of Educational Psychology*, 67 (1975), 307-11. On the value of asking your own questions, see Frase and Schwartz, "Effect."

[37]Wayne H. Bartz, *Memory* (Dubuque, Iowa: William C. Brown Company, Publishers, 1968), pp. 30-31.

[38]J. P. Rickards and G. J. August, "Generative Underlining Strategies in Prose Recall,"*Journal of Educational Psychology*, 67 (1975), 860-65.

[39]L. R. Gay, "Temporal Position of Reviews and Its Effect on the Retention of Mathematical Rules,"*Journal of Educational Psychology*, 64 (1973), 171-82.

[40]See Robinson, *Effective Study.*

[41]Hunter, *Memory*, pp. 312-13; Bartz, *Memory*, p. 31.

[42]H. Woodrow, "The Effect of Type of Training Upon Transference,"*Journal of Educational Psychology*, 18 (1927), 159-72.

Chapter 5

[1]Donald A. Norman, *Memory and Attention* (New York: John Wiley & Sons, Inc., 1969), p. 98.

[2]G. H. Bower, "Analysis of a Mnemonic Device," *American Scientist,* 58 (1970), 496-510 (p. 496).

[3]Frances Yates, *The Art of Memory* (London: Routledge & Kegan Paul Ltd., 1966).

[4]Some of these examples are contained in *A Dictionary of Mnemonics* (London: Eyre Methuen, 1972); and in Peg Bracken, *The I Hate to Housekeep Book,* chap. 10 (New York: Harcourt Brace Jovanovich, 1962).

[5]K. A. Blick and C. J. Waite, "A Survey of Mnemonic Techniques Used by College Students in Free-recall Learning," *Psychological Reports,* 29 (1971), 76-78; C. E. Boltwood and K. A. Blick, "The Delineation and Application of Three Mnemonic Techniques," *Psychonomic Science,* 20 (1970), 339-41; M. M. Gruneberg, "The Role of Memorization Techniques in Finals Examination Preparation—A Study of Psychology Students," *Educational Research,* 15 (1973), 134-39.

[6]J. A. Adams and W. E. Montague, "Retroactive Inhibition and Natural Language Mediation," *Journal of Verbal Learning and Verbal Behavior,* 6, (1967), 528-35.

[7]Ian M. L. Hunter, *Memory,* rev., (Middlesex, England: Penguin Books Ltd., 1964), p. 72.

[8]For example, see F. N. Dempster and W. D. Rohwer, Jr., "Component Analysis of the Elaborative Encoding Effect in Paired-associate Learning," *Journal of Experimental Psychology,* 103 (1974), 400-408; and D. L. Foth, "Mnemonic Technique Effectiveness as a Function of Word Abstractness and Mediation Instruction," *Journal of Verbal Learning and Verbal Behavior,* 12 (1973), 239-45.

[9]For example, see G. H. Bower and D. Winzenz, "Comparison of Associative Learning Strategies," *Psychonomic Science,* 20 (1970), 119-20; J. L. Santa, A. B. Ruskin, and A. J. H. Yio, "Mnemonic Systems in Free Recall," *Psychological Reports,* 32 (1973), 1163-70; G. D. Powell, T. G. Hamon, and R. K. Young, "Selective Encoding Interference in Paired-associate Learning," *Journal of Experimental Psychology: Human Learning and Memory,* 104 (1975), 473-79; F. L. Prestianni and R. T. Zacks, "The Effects of Learning Instruction and Cueing on Free Recall," *Memory and Cognition,* 2 (1974), 194-200.

[10]For example, see E. J. Forbes and H. W. Reese, "Pictorial Elaboration and Recall of Multilist Paired Associates," *Journal of Experimental Psychology,* 102 (1974), 836-40; N. J. Kanak and B. Rabenou, "Incidentally Learned Associations and Imagery in Verbal Discrimination Transfer," *Bulletin of the Psychonomic Society,* 6 (1975), 177-80; G. Keppel and B. Zavortink, "Further Test of the Use of Images as Mediators," *Journal of Experimental Psychology,* 82 (1969), 190-92; and William E. Montague and John Carter, "The Loci Mnemonic Technique in Learning and Memory" (paper presented at the meeting of the American Educational Research Association, Chicago, April 1974).

[11]B. R. Bugelski, "Images as Mediators in One-trial Paired-associate Learning. II: Self-timing in Successive Lists," *Journal of Experimental Psychology,* 77 (1968),

328-34; B. R. Bugelski, "Words and Things and Images," *American Psychologist,* 25 (1970), 1002-12.

[12]For children, see P. B. Odom and N. H. Nesbitt, "Some Processes in Children ɩ Comprehension of Linguistically and Visually Depicted Relationships," *Journal of Experimental Child Psychology,* 17 (1974), 399-408; and Allan Paivio, "Imagery and Long-term Memory," in *Studies in Long Term Memory,* eds. Alan Kennedy and Alan Wilkes (New York: John Wiley & Sons, Inc., 1975), pp. 57-88. For college students, see S. A. Bobrow and R. D. Easton, "A Confirmation that Relational Organization Facilitates Memory," *Psychonomic Science,* 29 (1972), 256-57; K. A. Wollen and D. H. Lowry, "Effects of Imagery on Paired-associate Learning," *Journal of Verbal Learning and Verbal Behavior,* 10 (1971), 276-84; and K. A. Wollen and D. H. Lowry, "Conditions that Determine Effectiveness of Picture-mediated Paired-associate Learning," *Journal of Experimental Psychology,* 102 (1974), 181-83.

[13]For example, see G. H. Bower, "Imagery as a Relational Organizer in Association Learning," *Journal of Verbal Learning and Verbal Behavior,* 9 (1970), 529-33; P. E. Morris and R. Stevens, "Linking Images and Free Recall," *Journal of Verbal Learning and Verbal Behavior,* 13 (1974), 310-15; and V. Neisser and N. Kerr, "Spatial and Mnemonic Properties of Visual Images," *Cognitive Psychology,* 5 (1973), 138-50.

[14]I. Begg, "Imagery and Integration in the Recall of Words," *Canadian Journal of Psychology,* 27 (1973), 159-67; I. Begg and R. Robertson, "Imagery and Long-term Retention," *Journal of Verbal Learning and Verbal Behavior,* 12 (1973), 689-700.

[15]Neisser and Kerr, "Spatial and Mnemonic Properties."

[16]For vividness and paired-associates, see Gordon H. Bower, "Mental Imagery and Associative Learning," in *Cognition in Learning and Memory,* ed. Lee W. Gregg (New York: John Wiley & Sons, Inc., 1972), pp. 51-88. For sentences, see R. C. Anderson and J. L. Hidde, "Imagery and Sentence Learning," *Journal of Educational Psychology,* 62 (1971), 526-30. For word lists, see P. S. Delin, "Learning and Retention of English Words with Successive Approximations to a Complex Mnemonic Instruction," *Psychonomic Science,* 17 (1969), 87-88.

[17]For sentences and paragraphs, see P. J. Holmes and D. J. Murray, "Free Recall of Sentences as a Function of Imagery and Predictability," *Journal of Experimental Psychology,* 102 (1974), 748-50; and W. E. Montague and J. F. Carter, "Vividness of Imagery in Recalling Connected Discourse," *Journal of Educational Psychology,* 64 (1973), 72-75. For adjectives, see E. P. Kirchner, "Vividness of Adjectives and the Recall of Meaningful Verbal Material," *Psychonomic Science,* 15 (1969), 71-72. For pictures, see L. Standing, "Learning 10,000 Pictures," *Quarterly Journal of Experimental Psychology,* 25 (1973), 207-22.

[18]G. G. Briggs, S. Hawkins, and H. F. Crovitz, "Bizarre Images in Artificial Memory," *Psychonomic Science,* 19 (1970), 353-54; P. S. Delin, "Success in Recall as a Function of Success in Implementation of Mnemonic Instructions," *Psychonomic Science,* 12 (1968), 153-54; J. J. Persensky and R. J. Senter, "An Investigation of 'Bizarre' Imagery as a Mnemonic Device," *Psychological Record,* 20 (1970), 145-50.

[19]For paired-associate tasks, see G. W. Nappe and K. A. Wollen, "Effects of Instructions to Form Common and Bizarre Mental Images on Retention," *Journal of Experimental Psychology*, 100 (1973), 6-8; P. M. Wortman and P. B. Sparling, "Acquisition and Retention of Mnemonic Information in Long-term Memory," *Journal of Experimental Psychology*, 102 (1974), 22-26. For Loci system, see Bower, "Analysis." For Link and Peg systems, see G. Wood, "Mnemonic Systems in Recall," *Journal of Educational Psychology*, 58 (1967), 1-27.

[20]Howard S. Hock and Lorann Romanski, "Rules of Physical Plausibility and Recognition Memory for Multi-object Scenes: A Developmental Study" (paper presented at the meeting of the Psychonomic Society, Denver, November, 1975).

[21]K. A. Wollen, A. Weber, and D. H. Lowry, "Bizarreness Versus Interaction of Mental Images as Determinants of Learning," *Cognitive Psychology*, 3 (1972), 518-23.

[22]S. C. Collyer, J. Jonides, and W. Bevan, "Images as Memory Aids: Is Bizarreness Helpful?" *American Journal of Psychology*, 85 (1972), 31-38.

[23]For uniqueness, see A. M. Lesgold and A. R. Goldman, "Encoding Uniqueness and the Imagery Mnemonic in Associative Learning," *Journal of Verbal Learning and Verbal Behavior*, 12 (1973), 193-202. For time, see Nappe and Wollen, "Effects of Instructions;" and Wortman and Sparling, "Acquisition and Retention."

[24]Harry Lorayne and Jerry Lucas, *The Memory Book* (New York: Stein & Day Publishers, 1974), pp. 25-26.

[25]Delin, "Learning and Retention;" M. M. Gruneberg, J. Monks, R. N. Sykes, and D. J. Oborne, "Some Correlates of Rated Memorability of Sentences," *British Journal of Psychology*, 65 (1974), 519-27.

[26]K. A. Wollen and D. H. Lowry, "Effects of Imagery on Paired-associate Learning," *Journal of Verbal Learning and Verbal Behavior*, 10 (1971), 276-84.

[27]For abstract words, see, for example, B. R. Bugelski, "Words;" and William E. Montague, "Elaborative Strategies in Verbal Learning and Memory," in *The Psychology of Learning and Motivation*, ed. Gordon H. Bower (New York: Academic Press, 1972), 6, 225-302. For concepts, see A. N. Katz and A. Paivio, "Imagery Variables in Concept Identification," *Journal of Verbal Learning and Verbal Behavior*, 14 (1975), 284-93.

[28]R. C. Anderson, "Concretization and Sentence Learning," *Journal of Educational Psychology*, 66 (1974), 179-83.

[29]For example, see Herbert F. Crovitz, "Mnemonics and the Total-time Hypothesis" (paper presented at the meeting of the Psychonomic Society, Denver, November 1975); D. Griffith, "Comparison of Control Processes for Recognition and Recall," *Journal of Experimental Psychology: Human Learning and Memory*, 104 (1975), 223-28; J. R. Levin and P. Divine-Hawkins, "Visual Imagery as a Prose-learning Process," *Journal of Reading Behavior*, 6 (1974), 23-30; and V. Modigliani and J. G. Seamon, "Transfer of Information from Short- to Long-term Memory," *Journal of Experimental Psychology*, 102 (1974) 768-72.

[30]B. R. Bugelski, E. Kidd, and J. Segmen, "Imagery as a Mediator in One-trial Paired-associate Learning," *Journal of Experimental Psychology,* 76 (1968), 69-73.

[31]B. R. Bugelski, "The Image as Mediator in One-trial Paired-associate Learning: III. Sequential Functions in Serial Lists," *Journal of Experimental Psychology,* 103 (1974), 298-303.

[32]Bugelski, "Words."

[33]T. Y. Arbuckle, "Mediational Instructions, Stage of Practice, Presentation Rate, and Retrieval Cue in Paired-associate Learning," *Journal of Experimental Psychology,* 88 (1971), 396-402; Eugene Winograd, Michael A. Karchmer, and Richard Tucker, "Strolling Down Memory Lane with the Method of Locations" (paper presented at the meeting of the Psychonomic Society, San Antonio, November 1970).

[34]Arbuckle, "Mediational Instructions;" C. McCauley and G. Kellar, "Induced Chunking: Temporal Aspects of Storage and Retrieval," *Journal of Experimental Psychology,* 102 (1974), 260-65.

[35]J. C. Yuille and S. Pritchard, "Noun Concreteness and Verbal Facilitation as Factors in Imaginal Mediation and PA Learning in Children," *Journal of Experimental Child Psychology,* 7 (1969), 459-66.

[36]J. A. Schnorr and R. C. Atkinson, "Study Position and Item Differences in the Short- and Long-term Retention of Paired-associates Learning by Imagery," *Journal of Verbal Learning and Verbal Behavior,* 9 (1970), 614-22.

[37]Wortman and Sparling, "Acquisition and Retention."

[38]For example, see F. J. Di Vesta and P. M. Sunshine, "The Retrieval of Abstract and Concrete Materials as Functions of Imagery, Mediation, and Mnemonic Aids," *Memory and Cognition,* 2 (1974), 340-44; Wortman and Sparling, "Acquisition and Retention;" and J. C. Yuille, "A Detailed Examination of Mediation in PA Learning," *Memory and Cognition,* 1 (1973), 333-42.

[39]For example, see L. Postman, "Does Imagery Enhance Long-term Retention?" *Bulletin of the Psychonomic Society,* 3 (1974), 385-87.

[40]For the fifth-graders, see R. M. Olton, "The Effect of a Mnemonic Upon the Retention of Paired-associate Verbal Material," *Journal of Verbal Learning and Verbal Behavior,* 8 (1969), 43-48. For college students, see L. Hasher, B. Riebman, and F. Wren, "Imagery and the Retention of Free-Recall Learning," *Journal of Experimental Psychology: Human Learning and Memory,* 2 (1976), 172-81; and D. H. Lowry, "The Effects of Mnemonic Learning Strategies on Transfer, Interference, and 48-hour Retention," *Journal of Experimental Psychology,* 103 (1974), 16-20.

[41]For example, see I. Begg and R. Robertson, "Imagery and Long-term Retention," *Journal of Verbal Learning and Verbal Behavior,* 12 (1973), 689-700; L. D. Groninger, "Mnemonic Imagery and Forgetting," *Psychonomic Science,* 23 (1971), 161-63; and L. D. Groninger, "Imagery and Subjective Categorization Effects on Long-term Recognition and Retrieval," *Bulletin of the Psychonomic Society,* 3 (1974), 261-63.

⁴²Paivio, "Long-term Memory."

⁴³Blick and Waite, "A Survey;" Boltwood and Blick, "The Delineation."

⁴⁴R. J. Weber and J. Castleman, "The Time it Takes to Imagine," *Perception and Psychophysics,* 8 (1970), 165-68.

⁴⁵Alan Richardson, *Mental Imagery* (New York: Springer-Publishing Co., Inc., 1969).

⁴⁶R. R. Holt, "Imagery: The Return of the Ostracised," *American Psychologist,* 19 (1964), 254-64.

⁴⁷S. M. Kosslyn and G. H. Bower, "The Role of Imagery in Sentence Memory: A Developmental Study," *Child Development,* 45 (1974), 30-38.

⁴⁸Di Vesta and Sunshine, "The Retrieval."

⁴⁹David F. Marks, "Individual Differences in the Vividness of Visual Imagery and Their Effect on Function," in *The Function and Nature of Imagery,* ed. Peter W. Sheehan (New York: Academic Press, 1972), pp. 83-108.

⁵⁰For disadvantaged children, see J. J. Russell, "Mental Elaboration and Cognitive Performance," *Journal of Negro Education,* 43 (1974), 202-11. For young children, see, for example, Jean B. Chandler and Larry Greeson, "Modeling, Imagery, and Verbal Mediation in Children's Associative Learning" (paper presented at the meeting of the American Psychological Association, Chicago, September 1975); and J. C. Yuille and M. J. Catchpole, "The Effects of Delay and Imagery Training on the Recall and Recognition of Object Pairs," *Journal of Experimental Child Psychology,* 17 (1974), 474-81. For retarded children, see, for example, Ann L. Brown, "The Role of Strategic Behavior in Retardate Memory," in *International Review of Research in Mental Retardation,* ed. Norman R. Ellis (New York: Academic Press, 1974), 7, 55-111.

⁵¹Bugelski, "Words."

⁵²Bugelski, "The Image;" Allan Paivio, "A Theoretical Analysis of the Role of Imagery in Learning and Memory," in *The Function and Nature of Imagery,* ed. Peter W. Sheehan (New York: Academic Press, 1972), pp. 253-79; Paivio, "Long-term Memory."

⁵³Gordon H. Bower, "Educational Applications of Mnemonic Devices," in *Interaction: Readings in Human Psychology,* ed. Kenneth O. Doyle, Jr. (Lexington, Mass.: D. C. Heath & Company, 1973), pp. 201-10, p. 209.

⁵⁴H. Klee and M. W. Eysenck, "Comprehension of Abstract and Concrete Sentences," *Journal of Verbal Learning and Verbal Behavior,* 12 (1973), 522-29; J. R. Levin, "Comprehending What We Read: An Outsider Looks In," *Journal of Reading Behavior,* 4 (1972), 18-28; J. R. Levin, "Inducing Comprehension in Poor Readers: A Test of a Recent Model," *Journal of Educational Psychology,* 65 (1973), 19-24.

⁵⁵Gordon H. Bower, "How to . . . uh . . . Remember!," *Psychology Today,* 7, no. 5 (October 1973), 63-70, p. 70.

⁵⁶J. Ross and K. A. Lawrence, "Some Observations on Memory Artifice," *Psychonomic Science,* 13 (1968), 107-8, p. 108.

[57]Laird S. Cermak, *Human Memory: Research and Theory* (New York: The Ronald Press Company, 1972).

[58]*Psychology Today: An Introduction,* 2nd ed. (Del Mar, CA.: CRM Books, 1972), p. 97.

[59]F. Stephan Hamilton, *Mastering Your Memory* (New York: Gramercy Publishing Company, 1947), p. 127.

[60]Allan Paivio, *Imagery and Verbal Processes* (New York: Holt, Rinehart, and Winston, Inc., 1971), p. 532.

[61]W. D. Rohwer, Jr., "Images and Pictures in Children's Learning: Research Results and Educational Implications," *Psychological Bulletin,* 73 (1970), 393-403; Russell, "Mental Elaboration."

[62]For 3rd-4th graders, see A. M. Lesgold, C. McCormick, and R. M. Golinkoff, "Imagery Training and Children's Prose Learning," *Journal of Educational Psychology,* 76 (1975), 663-67. For 4th-5th graders, see Levine and Divine-Hawkins, "Visual Imagery." For 5th-6th graders, see R. W. Kulhavy and I. Swenson, "Imagery Instructions and the Comprehension of Text," *British Journal of Educational Psychology,* 45 (1975), 47-51. For high school, see R. C. Anderson and R. W. Kulhavy, "Imagery and Prose Learning," *Journal of Educational Psychology,* 63 (1972), 242-43.

[63]Paivio, *Verbal Processes.*

Chapter 6

[1]For example, see G. H. Bower and D. Winzenz, "Comparison of Associative Learning Strategies," *Psychonomic Science,* 20 (1970), 119-20; B. R. Bugleski, "Words and Things and Images," *American Psychologist,* 25 (1970), 1002-12; D. Griffith, "The Attentional Demands of Mnemonic Control Processes," *Memory and Cognition,* 4 (1976), 103-8; Ronald Ley and Mary Huba, "Effects of Subject-generated and Experimenter-supplied Associations on Storage in Cued Recall" (paper presented at the meeting of the Psychonomic Society, Denver, November 1975); and M. Schwartz and M. F. Walsh, "Identical Subject-generated and Experimenter-supplied Mediators in Paired-associate Learning," *Journal of Experimental Psychology,* 103 (1974), 878-84.

[2]J. P. Robinson and P. London, "Labeling and Imaging as Aids to Memory," *Child Development,* 42 (1971), 641-44; John G. Borkowski and Patricia B. Wanschura, "Mediational Processes in the Retarded," in *International Review of Research in Mental Retardation,* ed. Norman R. Ellis (New York: Academic Press, 1974), 7, 1-54.

[3]B. R. Bugelski, "The Image as Mediator in One-trial Paired-associate Learning: III. Sequential Functions in Serial Lists," *Journal of Experimental Psychology,* 103 (1974), 298-303.

[4]D. L. Foth, "Mnemonic Technique Effectiveness as a Function of Word Abstractness and Mediation Instruction," *Journal of Verbal Learning and Verbal Behavior,* 12(1973), 239-45.

[5]W. A. Roberts, "Alphabetic Coding and Individual Differences in Modes of Organization in Free-recall Learning," *American Journal of Psychology,* 81 (1968), 433-38.

[6]K. A. Blick and C. J. Waite, "A Survey of Mnemonic Techniques Used by College Students in Free-recall Learning," *Psychological Reports,* 29 (1971), 76-78; C. E. Boltwood and K. A. Blick, "The Delineation and Application of Three Mnemonic Techniques," *Psychonomic Science,* 20(1970), 339-41.

[7]P. S. Delin, "Learning and Retention of English Words with Successive Approximations to a Complex Mnemonic Instruction," *Psychonomic Science,* 17 (1969), 87-89; P. S. Delin, "The Effects of Mnemonic Instruction and List Length on Serial Learning and Retention," *Psychonomic Science,* 17 (1969), 111-13; P. S. Delin, "The Learning to Criterion of a Serial List With and Without Mnemonic Instruction," *Psychonomic Science,* 16(1969), 169-70.

[8]Bugelski, "The Image as Mediator."

[9]J. H. Mueller and E. M. Jablonski, "Instructions, Noun Imagery, and Priority in Free Recall," *Psychological Reports,* 27 (1970), 559-66; G. Wood, "Mnemonic Systems in Recall," *Journal of Educational Psychology,* 58(1967), 1-27.

[10]F. S. Murray, "Effects of Narrative Stories on Recall," *Bulletin of the Psychonomic Society,* 4(1974), 577-79.

[11]G. H. Bower and M. C. Clark, "Narrative Stories as Mediators for Serial Learning," *Psychonomic Science,* 14(1969), 181-82.

[12]B. A. Manning and R. H. Bruning, "Interactive Effects of Mnemonic Techniques and Word-list Characteristics," *Psychological Reports,* 36(1975), 727-36.

[13]For 8-week recall see Boltwood and Blick, "Three Mnemonic Techniques." For sentences see P. A. DeVilliers, "Imagery and Theme in Recall of Connected Discourse," *Journal of Experimental Psychology,* 103(1974), 263-68.

[14]G. H. Bower, "How to . . . uh . . . Remember!," *Psychology Today,* 7, no. 5 (October, 1973), 63-70 (p. 63).

[15]Dale Carnegie, *Public Speaking and Influencing Men in Business* (New York: Association Press, 1926), p. 60.

[16]Douglas W. Matheson, *Introductory Psychology: The Modern View* (Hinsdale, IL.: The Dryden Press, Inc., 1975), p. 233.

[17]Several examples of how to do this are provided in Bruno Furst, *Stop Forgetting,* chap. 10, rev. by Lotte Furst and Gerrit Storm (Garden City, N. Y.: Doubleday & Company, Inc., 1972).

[18]Chesley V. Young, *The Magic of a Mighty Memory* (West Nyack, NY: Parker Publishing Co., 1971).

[19]Some examples are Tony Buzan, *Speed Memory* (London: Sphere Books Limited, 1971); William D. Hersey, *How to Cash in on Your Hidden Memory Power* (Englewood Cliffs, N. J.: Prentice-Hall, Inc., 1963); Harry Lorayne and Jerry Lucas, *The Memory Book* (New York: Stein & Day Publishers, 1974), published in paperback by Ballentine Books, Inc., 1975; Truman G. Madsen, *How to Stop Forgetting and Start Remembering* (Provo, UT: Brigham Young University Press, 1970); Young, *Mighty Memory;* Morris N. Young and Walter B. Gibson, *How to Develop an Exceptional Memory,* 1974 ed., (No. Hollywood, CA: Wilshire Book Co., 1974).

Chapter 7

[1]Frances A. Yates, *The Art of Memory* (London: Routledge & Kegan Paul Ltd., 1966).

[2]G. Lea, "Chronometric Analysis of the Method of Loci," *Journal of Experimental Psychology: Human Perception and Performance,* 104 (1975), 95-104.

[3]G. H. Bower, "Analysis of a Mnemonic Device," *American Scientist,* 58 (1970), 496-510.

[4]B. R. Bugelski, "The Image as Mediator in One-trial Paired-associate Learning: III. Sequential Functions in Serial Lists," *Journal of Experimental Psychology,* 103 (1974), 298-303.

[5]Alexandr R. Luria, *The Mind of a Mnemonist* (New York: Basic Books, Inc., Publishers, 1968), pp. 31-33.

[6]E. Z. Rothkopf, "Incidental Memory for Location of Information in Text," *Journal of Verbal Learning and Verbal Behavior,* 10 (1971), 608-13; E. B. Zechmeister and J. McKillip, "Recall of Place on the Page," *Journal of Educational Psychology,* 63 (1972), 446-53; E. B. Zechmeister, J. McKillip, S. Pasko, and D. Bespalec, "Visual Memory for Place on the Page," *Journal of General Psychology,* 92 (1975), 43-52.

[7]A. I. Schulman, "Recognition Memory and the Recall of Spatial Location," *Memory and Cognition,* 1 (1973), 245-60; J. M. von Wright, P. Gebhard, and M. Karttunen, "A Developmental Study of the Recall of Spatial Location," *Journal of Experimental Child Psychology,* 20 (1975), 181-90.

[8]For organization on a page, see B. Byrne, "Item Concreteness vs. Spatial Organization as Predictors of Visual Imagery," *Memory and Cognition,* 2 (1974), 53-59. For organization in a picture, see J. M. Mandler and R. E. Parker, "Memory for Descriptive and Spatial Information in Complex Pictures," *Journal of Experimental Psychology: Human Learning and Memory,* 2 (1976), 38-48.

[9]L. P. Acredolo, H. L. Pick, Jr., and M. G. Olsen, "Environmental Differentiation and Familiarity as Determinants of Children's Memory for Spatial Location," *Developmental Psychology,* 11 (1975), 495-501.

[10]Allan Paivio, *Imagery and Verbal Processes* (New York: Holt, Rinehart, and Winston, Inc., 1971).

[11]J. D. Read and R. H. Peterson, "Individual Differences in the Ease of Imagining the Faces of Others," *Bulletin of the Psychonomic Society,* 5 (1975), 347-

49; A. D. Yarmey, "I Recognize Your Face but I can't Remember Your Name: Further Evidence on the Tip-of-the-tongue Phenomenon," *Memory and Cognition,* 1 (1973), 287-90.

[12]Alan M. Lesgold, Mary E. Curtis, and Hildrene De Good, "Effects of Pictures and Imagery on Prose Recall" (paper presented at the meeting of the Psychonomic Society, Denver, November 1975).

[13]Eugene Winograd, Michael Karchmer, and Richard Tucker, "Strolling Down Memory Lane with the Method of Locations" (paper presented at the meeting of the Psychonomic Society, San Antonio, November 1970).

[14]A. L. Brown, "Mnemonic Elaboration and Recency Judgments in Children," *Cognitive Psychology,* 5 (1973), 233-48.

[15]A. Kobasigawa, "Effects of Retrieval Cues on Children's Recall Following Free- or Cued-recall Instructions," *Perceptual and Motor Skills,* 40 (1975), 187-91.

[16]J. Ross and K. A. Lawrence, "Some Observations on Memory Artifice," *Psychonomic Science,* 13 (1968), 107-8.

[17]G. H. Bower, "How to...uh...Remember!," *Psychology Today,* 7, no. 5 (October, 1973), 63-70.

[18]L. D. Groninger, "Mnemonic Imagery and Forgetting," *Psychonomic Science,* 23 (1971), 161-63; L. D. Groninger, "Imagery and Subjective Categorization Effects on Long-term Recognition and Retrieval," *Bulletin of the Psychonomic Society,* 3 (1974), 261-63.

[19]H. F. Crovitz, "Memory Loci in Artificial Memory," *Psychonomic Science,* 16 (1969), 82-83.

[20]G. G. Briggs, S. Hawkins, and H. F. Crovitz, "Bizarre Images in Artificial Memory," *Psychonomic Science,* 19 (1970), 353-54.

[21]William E. Montague and John Carter, "The Loci Mnemonic Technique in Learning and Memory" (paper presented at the meeting of the American Educational Research Association, Chicago, April 1974).

[22]Herbert F. Crovitz, "Mnemonics and the Total-time Hypothesis" (paper presented at the meeting of the Psychonomic Society, Denver, November 1975).

[23]P. McKellar, D. F. Marks, and B. F. Barron, "The Mnemonic Walk and Visual Imagery Differences," cited by David F. Marks, "Individual differences in the vividness of visual imagery and their effect on function," in Peter W. Sheehan ed., *The Function and Nature of Imagery* (New York: Academic Press, 1972), 83-108.

[24]G. H. Bower and J. S. Reitman, "Mnemonic Elaboration in Multilist Learning," *Journal of Verbal Learning and Verbal Behavior,* 11 (1972), 478-85.

[25]For college, see E. J. Forbes and H. W. Reese, "Pictorial Elaboration and Recall of Multilist Paired Associates," *Journal of Experimental Psychology,* 102 (1974), 836-40. For grade-school, see A. L. Brown, "Progressive Elaboration and Memory for Order in Children," *Journal of Experimental Child Psychology,* 19 (1975), 383-400. For preschool, see H. W. Reese, "Imagery and Multiple-list Paired-associate Learn-

ing in Young Children,"*Journal of Experimental Child Psychology,* 13 (1972), 310-23.

²⁶Herbert F. Crovitz, *Galton's Walk* (New York: Harper & Row, Publishers, 1970).

Chapter 8

¹Allan Paivio, *Imagery and Verbal Processes* (New York: Academic Press, 1971), p. 173.

²G. H. Bower and J. S. Reitman, "Mnemonic Elaboration in Multilist Learning,"*Journal of Verbal Learning and Verbal Behavior,* 11 (1972), 478-85.

³Some of these examples were suggested by Dale Carnegie, *Public Speaking and Influencing Men in Business* (New York: Association Press, 1926).

⁴Bower and Reitman, "Mnemonic Elaboration."

⁵Gordon H. Bower, "A Selective Review of Organizational Factors in Memory," in *Organization and Memory,* ed. Endel Tulving and Wayne Donaldson (New York: Academic Press, 1972), pp. 93-137.

⁶George A. Miller, Eugene Galanter, and Karl H. Pribram, *Plans and the Structure of Behavior* (New York: Henry Holt & Co., 1960), pp. 135-36.

⁷B. R. Bugelski, "Words and Things and Images," *American Psychologist,* 25 (1970), 1002-12.

⁸Bugelski, "Words;" G. Wood, "Mnemonic Systems in Recall,"*Journal of Educational Psychology,* 58 (1967), 1-27.

⁹Ian M. L. Hunter, *Memory,* rev. (Middlesex, England: Penguin Books, Ltd., 1964).

¹⁰B. R. Bugelski, E. Kidd, and J. Segman, "The Image as a Mediator in One-trial Paired-associate Learning,"*Journal of Experimental Psychology,* 76 (1968), 69-73.

¹¹Wood, "Mnemonic Systems."

¹²B. R. Bugelski, "Images as Mediators in One-trial Paired-associate Learning. II: Self-Timing in Successive Lists,"*Journal of Experimental Psychology,* 77 (1968), 328-34. Similar results were obtained by G. Keppel and B. Zavortink, "Further Test of the Use of Images as Mediators,"*Journal of Experimental Psychology,* 82 (1969), 190-92.

¹³Bugelski, "Words."

¹⁴Gordon H. Bower, "Mental Imagery and Associative Learning," in *Cognition in Learning and Memory,* ed. Lee W. Gregg (New York: John Wiley & Sons, Inc., 1972), pp. 51-88; also see Bower and Reitman, "Mnemonic Elaboration."

¹⁵Paivio, *Imagery.*

¹⁶First two studies were Allan Paivio, "Effects of Imagery Instructions and Concreteness of Memory Pegs in a Mnemonic System" (paper presented at the meeting of the American Psychological Association, 1968), as described in Paivio, *Imagery;* and

J. L. Santa, A. B. Ruskin, and A. J. H. Yio, "Mnemonic Systems in Free Recall," *Psychological Reports*, 32 (1973), 1163-70. Third study was D. J. Delprato and E. J. Baker, "Concreteness of Pegwords in Two Mnemonic Systems," *Journal of Experimental Psychology*, 102 (1974), 520-22. Fourth study was F. J. DiVesta and P. M. Sunshine, "The Retrieval of Abstract and Concrete Materials as Functions of Imagery, Mediation, and Mnemonic Aids," *Memory and Cognition*, 2 (1974), 340-44.

[17]J. J. Russell, "Mental Elaboration and Cognitive Performance," *Journal of Negro Education*, 43 (1974), 202-11.

[18]Bower and Reitman, "Mnemonic Elaboration."

[19]Gordon H. Bower, "Educational Applications of Mnemonic Devices," in *Interaction: Readings in Human Psychology*, ed. Kenneth O. Doyle, Jr. (Lexington, Mass.: D. C. Heath & Company, 1973), pp. 201-10, p. 207.

Chapter 9

[1]Richard Grey, *Memoria Technica* (London, 1730).

[2]M. Gregor von Feinaigle, *The New Art of Memory*, 2nd ed. (London: Sherwood, Neely, and Jones, 1813).

[3]William James, *Principles of Psychology*, Vol. I, (New York: Henry Holt and Company, 1890), p. 669; A. Loisette, *Assimilative Memory, or How to Attend and Never Forget* (New York: Funk & Wagnalls, Inc., 1899).

[4]Tony Buzan, *Speed Memory* (London: Sphere Books Limited, 1971); Francis Fauvel-Gouraud, *Phreno-Mnemotechnic Dictionary: A Philosophical Classification of all the Homophonic Words of the English Language*. Part First (New York: Houel & Macoy, 1844); Bruno Furst, *Number Dictionary*, rev. and enl. by Lotte Furst and Gerrit Storm (Mundelein, Ill.: Memory and Concentration Studies, 1972); William D. Hersey, *How to Cash in on Your Hidden Memory Power* (Englewood Cliffs, N. J.: Prentice-Hall, Inc., 1963).

[5]R. K. Smith and C. E. Noble, "Effects of a Mnemonic Technique Applied to Verbal Learning and Memory," *Perceptual and Motor Skills*, 21 (1965), 123-34.

[6]R. J. Senter and G. K. Hauser, "An Experimental Study of a Mnemonic System," *Psychonomic Science*, 10 (1968), 289-90.

[7]E. Berla, J. J. Persensky, and R. J. Senter, "Learning Time with a Mnemonic System," *Psychonomic Science*, 16 (1969), 207-8.

[8]J. J. Persensky and R. J. Senter, "An Experimental Investigation of A Mnemonic System in Recall," *Psychological Record*, 19(1969), 491-99.

[9]J. J. Persensky and R. J. Senter, "An Investigation of 'Bizarre' Imagery as a Mnemonic Device," *Psychological Record*, 20 (1970), 145-50.

[10]D. L. Foth, "Mnemonic Technique Effectiveness as a Function of Word Abstractness and Mediation Instruction," *Journal of Verbal Learning and Verbal Behavior*, 12 (1973), 239-45.

[11]S. Slak, "Phonemic Recoding of Digital Information," *Journal of Experimental Psychology*, 86 (1970), 398-406.

[12]Loisette, *Assimilative Memory*.

[13]F. Stephen Hamilton, *Mastering Your Memory*, chap. 17 (New York: Gramercy Publishing Company, 1947); Harry Lorayne, *How to Develop a Super-power Memory* (New York: Frederick Fell, Inc., 1957), pp. 104-13, published in paperback by The New American Library Inc., 1974; Young and Gibson in footnote 19 of Chapter 6, pp. 100-103; Buzan, *Speed Memory*, chap. 15.

[14]See footnote 19, Chapter 6.

Chapter 10

[1]Earl Hunt and Tom Love, "How Good Can Memory Be?" In *Coding Processes in Human Memory*, eds. Arthur Weever Melton and Edwin Martin (Washington, D.C.: V. H. Winston & Sons, 1972), p. 255.

[2]*Family Weekly*, September 1975.

[3]Joyce Brothers and Edward P. F. Eagan, *Ten Days to a Successful Memory* (Englewood Cliffs, N. J.: Prentice-Hall, Inc., 1957), p. 104.

[4]Kenneth Deffenbacher, Evan Brown, and William Sturgill, "Memory for Faces and the Circumstances of their Encounter" (paper presented at the meeting of the Psychonomic Society, Denver, November 1975); J. Hochberg and R. E. Galper, "Recognition of Faces: 1. An Exploratory Study," *Psychonomic Science*, 9 (1967), 619-20.

[5]H. P. Bahrick, P. O. Bahrick, and R. P. Wittlinger, "Fifty Years of Memory for Names and Faces: A Cross-sectional Approach," *Journal of Experimental Psychology: General*, 104 (1975), 54-75.

[6]H. M. Clarke, "Recall and Recognition for Faces and Names," *Journal of Applied Psychology*, 18 (1934), 757-63.

[7]J. D. Read and R. G. Wilbur II, "Availability of Faces and Names in Recall," *Perceptual and Motor Skills*, 41 (1975), 263-70.

[8]Bahrick, Bahrick, and Wittlinger, "Fifty years."

[9]A. Paivio and I. Begg, "Pictures and Words in Visual Search," *Memory and Cognition*, 2 (1974), 515-21.

[10]H. Ellis, J. Shepherd, and G. Davies, "An Investigation of the Use of the Photofit Technique for Recalling Faces," *British Journal of Psychology*, 66 (1975), 29-37.

[11]A. D. Yarmey, "I Recognize Your Face but I can't Remember Your Name: Further Evidence on the Tip-of-the-tongue Phenomenon," *Memory and Cognition*, 1 (1973), 287-90.

[12]J. E. May and K. N. Clayton, "Imaginal Processes During the Attempt to Recall Names," *Journal of Verbal Learning and Verbal Behavior*, 12 (1973), 683-88.

[13]Harry Lorayne, *Remembering People: The Key to Success* (New York: Stein & Day Publishers, 1975).

¹⁴See footnote 19, chap. 6.

¹⁵J. D. Read and R. H. Peterson, "Individual Differences in the Ease of Imagining the Faces of Others," *Bulletin of the Psychonomic Society*, 5 (1975), 347-49; Ellis, Shepherd, and Davies, "An Investigation."

¹⁶Bahrick, Bahrick, and Wittlinger, "Fifty Years"; J. F. Cross, J. Cross, and J. Daly, "Sex, Race, Age, and Beauty as Factors in Recognition of Faces," *Perception and Psychophysics*, 10 (1971), 393-96; H. Ellis, J. Shepherd, and A. Bruce, "The Effects of Age and Sex Upon Adolescents' Recognition of Faces," *Journal of General Psychology*, 123 (1973), 173-74; K. R. Laughery, J. F. Alexander, and A. B. Lane, "Recognition of Human Faces: Effects of Target Exposure Time, Target Position, Pose Position, and Type of Photgraph," *Journal of Applied Psychology*, 55 (1971), 477-83.

¹⁷G. H. Bower and M. B. Karlin, "Depth of Processing Pictures of Faces and Recognition Memory," *Journal of Experimental Psychology*, 103 (1974), 751-57, pp. 756-57.

¹⁸For attractiveness, see Cross, Cross, and Daly, "Sex, race, age"; and J. W. Shepherd and H. D. Ellis, "The Effect of Attractiveness on Recognition Memory for Faces," *American Journal of Psychology*, 86 (1973), 627-33. For race, see Cross, Cross, and Daly, "Sex, race, age"; R. S. Malpass and J. Kravitz, "Recognition for Faces of Own and Other Races," *Journal of Personality and Social Psychology*, 13 (1969), 330-34; and J. W. Shepherd, J. B. Deregowski, and H. D. Ellis, "A Cross-cultural Study of Recognition Memory for Faces," *International Journal of Psychology*, 9 (1974), 205-12. For smile, see R. E. Galper and J. Hochberg, "Recognition Memory for Photographs of Faces," *American Journal of Psychology*, 84 (1971), 351-54.

¹⁹L. D. Harmon, "The Recognition of Faces," *Scientific American*, 229 (1973), 70-82.

²⁰G. H. Fisher and R. L. Cox, "Recognizing Human Faces," *Applied Ergonomics*, 6 (1975), 104-9; Laughery, Alexander, and Lane, "Recognition" vs. A. G. Goldstein and E. J. Mackenberg, "Recognition of Human Faces from Isolated Facial Features: A Developmental Study," *Psychonomic Science*, 6 (1966), 149-50; L. D. Harmon, "The Recognition of Faces," *Scientific American*, 229 (1973), 70-82; T. H. Howells, "A Study of Ability to Recognize Faces," *Journal of Abnormal and Social Psychology*, 33 (1938), 124-27.

²¹Laughery, Alexander, and Lane, "Recognition," found that the longer people can look at a face, the better they remember it.

²²Laughery, Alexander, and Lane, "Recognition"; A. D. Yarmey, "Proactive Interference in Short-term Retention of Human Faces," *Canadian Journal of Psychology*, 28 (1974), 333-38.

²³For seeing and hearing, see B. M. Gadzella and D. A. Whitehead, "Effects of Auditory and Visual Modalities in Recall of Words," *Perceptual and Motor Skills*, 40 (1975), 255-60. For spelling words, see S. Farnham-Diggory and H. A. Simon,

"Retention of Visually Presented Information in Children's Spelling," *Memory and Cognition*, 3 (1975), 599-608.

[24] Wayne H. Bartz, *Memory* (Dubuque, Iowa: William C. Brown Company, Publishers, 1968), p. 29.

[25] Lorayne, *Remembering People*.

[26] J. C. Cooper, "Some Relationships Between Paired-associate Learning and Foreign Language Aptitude," *Journal of Educational Psychology*, 55 (1964), 132-38.

[27] R. C. Atkinson, "Mnemotechnics in Second-language Learning," *American Psychologist*, 30 (1975), 821-28; R. C. Atkinson and M. R. Raugh, "An Application of the Mnemonic Keyword Method to the Acquisition of a Russian Vocabulary," *Journal of Experimental Psychology: Human Learning and Memory*, 1 (1975), 126-33; M. R. Raugh and R. C. Atkinson, "A Mnemonic Method for Learning a Second-language Vocabulary," *Journal of Educational Psychology*, 67 (1975), 1-16.

[28] C. E. Ott, R. S. Blake, and D. C. Butler, "Implications of Mental Elaboration for the Acquisition of Foreign Language Vocabulary," *International Review of Applied Linguistics*, 14 (1976), 37-48.

[29] C. E. Ott, D. C. Butler, R. S. Blake, and J. P. Ball, "The Effect of Interactive-image Elaboration on the Acquisition of Foreign Language Vocabulary," *Language Learning*, 3 (1973), 197-206.

[30] C. K. Knop, "Mnemonic Devices in Teaching French," *The French Review*, 45 (1971), 337-42, p. 342.

[31] First study is Chien-Shu Chuang, "The Effect of Elaboration and Response Mode upon Acquisition of Chinese Ideographs" (Unpublished masters' thesis, Brigham Young University, 1974). Second study is Roy B. Bennion, "Response Mode and Memory Coding Strategies: A Study in Learning of Chinese-English Pairs" (Unpublished doctoral dissertation, Brigham Young University, 1974).

[32] John A. Meacham and Burt Leiman, "Remembering to Perform Future Actions" (paper presented at the meeting of the American Psychological Association, Chicago, September 1975).

[33] Peg Bracken, *The I Hate To Housekeep Book* (New York: Harcourt Brace Jovanovich, 1962).

[34] Meacham and Leiman, "Remembering."

Index